The Cambridge Introduction to
Gabriel García Márquez

The Colombian Nobel Prize winner Gabriel García Márquez (b. 1927) wrote two of the great novels of the twentieth century, *One Hundred Years of Solitude* and *Love in the Time of Cholera*. As novelist, short story writer and journalist, García Márquez has one of literature's most instantly recognisable styles and since the beginning of his career has explored a consistent set of themes, revolving around the relationship between power and love. His novels exemplify the transition between modernist and postmodernist fiction and have made magical realism one of the most significant and influential phenomena in contemporary writing. Aimed at students of Latin American and comparative literature, this book provides essential information about García Márquez's life and career, his published work in literature and journalism, and his political engagement. It connects the fiction effectively to the writer's own experience and explains his enduring importance in world literature.

Gerald Martin is Andrew W. Mellon Professor Emeritus of Modern Languages in the Department of Hispanic Languages and Literatures at the University of Pittsburgh.

D1521360

The Cambridge Introduction to
Gabriel García Márquez

GERALD MARTIN

CAMBRIDGE
UNIVERSITY PRESS

CAMBRIDGE UNIVERSITY PRESS
Cambridge, New York, Melbourne, Madrid, Cape Town,
Singapore, São Paulo, Delhi, Mexico City

Cambridge University Press
The Edinburgh Building, Cambridge CB2 8RU, UK

Published in the United States of America by Cambridge University Press, New York

www.cambridge.org
Information on this title: www.cambridge.org/9780521895613

First published 2012

Printed in the United Kingdom at the University Press, Cambridge

A catalogue record for this publication is available from the British Library

Library of Congress Cataloguing in Publication data
Martin, Gerald, 1944–
The Cambridge introduction to Gabriel García Márquez / Gerald Martin.
pages cm
Includes bibliographical references and index.
ISBN 978-0-521-89561-3 (hardback) – ISBN 978-0-521-71992-6 (paperback)
1. García Márquez, Gabriel, 1928– I. Title.
PQ8180.17.A73Z717 2012
863′.64–dc23
2012002117

ISBN 978-0-521-89561-3 Hardback
ISBN 978-0-521-71992-6 Paperback

To my friend John King

Contents

Introduction   *page* 1

Chapter 1 The life and work in
historical context   3

Chapter 2 Early short stories,
journalism and a first (modernist)
novel, *Leaf Storm* (1947–1955)   11

The first short stories   12
The early journalism   16
Leaf Storm   21

Chapter 3 The neorealist turn:
*In Evil Hour, No One Writes to the
Colonel* and *Big Mama's
Funeral* (1956–1962)   29

In Evil Hour   32
No One Writes to the Colonel   36
Big Mama's Funeral (published 1962)   40

Chapter 4 *One Hundred Years of
Solitude* (1967): the global village   45

'The Sea of Lost Time'   45
One Hundred Years of Solitude   47

Chapter 5 *The Autumn of the Patriarch* (1975): the love of power   61

Innocent Eréndira and Other Stories (1972)   61

The Autumn of the Patriarch   63

Chapter 6 *Chronicle of a Death Foretold* (1981): postmodernism and Hispanic literature   75

Militant journalism: *Alternativa*, Bogotá (1974–1980)   75

A return to the newspaper 'chronicle' (1980)   77

Chronicle of a Death Foretold (1981)   78

Chapter 7 *Love in the Time of Cholera* (1985): the power of love   90

Chapter 8 More about power: *The General in His Labyrinth* (1989) and *News of a Kidnapping* (1996)   102

The General in His Labyrinth (1989)   102

News of a Kidnapping (1996)   107

Epilogue: the later journalism   114

Chapter 9 More about love: *Of Love and Other Demons* (1994) and *Memories of My Melancholy Whores* (2004)   117

Memories of My Melancholy Whores   120

Chapter 10 Memoirs: *Living to Tell the Tale* (2002)   128

Strange Pilgrims   129

Living to Tell the Tale   133

Conclusion: the achievement of the universal Colombian

143

Notes   150
Further reading   160
Index   165

Introduction

Gabriel García Márquez may be the best-known, best-loved and most widely read serious writer of the last five decades. He is not only a major figure in world literature, and the most popular Nobel Prize winner of the last third of the twentieth century, but also a writer who exemplifies better than almost any other the world-historical transition between 'modernist' and 'postmodernist' fiction and the author whose work made 'magical realism' one of the most significant phenomena in 'Third World' or 'postcolonial' writing after the 1960s.

García Márquez's writing is notable for its ability to reconcile things that do not usually go together. Like all great works of literature, his novels and short stories explore, both in breadth and in depth, what it is to be a human being and yet they also address specific historical moments and specific political circumstances. They are carefully structured, yet they give a sense of spontaneity and creativity. Few modern works are more evocative and more poetic, yet García Márquez's powers as a traditional storyteller are unsurpassed in contemporary fiction. Moreover, his works refer to a world that is often grim and even sordid, yet no body of twentieth-century fiction has persuaded so many readers of the simple but sometimes elusive truth that life, despite everything, is beautiful and absolutely worth living. This book seeks to explain how this writer became the author of that world-changing novel, *One Hundred Years of Solitude* (1967), and thereafter a Nobel Prize winner and a contemporary classic.

Many writers and critics have attempted to sum up García Márquez's life and work, with varying degrees of success. Even those who have succeeded in evoking the flavour of the prose and the reach of the oeuvre have only intermittently managed a coherent exposition of the writer's recurrent obsessions (childhood, solitude, politics, love) and the interlocking nature of his works. García Márquez himself has contributed to the difficulties by persistently mythologising and indeed mystifying both his life experience and his narrative fiction in ways which lead all but the most tenacious readers down the novelist's own garden path. Few writers have succeeded so completely in shaping their own public image and in prearranging the critical reception of their works.

For these reasons there is a pressing need for a book which goes beyond the conventional interpretations and explanations and relates the fiction more effectively both to the writer's own experience and to the different worlds – Aracataca ('Macondo'), Colombia, Latin America, the planet itself – in and against which it was elaborated. That is the task I have set myself here: to outline García Márquez's historical trajectory; to examine, explain and hopefully throw new light on his written oeuvre; and to assess his achievement.

Chapter 1

The life and work in historical context

Gabriel José García Márquez is a Caribbean writer. He was born in Aracataca, a small banana plantation town close to the northern coast of tropical Colombia ('la Costa'), on 6 March 1927.* His mother, Luisa Santiaga Márquez Iguarán, was from a family which originated in the wild Guajira Indian territory to the east, across the Sierra Nevada, and which had emigrated to Aracataca after her father, Colonel Nicolás Márquez, had killed a former comrade from the War of the Thousand Days between the Liberal and Conservative parties (1899–1902). By the time of García Márquez's birth his grandfather, a Liberal, was one of the leading figures in the town, even though the Liberals had lost the war. By contrast, his father, Gabriel Eligio García, was a telegraphist from Bolívar province, to the west, a region more associated with Afro-Colombian than Indian culture, and had been born illegitimate to a girl of fourteen who was seduced by a schoolteacher. Gabriel Eligio, perhaps surprisingly, was a Conservative. The courtship of Gabriel Eligio and Luisa Santiaga was vigorously opposed by her parents. (They had a skeleton in their own closet: they were first cousins.) They sent her away for a year, but love triumphed in the end and their daughter's open rebellion eventually forced the colonel and his wife Tranquilina Iguarán to relent. The young couple were married in 1926 and moved to the coastal town of Riohacha, in the Guajira.

A few months later Luisa Santiaga returned to her parents' house in Aracataca for the birth of her first child. By now her husband had tired of telegraphy and had set up as a homeopathic doctor. When the baby – known as Gabito – was less than a year old the young couple left him behind with his grandparents and moved with their second baby, Luis Enrique, to another Caribbean coastal city, Barranquilla, at the mouth of the Magdalena River. Until the age of seven

---

* Geographical terms relating to northern Colombia can be confusing. Its seaboard is known, indiscriminately, both as the 'Atlantic Coast' and the 'Caribbean Coast'. However, this entire region of Colombia (including the departments of Bolívar, Atlántico, Magdalena, Cesar and Guajira) is commonly referred to as the 'Colombian Caribbean' but not as the 'Colombian Atlantic'.

Gabito saw his mother and father no more than two or three times and effectively forgot them: their place was taken by his grandfather, the colonel, and his wife Tranquilina, as well as several aunts and a collection of servants. Later his sister Margot, a sickly child, was also sent to live with him in Aracataca.

During these seven years Gabito became his grandfather's pride and joy and the boy, in return, idolised Don Nicolás and learned about life in general, and Aracataca in particular, through the old man's eyes. In particular he absorbed the lessons of two historical events which took on mythical status in his later life: the War of the Thousand Days, in which his grandfather had taken on a heroic responsibility; and the massacre of the striking United Fruit Company workers in Ciénaga by the Colombian military in December 1928, which took place when the child was eighteen months old. Both events would be key points of reference in his literary works down the years.

He was also strongly influenced by his rather eccentric grandmother, whose world view was a mixture of Catholic folklore and local superstition, allowing him to combine the rational world view of Nicolás with the mythological perspective of Tranquilina. Two decades later García Márquez would recreate Aracataca in his fiction under the name of 'Macondo' and would use his extraordinary childhood experiences to breathe magical life into his representation of that small, forgotten town; and give birth to his best-known character, the incorrigible Colonel Aureliano Buendía.

Gabito had recently started his education at the local Montessori school when in 1934 Luisa and Gabriel Eligio returned to Aracataca from Barranquilla – none of Gabriel Eligio's economic ventures ever prospered for long – with another son and daughter. By then Colonel Márquez was ailing and in 1937 he died: later García Márquez would famously comment that after his death, 'nothing else of importance ever happened to me'. Now he and Margot had to adjust to life with a family they barely knew.

That family – now a mother and a father and five children – returned to Barranquilla. Gabriel Eligio set up another homeopathic pharmacy, which soon failed, and set off around the interior as a peripatetic quack doctor to keep the family finances afloat. Gabito, as the eldest, had to assist his mother in every way possible at a time when they were living in real poverty. Eventually Gabriel Eligio found a river town called Sucre where he could set up as a practitioner, and the family moved there in 1940 and stayed for the next eleven years. Gabito, however, was sent back to school in Barranquilla and then in 1943 won a scholarship to study at a national boarding school in the highland town of Zipaquirá, near the capital Bogotá. It was in the light of these experiences that he would later insist that he barely knew his family, which, by the time he had finished in Zipaquirá, in 1946, had almost grown to its final total of eleven sons and daughters – without counting Gabriel Eligio's separate brood of four illegitimate children.

At the national college in Zipaquirá, García Márquez lived and studied with boys from all over Colombia and noted the difference between his own *costeño* (coastal) culture and the cultures of other parts of the country, most notably the highland culture of Bogotá, whose inhabitants were known, pejoratively, as *cachacos* (fops, dandies). Like most *costeños*, he would always insist that the *cachacos* were devious and pretentious and that Bogotá's Andean climate was unbearably cold and forbidding. He was always relieved when the summer vacations came and he could travel back down the River Magdalena by steamboat and re-encounter his beloved Caribbean world. Nevertheless, in Zipaquirá he received an excellent education, and although he was an erratic student his intelligence soon became evident and he was recognised as one of the most talented boys in the school.

In January 1947, very reluctantly, he returned to Bogotá to study Law at the National University. (Law and Medicine were really the only options in most Latin American universities of that era.) He had already started writing poetry in Zipaquirá and now he began to write short stories, one of which, 'The Third Resignation' ('La tercera resignación'), was published in one of Bogotá's leading newspapers, *El Espectador*, in September of that year. At the age of twenty he had suddenly become one of the country's most promising literary talents, an extraordinary experience for a boy from his background who was finding it difficult to make ends meet in the chilly and somewhat intimidating capital city. Other stories followed, but in April 1948 García Márquez's stay in Bogotá was curtailed by the *Bogotazo*, the extraordinary insurrection which followed the assassination of Colombia's most charismatic politician, the Liberal populist Jorge Eliécer Gaitán. This inaugurated almost twenty years of undeclared civil war known as the *Violencia*. The university was closed and García Márquez moved back to the Costa, to the old colonial city of Cartagena, with its faded grandeur, where he found a job on a recently founded Liberal newspaper, *El Universal*. For the next thirteen years he would earn his living as a journalist, both in Colombia and abroad, while writing his stories and novels in his spare time.

Cartagena was really too traditional and conservative for his taste and he moved in 1950 to Barranquilla, at that time Colombia's most dynamic city, to work on *El Heraldo*. There he found a bohemian literary set later known as the 'Barranquilla Group', which provided a stimulating and fun-filled background for his intellectual development. Soon after his arrival, a visit with his mother to try to sell the old house in Aracataca had an extraordinary effect on his view of the world. He had been working for some time on a novel called 'The House' – which would never be completed – but now he set about a new work which he would entitle *La hojarasca* (translated into English as *Leaf Storm*). It was a story about a man something like his grandfather who finds himself in conflict over a moral issue with the inhabitants of the small town in which he lives (the town is called Macondo and is based quite directly on Aracataca); the other main characters have an unmistakable likeness to García Márquez himself and his mother. The novel would be published in May 1955.

In 1951 the García Márquez family left Sucre following the savage murder of a neighbour's son, seen by them as the last straw in an increasingly threatening environment. They installed themselves in Cartagena and Gabito briefly accompanied them but later returned to Barranquilla and in 1953 took a job as a travelling salesman touting encyclopedias around the Guajira, where his maternal grandparents had been born. This experience would be crucial in his understanding of his identity and of the culture in which he had been raised. The next year a Bogotá friend, the writer Alvaro Mutis, got him a job in Bogotá working for another Liberal newspaper, *El Espectador*. By now there was a dictatorship in charge of the country. García Márquez worked first as a film critic and then as a reporter and in just a few months, in difficult political circumstances, was recognised as one of the most talented investigative journalists in the country.

In July 1955 the newspaper sent him to Europe. After a brief visit to Geneva he moved to Rome, where he was interested in studying cinema, especially Italian neorealism; he also made a clandestine trip to Eastern Europe (by now he was taking a serious interest in socialist politics) and then moved to Paris at the beginning of 1956. Only weeks into his stay the government closed down *El Espectador* and García Márquez cashed in his return ticket, determined to scrape by in Paris while trying to write more novels. He began with a work which would eventually be entitled *La mala hora* (*In Evil Hour*) but set it aside for another more focused novel, to be entitled *El coronel no tiene quien le escriba* (*No One Writes to the Colonel*), which he completed by the end of the year though it would not be published until 1961. Set in an unnamed town closely based on Sucre, it was a book whose claim to classic status would not be recognised for many years.

After completing the novel García Márquez made an extended visit to Eastern Europe, including the Soviet Union, and then spent a few weeks in London where he wrote some of the stories which would eventually make up the collection *Los funerales de la Mamá Grande* (*Big Mama's Funeral and Other Stories*). After that he moved to Caracas, Venezuela, where his friend Plinio Mendoza had found him a job on a magazine called *Momento*. His first days coincided with the overthrow of the notorious dictator Pérez Jiménez and at the end of the year the most momentous event in twentieth-century Latin American history was to take place: the Cuban Revolution. By then García Márquez had married his childhood sweetheart, Mercedes Barcha.

Nevertheless, he flew to Cuba in the early weeks of the revolution and accepted a job as a representative of its new press agency, Prensa Latina, in Bogotá. He spent several months in Cuba and was then sent to the Prensa Latina office in New York at the time when US-backed mercenaries were about to launch an unsuccessful invasion at the Bay of Pigs.

Despite the revolution's triumph, García Márquez had difficulties with the communist hard-liners in the office and eventually opted to leave Prensa Latina and look for work – hopefully in the cinema – in Mexico. There he, Mercedes and their sons Rodrigo and Gonzalo, born in 1958 and 1962, lived a difficult existence – he worked in tabloid-style journalism, public relations and eventually script-writing – until finally, in mid 1965, he had an epiphanic experience while driving his car to Acapulco and returned to Mexico City, inspired, to write what he would later call *Cien años de soledad* (*One Hundred Years of Solitude*), one of the twentieth century's most important novels and undoubtedly the most celebrated book ever published in Latin America. It took him a year to write, full time, with Mercedes pawning many of the family's possessions while he did it, but by the time the novel was finished friends of his like the Mexican writer Carlos Fuentes, a leader of Latin America's so-called literary 'Boom', were hailing it as one of the masterworks of the continent.

The novel was published in Buenos Aires in 1967 and caused an immediate sensation. Realising that he was going to be able to live off his writing, one of the first Latin American writers ever to do so, García Márquez took his family to live in Barcelona, Spain, where his literary agent lived and where the Franco dictatorship was in its last decade. A new friend, the Peruvian novelist Mario Vargas Llosa, would soon follow him to the city. García Márquez, now a celebrity, began to write his next novel, about an ancient Latin American dictator, and this book, *El otoño del patriarca* (*The Autumn of the Patriarch*), with hundreds of thousands of readers impatiently waiting for it, was finally published in 1975. By the end of the 1960s Latin America had fallen prey to a new era of dictatorship and García Márquez's novel, produced under the pressure of huge expectation, was not only a portrait of a Latin American tyrant but also an autobiographical work written by a man who had been sucked from one day to the next into a whirlwind of celebrity previously unknown in the continent.

By that time the so-called Padilla Affair in Cuba (1971), a litmus test for the relation between literature and politics in Latin America, had divided the continent's writers into two hostile camps and helped to put an end to the 'Boom', of which García Márquez was the brightest star. He took the side of the Cuban communist regime during the Padilla Affair, a decision which would have far-reaching effects on the rest of his life. In 1973, when Salvador Allende's socialist government was overthrown in Chile, García Márquez vowed that he would publish no more fiction after *The Autumn of the Patriarch* until the leaders of the coup were themselves overthrown. He turned to political journalism and campaigning and founded a radical socialist magazine in Bogotá called *Alternativa*; he also left Europe and took up residence again in Mexico City, this time for good.

In 1975 – shortly after the time, ironically enough, when he completed *The Autumn of the Patriarch* – García Márquez forged a relationship with Fidel Castro, the leader of the Cuban regime, and put his pen at the service of Latin America's leftist revolutions, including the Sandinista movement in Nicaragua (1979). But this was an era of counter-revolution almost everywhere in the world and by 1981 he had recognised that his contribution had to be more subtle: he published a new, brief novel, *Crónica de una muerte anunciada* (*Chronicle of a Death Foretold*), apparently devoid of political militancy, whose first edition sold more copies than that of any previous novel in history and whose title is quoted or paraphrased in newspaper headlines every day. At the same time he began to seek a more discreet political role behind the scenes. He was assisted in this transition from politics to diplomacy by the award in 1982 of the Nobel Prize in Literature. His journey to Stockholm was nothing short of an apotheosis and he was recognised as perhaps the most popular winner of the accolade in recent times.

Up to this point he had concentrated in his fiction on the themes of power, solitude and political violence. Now, aware of the need to keep up morale in an exceptionally bleak era for socialists, and thus complementing his move away from overt political militancy, he turned to writing about personal relationships and more specifically about love, a theme largely absent from his earlier work. Late in 1985 he published perhaps his most popular book, *El amor en los tiempos del cólera* (*Love in the Time of Cholera*), an historical novel inspired in part by his parents' anecdotes about their dramatic courtship in the 1920s. With this he demonstrated that he was not going to be one of those writers distracted or intimidated by the Nobel award.

In 1989, as the events leading to the fall of the Berlin Wall began to develop, García Márquez published one of his most risky and ambitious books, a novel entitled *El general en su laberinto* (*The General in His Labyrinth*) about the last months in the life of the great Liberator, Simón Bolívar, a Latin American leader even more famous and influential than García Márquez's friend Fidel Castro. Some readers protested that the book distorted Bolívar's profile by turning him into a Caribbean personality like García Márquez himself but most critics were astonished by the work's achievement in painting a convincing and eventually influential portrait of so notable a central character.

By now García Márquez was one of the four or five best-known and most admired writers in the world. He counted many presidents and other celebrities among his friends, including Spain's Felipe González and France's François Mitterrand. To coincide with the celebrations in 1992 marking the five hundredth anniversary of Spain's 'discovery' of the Americas, he published a collection of stories, *Cuentos peregrinos* (*Strange Pilgrims*), which took an ironic view of the relation between the New World and the Old. He followed this up in 1994 with another historical novel about love, *Del amor y otros demonios* (*Of Love and Other Demons*), a drama about the affair between a teenager accused of witchcraft and a Catholic priest in late eighteenth-century Cartagena.

Meanwhile Colombia, as if its twentieth-century experience were not already dark enough, was undergoing one of the worst periods in its entire history: a time of drug traffickers, guerrilla movements, paramilitary atrocities, a national army barely under civilian control and countless bomb explosions and political assassinations. García Márquez, who never had much faith that Colombia could reform itself, as Mexico had done, still less revolutionise itself, as Cuba had done, broke the habit of almost forty years and once again wrote a work (like *In Evil Hour*, or *The Colonel*) about the contemporary situation. *Noticia de un secuestro* (*News of a Kidnapping*) was a kind of documentary novel about the wave of political kidnappings which had hit the country at the beginning of the 1990s and was another international success for its author.

In 1999 García Márquez was stricken with lymphoma – he had had an earlier brush with cancer in 1992 – and retired from public life for almost three years while recovering from the illness. He began to write a more nostalgic kind of work suffused in part by the sense that his vital trajectory was coming to a close and in part by his tacit renunciation of political activism in the era of post-socialist globalisation. He had been talking for decades about writing his memoirs and concentrated now on the first volume, which he would entitle *Vivir para contarla* (*Living to Tell the Tale*). The work became an international bestseller on its publication in 2002. In the following years García Márquez began to appear again in public but no longer gave interviews to the always insatiable press. He worked on what appears to be his last novel, *Memoria de mis putas tristes* (*Memories of My Melancholy Whores*), a somewhat startling account of the relationship between a ninety-year-old bachelor and a fourteen-year-old virgin procured as a prostitute for the purpose of satisfying the old reprobate. Even this book was well received, on the whole, when it appeared in 2004, though it lacked the brilliance and the hypnotic power of earlier works.

In 2007 the Spanish Royal Academy marked García Márquez's eightieth birthday with a special homage at its conference in Cartagena, Colombia, where the writer had had a large house built as a Caribbean holiday home. Explicitly comparing him to Cervantes, the academy published a special edition of a million copies of *One Hundred Years of Solitude*. The king of Spain, ex-president Bill Clinton of the United States and several ex-presidents of Colombia were in attendance, as well as literary friends such as Carlos Fuentes and the Argentinian writer Tomás Eloy Martínez. García Márquez made a speech in which he recalled the hard times during which he had written his most famous novel and expressed astonishment at the direction his life had taken. By now his memory was failing and after this he never again subjected himself to such public challenges.

Chapter 2

Early short stories, journalism and a first (modernist) novel, *Leaf Storm* (1947–1955)

The first short stories   *12*
The early journalism   *16*
Leaf Storm   *21*

How does a child born in a small tropical town grow up to become a great writer?

As a small boy Gabriel García Márquez drew accomplished pictures well before he could read and write, and his early experience in a Montessori school may have helped him acquire the remarkable sensuality and plasticity so evident in his literary art. The first work he remembered reading was the *One Thousand and One Nights*, in which Scheherazade manages to survive by enchanting the murderous caliph with the hypnotic beauty of her storytelling – an appropriate antecedent, perhaps, for any Latin American child wishing to be a writer in that most politically risky of continents. Later, adding to the exotic impact of that magical serial, he read such typical boyish adventure stories as *The Count of Monte Cristo*, *Treasure Island* and the tales of Salgari, novels written by masters of narrative, the sort of books which some writers forswear as they become more sophisticated but which for him remained eternal classics of the storyteller's art.

In high school in Zipaquirá, as a romantic adolescent, he turned to poetry. Few countries in Latin America were traditionally more committed to poetry, as against the novel, than Colombia. (Chile and Nicaragua would be two further examples.) In the 1940s, when García Márquez was a student, Colombian poetry boasted a movement called Piedra y Cielo (Stone and Sky), effectively a national continuation of the avant-garde movements in Spain and Latin America in the 1920s and 1930s, whose most notable representatives were Spain's Federico García Lorca and Chile's Pablo Neruda – though all the poets of their generation owed a vast debt to the end-of-the-century Nicaraguan modernist Rubén Darío, whom García Márquez himself would always revere.

Those movements, at the same time that they carved out a new internationalist aesthetic, also rehabilitated the great poets of the Spanish Golden Age (Garcilaso and Quevedo, but most of all Luis de Góngora), writers whom García Márquez would quote throughout his life. Although he would later renounce his own early efforts as immature and unoriginal, García Márquez was a talented adolescent poet and could probably have made his name in the genre. Certainly he worked hard enough at it, in this very favourable cultural climate, to give himself a personal poetics, with a gift for striking images and an elegance of balance and rhythm, which, although always under firm control, would make him at once one of the most original as well as one of the most classical exponents of Latin American narrative prose.

The school in Zipaquirá encouraged poetry, certainly; but many of its teachers were left-wing Liberals and even Marxists, and García Márquez also acquired a materialist world view which gave him a purchase, from an early age, on the nature of politics and the direction of history. This would be invaluable not only in his fiction but in his work as a journalist. He also explored some of the works of Freud. However rudimentary these appreciations may have been, his secondary education gave him a significant early insight into some of the most influential works of the twentieth century combined with a profound sense of the different functions of 'poetry' and 'prose' and the potential for their fusion in literary expression.

García Márquez, by then a first-year law student at the National University, began writing his first short stories in September 1947 in response to a challenge famously issued in one of the capital city's leading Liberal newspapers, *El Espectador*, by the writer Eduardo Zalamea Borda. Zalamea said that Colombia had never been a home of the short story and he would like to see the new generation improve on the undistinguished performance of previous writers. García Márquez sat straight down, quickly produced a story entitled 'The Third Resignation', and found himself lionised in the national press at the age of twenty. A second story, 'The Other Side of Death', was published within a few weeks.

The first short stories

We can say now, all these years later, that García Márquez would be well known in Latin America as a great short story writer even if he had never written a novel. It would be difficult to argue, as many do argue in the case of his fellow 'Boom' writer Julio Cortázar (Argentina, 1914–84, author of *Hopscotch*, 1963), that García Márquez's stories are even better than the undeniably outstanding novels; but they are certainly more distinguished than the stories of either of his other 'Boom' colleagues, Carlos Fuentes (Mexico, 1928–) or Mario Vargas Llosa (Peru, 1936–). Indeed, simply as a short story writer, García Márquez can compete with top-rank exponents such as Machado de Assis (Brazil, 1839–1908), Horacio Quiroga (Uruguay, 1878–1937), Jorge Luis Borges (Argentina, 1899–1986), Juan Rulfo (Mexico, 1917–86) or Cortázar himself, and stands above almost all other Latin American short story writers of the twentieth century.

García Márquez has said that from the very beginning he believed the short story was the superior genre: 'I thought that the short story and the novel were not only two quite different literary genres but two such different organisms that it would be dangerous to confuse them. I still think the same today and I am more convinced than ever of the supremacy of the short story over the novel.'[1] The short story, he thought, was a more difficult and more artistic form, and a serious writer had to invest just as much effort and invention into starting and finishing a short story as – for example – Tolstoy had in starting and finishing *War and Peace*.

By now there are some thirty-eight stories published in four collections, all of which have been translated into English.[2] Taken as a whole, they reflect their writer's journeys around Colombia, Latin America and Europe: over the years he would write stories everywhere he went. Those of the first collection, *Eyes of a Blue Dog* (*Ojos de perro azul*), all written in Colombia, are set not so much in places (even though García Márquez must have had Bogotá, Cartagena and Barranquilla in mind) as in literary zones of influence: they recall Poe, Kafka, Woolf, Faulkner or Hemingway. At this time García Márquez was still a literary apprentice learning his trade. By contrast, the stories of the second collection, *Big Mama's Funeral* (*Los funerales de la Mamá Grande*, 1962), mainly written in London and Caracas, would be fully mature compositions, markedly realist works set in two literary communities, 'Macondo' (largely based on Aracataca) and 'the Town' (largely based on Sucre). The third collection, *Eréndira and Other Stories* (*La increíble y triste historia de la cándida Eréndira y de su abuela desalmada*, 1972), mainly written in Barcelona, would comprise 'magical realist' works set on Colombia's Caribbean coast and in the Guajira. And the stories of the fourth collection, *Strange Pilgrims* (*Cuentos peregrinos*, 1992), written in many different places over a long period of time, would be whimsical or fantastic works set in Europe.[3]

The earliest stories, eventually collected together in 1975, after García Márquez became famous, under the title *Eyes of a Blue Dog*, had been published in newspapers between 1947 and 1952 and would never have been anthologised by the writer himself. He was reluctant to allow the publication of what he considered novice works (he exempted 'The Night of the Curlews' from this description) and was only persuaded when his agent in Barcelona convinced him that if he didn't publish them, others – mainly pirates – undoubtedly would. These first stories were written in Bogotá in 1947–8, Cartagena 1948–9, and Barranquilla in 1950.* They are a wonderfully revealing guide to the first experimental steps taken by a great author in an unknown Third World country midway through the twentieth century.

In general, these very early stories show us a writer who is exploring the universe (time, space, matter, spirit, idea, life, death, corruption, burial) and, more specifically, the relation of human perception – our senses – to that surrounding world. This is what the modernists of the early twentieth century – Proust, Kafka, Joyce, Woolf, Faulkner, Huxley – taught writers to do. Thus García Márquez is learning narrative technique but in order to do so he is exploring the relation between the world and our body, between sense perceptions and ideas, materiality and thought, sensation and emotion, metaphysics and surrealism. And this structure of knowledge and literary strategy, once explicitly explored and elaborated, will become *implicit* later, and he will use aspects of it at will, for maximum effect.

To the exploration of the universe and humanity in their abstract materiality García Márquez, alone and without any help from Hispanic literature, attaches the essential Latin American questions of *genealogy* (*estar*: being as existence, history) and *identity* (*ser*: being as essence, myth): between them they make up *the* Latin American problematic of the nineteenth and twentieth centuries. Genealogy – and its corollary, legitimacy – is inevitably a crucial problem in a continent whose identity has been vitiated, where everything seems up for grabs. It is impossible to escape from our biological, family destiny; yet it is impossible to fully know it or control it. García Márquez in Bogotá feels totally isolated, yet he knows he is tied to others by blood – giving his quest a Darwinian twist – and by history and seeks to explore the implications. These first stories, then, are explorations, exercises, excursions in which García Márquez tries to find out who he is as a person, as a writer and as an inhabitant of the cosmos.

---

* The stories of *Eyes of a Blue Dog* are 'The Third Resignation' (*El Espectador*, Bogotá, 13 September 1947), 'Eva is Inside Her Cat' (*EE*, 25 October 1947), 'The Other Side of Death' (*EE*, 25 July 1948), 'Dialogue with the Mirror' (*EE*, 23 January 1949), 'Bitterness for Three Sleepwalkers' (*EE*, 13 November 1949), 'Eyes of a Blue Dog' (*EE*, 18 June 1950), 'The Night of the Curlews' (*Crónica*, 29 June 1950), 'Someone Has Been Disarranging These Roses' (*Crónica*, 2 December 1950), 'Nabo: The Black Man Who Made the Angels Wait' (*EE*, 18 March 1951), 'The Woman Who Came at Six O'Clock' (*Crónica*, Barranquilla, 24 June 1950) and 'Monologue of Isabel Watching it Rain in Macondo' (published 24 December 1952 in *El Heraldo* and announced as a fragment of *Leaf Storm*).

'The Third Resignation' (1947), the first story, about a young man who died at the age of seven but has never decayed or been buried, is a remarkable beginning. The protagonist is dead in his coffin but still conscious, still growing and preparing himself, in a state of terror, to die all over again. Although clearly a novice work, the story is strikingly ambitious and already sounds something like the future 'García Márquez'. It is, however, a García Márquez influenced by Kafka and Poe, writing in a cold – and cold-hearted – city from which he feels alienated and which, in general, he will, as far as possible, exclude from his later writing. The story is based on what will become a twin obsession in García Márquez's fiction: first, the idea that people may be dead yet still alive; and second, logically connected to this, the theme of burial and, in particular, the terror of being buried alive. (Before being born, of course, we are 'buried' inside our mother: the protagonist of this story finds himself 'swimming in his own sweat, in a thick, viscous liquid, just as he swam in his mother's womb before he was born'.)[4]

If the first story is a reflection on one's own death, the second, 'The Other Side of Death' (1948), is more a reflection on the death of others (or the death of one's own other, one's double). Appropriately, therefore, the narrative voice alternates between a 'he' and an 'I'. Again we are implicitly in a city, but now the theme of the twin, the double identity, the mirror (including that internal mirror, our consciousness), predominates. But again death prevails over all and the smell of formaldehyde appears in the second sentence: there is a strong emphasis on the body as a site of horror. The idea of a recurrent dream, impossible to interpret, appears. External sense perceptions are contrasted with inner ones, as the nightmarish brother emerges, 'another body, rather, that was coming from beyond his, that had been sunken with him in the liquid night of the maternal womb and was climbing up with him through the branches of an ancient genealogy; that was with him in the blood of his four pairs of great-grandparents and that came from way back, from the beginning of the world, sustaining with its weight, with its mysterious presence, the whole universal balance'.[5]

In the simplest terms one might say that the first five early stories – 'The Third Resignation', 'Eva is Inside Her Cat', 'The Other Side of Death', 'Dialogue with the Mirror' and 'Eyes of a Blue Dog' – are absurdist or existentialist works: all are strange, ghostly, dreamlike, about people who don't know who or where they are, whether they are awake or dreaming, alive or dead, encoded versions of García Márquez's anguished quest for *personal* identity in the alien environment of Bogotá while looking back at his childhood and adolescence on the Costa in the light of his reading of Dostoyevsky, Kafka and possibly Edgar Allen Poe.[6]

The remaining stories in the collection are similarly encoded versions of his quest for *literary* identity: there is already something Faulknerian about 'Bitterness for Three Sleepwalkers', 'Someone Has Been Disarranging These Roses' and 'Nabo: The Black Man Who Made the Angels Wait'; while 'The Woman Who

Came at Six O'Clock', about a prostitute who has just killed an abusive client and is hoping to establish an alibi in the restaurant she visits every evening, is much more realistic and directly reminiscent of Hemingway. 'The Night of the Curlews', inspired by a Colombian superstition, is a brilliant harbinger of the magical realist mode to come: in it, three drunkards are left blind after having their eyes pecked out by curlews in a patio. The last story, 'Monologue of Isabel Watching it Rain in Macondo', is a long section excluded from the novel *Leaf Storm*. It shows how ruthless the writer always was in terms of securing the unity and coherence of his works, because in and of itself this is one of the most striking texts he ever wrote but it was discarded because it was surplus to requirements in the novel for which it was written. Reminiscent of nothing and no one as much as the mature García Márquez, one feels that it should really have been included in his second collection, *Big Mama's Funeral*, not this first one.[7]

The early journalism

It was due to the violent consequences of the *Bogotazo* that García Márquez became a journalist in May 1948, only six months after his first short stories were published. Those first stories had been printed, as we have noted, in a newspaper: the normal practice in those days in countries where relatively few people were fully literate and it was difficult to get books published. Indeed, since the '*modernista*' period of the late nineteenth century,[8] the journalism of the majority of Latin American writers has been closer to 'literature' than newspaper writing as usually understood in Europe and the United States – largely restricted, since the Second World War, to investigative reporting or opinion columns, especially political ones. In fact, the form most Latin American writers have traditionally employed is the *crónica* (chronicle), a short essentially literary piece involving a variable mixture of genres: an article, a commentary, an interview turned into a story, a portrait of a writer, a book review, an imaginative or openly literary essay, an autobiographical note or travel diary – in short, a potpourri, a bridge between literature and journalism proper.

García Márquez's journalism has involved many different genres and styles, from traditional *crónicas* of the kind just mentioned to investigative reporting, from political interventions to film criticism. It is an activity which, like his narrative fiction, has stretched over sixty years, and it must be considered extraordinary that one of Latin America's greatest novelists and short story writers is also one of the most notable journalists that Latin America – and not only Latin America – has known. (Almost none of this journalism, unfortunately, has been translated into English.)

In effect, unlike most writers, who mainly live quite solitary and self-absorbed lives, García Márquez has been an activist. Indeed, such an activist personality has he been that in terms of journalism he eventually founded his own organisation, the Foundation for New Latin American Journalism (the FNPI), in Cartagena in 1994; he has also run several magazines, starting when he was twenty-three; helped to fund the political journal *Alternativa* in Bogotá in 1974; tried to start his own newspaper, *El Otro*, after winning the Nobel Prize in 1982; and bought the Colombian weekly magazine *Cambio* in 1999. In terms of cinema, he founded two international film organisations, the Foundation for New Latin American Cinema and the International School for Cinema and Television in Havana in 1986, and also his own film company. Moreover, after writing his first historical novel, *The General in His Labyrinth*, in 1989, he gave serious thought to creating a foundation for the study of history as well as beginning to give the occasional workshop about storytelling.

Storytelling, indeed, is García Márquez's most obvious talent. It is a much rarer ability than one might think. All writers have to have a more or less coherent world view, which is the structure, or, to put it more diffusely, the magma, behind or beneath their works. In a way, this 'magma' connects the structure of the world with the experience of the person, notably the writer. Some writers, more given to experimentalism, spend their entire time, or most of their time, exploring – and hence deepening, broadening – this magma. Others leave it unspoken and prefer to concentrate upon telling a story in a more or less straightforward way. One might remark that back in Cervantes's era the structure or magma was mainly explored by poetry – Quevedo, Góngora – whereas he, Cervantes, initiated a form of writing in which structure was mainly subordinate to narrative, society to history, synchrony to diachrony. In the nineteenth century the impressionists and in the twentieth century the modernists deconstructed the traditional – 'realist' or 'naturalist' – approach to narrative by showing how much every narrative emerges out of the magma which is the experience of life or reality stored and organised in our mind, or brain.

García Márquez's induction into journalism may seem casual, a mere matter of chance, and in a way it was (it happened as it did because of the 1948 *Bogotazo*); but it is also true that García Márquez had been a kind of journalist very early – he reported on school activities in the Colegio San José in Barranquilla – and that as a child, encouraged by his grandfather, he had always tried to convert or 'adapt' films he had seen into oral or graphic stories. In other words, he had the instincts of a journalist and he would probably have become a professional journalist sooner or later, in the Latin American situation, whatever the political context. Like Mark Twain or Ernest Hemingway, García Márquez, though as subtle as any other writer in terms of his underlying view of the world (his intuition of the 'magma'), was almost always more committed to 'story' than to 'structure' in the sense I am using here. (The great exception would be *The Autumn of the Patriarch*: see Chapter 5). This is why, in part, he decided, in a country of poets, not to be a poet.

Though it is true that, statistically speaking, most of García Márquez's newspaper work has been, inevitably, through the medium of 'chronicles', one of the most interesting things about him is that he has distinguished himself in almost every kind of journalism. In the mid 1950s he would become the most successful reporter in Colombia, with a series of sensational scoops and exposés, demonstrating in the process that reporting too can benefit from the virtues of the master storyteller – both in the choice, analysis and structuring of the subject and in the talent to narrate it without ever letting the reader's attention escape. It is this kind of journalism, not the literary kind, that García Márquez has always most enjoyed.

In practice, therefore, it is not easy to categorise García Márquez's journalism either in terms of chronological periods or in terms of activities or in terms of types or genres of writing. The truth is that he has done almost everything; his breadth of experience and expression is quite extraordinary.

We may identify three major periods of journalism, broadly defined, in García Márquez's life: what we may call the Formative Period: 1948–63;[9] the period of his Political Journalism: 1974–80; and the era of World-Wide Fame and Personal Freedom: 1980–*c*. 2000. The second period is uncomplicated and unambiguous but the first and last periods are complex and involve several or many different activities, many different newspapers and magazines, and many different kinds of journalism, as well as activities directly or indirectly connected to journalism. (In the 1970s, for example, he participated in the famous Russell Tribunals, founded a human rights organisation named Habeas and was a member of the MacBride Commission set up by Unesco to examine the ownership, control and bias of the international press.)

During the first period García Márquez depended on journalism for his living and wrote several hundred articles of every description.[10] Between May 1948 and December 1949 he wrote more than forty signed 'chronicles' for *El Universal*, a Liberal newspaper in Cartagena directed by a brilliant journalist, Clemente Manuel Zabala, and many times that number of unsigned contributions. One of the young man's tasks was to sift through the cables coming off the teletype machine in order to select news items and propose topics for the commentary pieces and literary extrapolations that were so important in the journalism of those times. This daily practice must have given him an experience of the way in which the events of everyday life are transmuted into 'news', into 'stories' – just as he had turned movies into both comic strips and verbal narratives for his grandfather as a child in Aracataca. Journalists almost everywhere at this time were obliged to adopt the hands-on, sleeves-rolled-up approach of US journalistic practices and from the beginning García Márquez took to this like a duck to water. It would make him a very different sort of writer from the majority of his Latin American contemporaries, for whom France and French ways of doing things were still the models to follow in an age when France itself was beginning to lose its grip on modernity.

García Márquez's first sentence as a journalist was: 'We the inhabitants of this city had become accustomed to the metal throat which announced the evening curfew' (21 May 1948). His second piece began: 'I don't know what it is about the accordion's way of communicating that when we hear it our feelings become wrinkled. Forgive me, dear reader, for this attempt at a *greguería*' (22 May 1948). Thus his first article starts with a political reference and, implicitly, a rejection of the political class of Colombia which has introduced a state of siege and shut the country down; the next one begins with a reference to Colombia's popular culture, viewed (in its second sentence) in counterpoint with high culture (via the *greguerías* or distinctive word-games invented by the Spanish avant-garde writer Ramón Gómez de la Serna). It is a remarkable fact that these topics – politics and popular culture – and these points of view would both remain fundamental throughout the rest of his career. Notice also that the first article assumes a collective attitude with its initial 'we'; that the second also addresses his readers directly; and that both are not only effecting communication – written by a young writer who will later complain obsessively about his continent's solitude – but are also *about* the nature of communication: the curfew siren has an intimidating metal throat while the accordion gets its message across through sentiment.

More specifically, one might suspect that García Márquez's warning later in the first article that he is not going to become 'a man of goodwill' – his generation has been deceived, so they too will deceive – means that he will not be either a Liberal or a Conservative, that he will not 'play the [national, two-party] game' but instead will adopt an international perspective (socialist, communist, or who knows what). Ironically enough, this confession of 'untrustworthiness' is profoundly honest of García Márquez, a sign of his surprising and disconcerting integrity: that so early in his literary career he feels the public need to make such a statement. In an article published on 22 June 1948, 'We agree, dear friend and comrade', he would repeat the idea – 'No one can oblige us to be men of good will' – and would end with an awful, prescient reflection on the condition of Colombia: '"A bad peace is even worse than war". We should remember at this time the words of Tacitus, though there is surely no need for us to say why we should remember them.'

The second article is equally provocative in another way: in general, it declares his faith in and identification with his region's popular culture; and in particular, it declares his affection for the accordion, which is *mestizo* (of mixed blood, implicit in his depiction, though he doesn't say this explicitly), *illegitimate* (he even says *'bastard'* at one point), *proletarian* (he actually uses the word), *bohemian* and *vagabond*. This is quite a package; and it conveys García Márquez's vision of *himself* here at the beginning of his literary career. Just a few months later, in an article on the Cartagena Afro-Colombian writer Jorge Artel, he was implicitly calling for a literature at once local and continental which would represent 'our race' – an astonishing perspective for Colonel Márquez's grandson to adopt at the age of twenty-one – and thus give the Atlantic Coast 'an identity of its own' ('Un Jorge Artel continental', *El Universal*, 15 September 1948).

In one sense there could have been no worse time to become a journalist in Colombia. Censorship was imposed immediately after the events of April 1948, though less brutally on the coast than in the interior of the country. García Márquez began to practise journalism because of the *Violencia* but the *Violencia* severely limited what a journalist could do. For the next seven years, albeit with variable intensity, there would be continuously active government censorship.

Internationally, this was also an extraordinary time, one of the most intense and decisive moments of the entire twentieth century. By the time García Márquez finally made the decision to take hold of his own life and move to Barranquilla at the end of 1949, the new international system which would organise the world throughout the recently declared Cold War and beyond was firmly in place and would shape his life and career for the next forty years.

In *El Heraldo*, in Barranquilla, he would write 450 articles (almost half the articles he ever wrote): they were more competent, lucid, confident, humorous and authoritative; also, generally speaking, more euphoric and celebratory. He was at last himself. Even so, he continued with the pseudonym 'Séptimus', which he had assumed in Cartagena, inspired by the mad but visionary protagonist of Virginia Woolf's *Mrs Dalloway* ('Here is a young man who carries in him the greatest message in the world, and is, moreover, the happiest man in the world and the most miserable'), a novel he greatly admired; Woolf's Septimus was, significantly, a young man mortally damaged by history and politics. More humorously, however, Séptimus's daily column was entitled 'The Giraffe' ('La Jirafa'), a secret tribute to his adolescent Muse and future wife, Mercedes Barcha, noted for her long slim neck. No doubt he was also inspired by a Gómez de la Serna *greguería*, which says that 'the giraffe is a horse elongated by curiosity'.

By the time he quit Barranquilla three years later, he had built up an impressive body of literary journalism; yet he was only twenty-five when he left. He has been characteristically hard upon these early efforts, commenting in his memoir that they were just a 'mental gymnasium for my formation as a writer,

safe in the knowledge that they were mere alimentary materials with no commitment to the future'. There is truth in this statement, but from the very start
the 'Giraffes' carried a new radiance, even if they were often very low on content;
after all, there was still a censorship regime in place. García Márquez nevertheless maintained his political perspective – and impertinence – as far as possible,
with insolent articles on Eva Perón's visit to Europe (11 January 1950) and the
daily temptation to which the president of Colombia's barber was surely subjected as he shaved the tyrant's throat (16 March 1950). What really excited him
about journalism, however, was the idea of becoming a reporter, but for this he
would have to wait. In the meantime, he worked on ideas for a novel.

Leaf Storm

His first novel was to have been entitled 'The House'. It is no exaggeration to
say that this concept – 'the house' – would obsess him for two decades, yet the
novel he wanted to erect around it would repeatedly fail to get itself written
until at last, with *One Hundred Years of Solitude* in 1967, he found a way of
relativising and universalising his childhood experience and perception of his
family, his region and his nation – which would mean a complete transformation of the original idea for 'The House' and both the apotheosis and, ironically, the end of 'Macondo' and a turn to other topics.

In fact he would write three short novels in the decade 1950–60, all slowly
and with great difficulty; all would be difficult to publish. *Leaf Storm* (*La hojarasca*), the first of the three, would be an offshoot of 'The House'. It was written under the influence of Virginia Woolf and William Faulkner. (A reading of
his *As I Lay Dying* and her *Mrs Dalloway* would be the most suitable prepar-
ation for a reading of *Leaf Storm*. Then, after finishing it, readers should remind
themselves that García Márquez, working just twenty years after those writers,
in a Third World country, was only twenty-three when he wrote most of this
remarkable first book.) The second novel, *In Evil Hour* (*La mala hora*), would
be a turn away from such 'modernist' influences to another form of writing
influenced by Hemingway's short works, especially *The Old Man and the Sea*,
but above all by the cinema, especially Italian neorealism. *No One Writes to the
Colonel* (*El coronel no tiene quien le escriba*), one of his best-loved books, would
in its turn be an offshoot of *In Evil Hour*, though completed and published
before it and a much more successful novel – indeed, the highest achievement
of the author's 'realist' or 'neorealist' (rather than 'magical realist') phase.

Leaf Storm, begun in 1950 and essentially completed by 1952 but not published until 1955, is the first major work by García Márquez set in the fictional
town of Macondo, which is based on his birthplace, Aracataca. The house

inhabited by the central characters of the novel is, to all intents and purposes, his grandfather's house in Aracataca, the house in which García Márquez was born. The writing of the novel was inspired by a supremely emotional and symbolic moment in the writer's personal life: the return he made to that house in early 1950 with the mother who left him there with her parents when he was still a baby and did not return for seven years. (The reminiscences of the house itself are extremely precise: the boy remarks that he knows every corner by its smell and that he can walk around it blindfold. It may be worth noting that a bisected anagram of the Spanish word *hojarasca* would be very close to the words *hogar*, home, and *casa*, house.) In the novel a character, looking at this building just across the road, remarks: 'it looks distant, unknown'. What we have then is, simultaneously, a *return* and a *distancing* – clearly an extraordinarily powerful and defining experience with a dialectical fusion of the emotional and the intellectual, the past and the present.

Literature and life thus come together in multiple, complex ways. It is possible to argue that García Márquez's recent readings of Faulkner and Virginia Woolf, writers preoccupied with time, consciousness and memory, not only allowed him to structure the novel once the return journey had inspired him to write it: they had already allowed him to *live* the experience differently, to see it in the cinematographic way that the most distinctive twentieth-century novelists had made possible in the 1920s and 1930s. (The walk with his mother through the hot dusty streets they had not seen for so many years would also be the inspiration for his memorable story 'Tuesday Siesta'.)

The three central characters of the novel, a retired colonel, his daughter Isabel (the Isabel of 'Monologue of Isabel Watching it Rain in Macondo'), who has been abandoned by her husband, and her ten-year-old son, are closely based upon García Márquez himself, his mother Luisa Márquez de García, and his maternal grandfather, Colonel Nicolás Márquez. Luisa and Nicolás were the two most important people in García Márquez's childhood. In the novel the boy's father, Martín, has disappeared. In reality García Márquez's mother and father moved away *together* to Barranquilla and left him with his grandfather and grandmother; the stepmother, Adelaida, is an invention. Obviously this imaginative reorganisation allows García Márquez, who was hostile to his father in real life, to imagine a childhood quite different from – and for him much better than – it really was. The boy in the novel never once thinks about his father, never once wonders about him; though Isabel, for her part, fears that the boy may turn out just like his father.

The novel is set very precisely between 2.30 p.m. and 3.00 p.m. on 12 September 1928.[11] The three main characters are sitting in the house – across the street from their own – of a fourth character known to us only as 'the doctor': a friend of the colonel's, a foreigner, the crippled and embittered survivor of some European war at the turn of the century. This doctor has died overnight and the trio are watching over his corpse prior to its removal to the cemetery.[12] However, there are two major obstacles. First, the local priest is unwilling to bury the body in holy ground because the doctor has committed suicide; and, still more dramatically, the town mayor is reluctant to remove him at all because the doctor has been deeply unpopular in Macondo for the last ten years, ever since he refused to attend to the wounded after the army fired on protesters following a fraudulent election. (This too is more complex than it appears, however, because there is evidence that the townspeople had turned against the doctor, through gossip and rumour, years before the unrest.) This means that the novel is also a work of suspense: the reader knows that at the end of the half-hour the central characters will have to walk out into the street, like characters in a Western, and confront the hostility of the townsfolk: their lives may change forever. (In the event, predictably enough, the novel ends at the very moment when they get to their feet and prepare to go out: we will never know what happens to them.)

The colonel, evidently the most respected person in the town, is prepared to risk unpopularity even though the doctor had let him down also by seducing and impregnating Meme, the family maid (some people think he may even have killed her). We discover that he owes the doctor some important favours and in any case considers that he has a 'debt of honour' to ensure that his former friend is decently buried: this is the least that a civilised society should undertake to do for its people. (Clearly the theme bears some relation to Sophocles's classic *Antigone*, and García Márquez added an epigraph from that drama after this was pointed out to him; the significance of this influence should not be exaggerated, however; burial is an important theme not only in García Márquez's work but also in his own collection of personal obsessions.) Nevertheless, the reader feels that the colonel, brave as he is, has shown a certain weakness of character and resolve in taking his daughter to the doctor's house in order, perhaps, to arm himself with a moral and perhaps even physical shield. The daughter certainly thinks this (and she, far from being impressed by her father's behaviour, is embarrassed and shamed by his actions, fearful of 'what people will think'); but then she is doing the same thing by taking her son along; and the child himself doesn't know what to think. 'I don't know' is a phrase he repeats many times, sometimes followed by a 'Now I see'. Of course, unlike the other characters, he will have a lifetime in which to find out what this event was all about.

The three characters are of different ages and experience, have different knowledge, different moral visions and different levels of authority and power.

The colonel knows all the things that men of position and influence can know: for him, for example, the civil wars are lived history whereas his daughter Isabel really only understands her own family and a woman's limited experience of the town: for her, the civil wars and the flight to Macondo reside in the world of myth. The boy, in contrast, lives more in the eternal present of the realm of nature, yet even he, an apparent innocent, already seems distant to his mother, seems to feel adolescent homosexual desire for his friend Abraham and – boys will be boys – has a predatory attitude to birds and, sexually, to the idiot woman Lucrecia.

We know what these three characters are thinking (even when they themselves 'don't know what to think') because the entire novel is narrated through their respective first-person narratives. There is no narrative in the third person, which is the usual convention in novels, and there is no other narrator outside of the three characters mentioned (except for the narrator of an anonymous two-page prologue, added retrospectively by García Márquez, which gives a strange, almost mythological explanation of the decline of Macondo and anticipates its eventual destruction). A problem with this device, of course, is that it sometimes obliges the characters to think things they might not have thought (at least in explicit words) or to think in words they might not have used, in order to get essential information across to us; but all narrative techniques have their problems and limitations. (The enormous advantage of this method is that by simply juxtaposing sections instead of having to *explain* their connections a brief novel like *Leaf Storm* can pack as much information in its pages as a conventional novel two or three times as long.) There are twenty-eight fragments distributed through eleven numbered parts or chapters. The grandfather narrates twelve of them, Isabel ten and the boy six. But the novel both begins and ends with sections narrated by the boy, and the author makes us aware that only he, the boy, is able to escape from the ties which bind the other characters, and think about the future. The others have all been worn down, and to some extent defeated, by life.

As we can see, modernist novels like this one are puzzles: the reader has to work out the plot, the dimensions of time, space and sequence as if she were a detective, at the same time as she attempts to understand the more general structure of themes and meanings and the abstract questions of ideology and morality. Thus the point of each section is not so much – or not only – what happens as what clues to understanding are revealed. Isabel communicates the author's awareness of this to the reader when she says, guiltily, that her son has no idea why he has been brought to this house and is waiting for someone to 'decipher this dreadful riddle'; she, on the contrary, hopes that nobody will 'open that invisible door that is preventing him from penetrating beyond the range of his senses.'[13] Novelists often give tacit explanations of how their books are to be read and this is a classic example; chapter 5, similarly, gives a brilliant interspersing, reminiscent of Virginia Woolf, of Isabel's thoughts, the thoughts and activities of all the other women of the town – many of them knitting or sewing – and the heat in the streets and houses. It is like a symphony of time and space and Isabel herself comments that the women are weaving an immense 'sheet of gossip'. She also notes implicitly that time itself is a patriarchal imposition, one which imposes history: women find themselves imprisoned by both society and nature. (This interweaving also initiates a process of intertextuality between books: in this novel, characters who will feature in other novels and stories appear – the colonel, the priest Father Angel, the widow Rebeca – while others are just mentioned, notably Colonel Aureliano Buendía and the Duke of Marlborough.)

Needless to say, as the characters sit thinking about what is happening in the room during those painful thirty minutes they are also thinking back into the past – in the colonel's case as far back as the early 1870s, when he himself was a child.[14] Sometimes that past is very recent – for example, life back in their own house across the road just a few minutes ago. In other words, there is a 'present' plane of action which covers this half-hour in September 1928 and moves gradually through it and there is a long 'past' which goes back from 1928 to the 1870s, though particularly from the 1870s to 1918. Towards the end of the most memorable piece of writing in the entire novel, Isabel notes that 'the two times become reconciled',[15] which is, once again, what this novel will do finally with its two different time planes on its very last page.

The colonel remembers his own childhood, his marriage and the birth of his children, the civil war in which he fought and lost, the reluctant migration from the Guajira to Macondo,[16] the arrival of the banana company and the railway, the doctor's arrival during the war and the bitter electoral riots of 1918 when, after a few positive years, the doctor lost the affections of the town. (We never know the colonel's name, nor – as mentioned above – the doctor's, nor the mayor's, nor even the boy's, though, curiously, we know the names of all the female characters.) The colonel's daughter Isabel knows less about the family history and anyway, as a woman and a daughter, has a different view; she remembers her relationship with her apparently cynical and irresponsible husband Martín with a mixture of bemusement and scarcely suppressed bitterness; and cannot understand why her father is making such a point of principle about the fate of the disagreeable doctor's corpse. As for the boy, he is trying to understand what is going on with no one trying very hard to explain it to him; he thinks about the day at school he is missing and looks forward to adventures with his friends among the trees and down by the river.

The boy tries not to look at the corpse but he can't help it. He is confronted with the horror, the mystery and the finality of death. No one helps him to understand it (even as far as anyone could). But this death is surrounded by a tissue of moral and political questions and no one helps him with those either. He exists, it might be said, in a 'Victorian' world where most things are closed to children and where children are seen but not heard and hardly talked to. The colonel is a figure both respected and feared who is no longer powerful but still influential; the doctor, an outsider, is hated because, already a surly figure who had alienated the townsfolk years before (his wartime experiences had left him bitter and cynical), he refused to help them in their hour of need when the authorities fired on the demonstrators. When the doctor was alive he and the colonel had wide-ranging conversations which showed that, though both were 'men of the world', they lived in totally different moral universes: the colonel, himself the survivor of a brutal but low-level war, nevertheless clings to certain illusions about the meaning of life, about the essential good-ness of most human beings, and one's duty to one's fellow man and woman; the doctor, from a more jaded continent and a much more horrifying war (he is like a character from Conrad or Greene), no longer believes that life has any meaning or that human beings are essentially good – indeed, he thinks they are worse than animals and for this reason is a vegetarian. (Even the boy, at his own intuitive level, is acutely aware that all the things we eat – both animals and fruits – are dead and decaying and that we ourselves will further convert them into excrement.)

As the mother and child sit waiting and the colonel, more anxious than he wishes to let on, gives orders to his four Indian servants, the mayor and his men come and go and the townsfolk, perhaps in an ugly mood, are appearing at their windows, having been deterred from gathering in the streets. The whis-tle of the 2.30 p.m. train is heard as it disappears down the line and the cries of birds are heard outside from time to time. This is to underline the immediacy of the narrative. These characters not only think *thoughts* and feel *emotions*, but also feel *sensations*: they feel hot in their Sunday best in the asphyxiating room of death, they feel uncomfortable on their hard chairs, they see things, hear things, smell things (not least the corpse), and the boy feels a strong and dismaying urge to defecate. (In many ways smell is his strongest sensation, giving the reader a repeated impression of an atmosphere of corruption, decay and disgust.)

And behind all that we have mentioned up to now is the neocolonial reality of Macondo, its former status as a plantation town in the hands of the North American banana company which came for a few years and then left, giving prosperity and taking it away, and above all bringing the hated *hojarasca*, or leaf storm, the nomadic lower-class workers who follow the onward movement of the global economy: the traders, the hustlers and the prostitutes with their sordid pursuits and their life of crime. *Hojarasca* really means 'leaf trash', the dead leaves blown around after harvesting, and therefore suggests the decay and corruption not only of economic systems but of all things. 'Leaf Storm' is a striking translation but a misleading one which deprives the original not only of its social dimension but also of the more general theme of decline and decay.[17]

But why is the novel called '*La hojarasca*' anyway? It ought to be called 'The Doctor' or 'The Burial'. By the time the events take place the human leaf trash has long since disappeared, though the colonel appears to blame them and not the banana company for the town's decline and the Prologue expresses a similar view – they are a mythical explanation, some kind of *fatal force* – though there the idea of economic decline fuses into natural decay and regeneration (or 'fermentation').[18] Clearly, García Márquez has a more *historical* interpretation and critics who have claimed the novel has an 'upper-class' standpoint (García Márquez identifying with his grandfather, presumably) have failed to see the full subtlety of this book's interweaving of history, myth and ideology. The *hojarasca* may be 'the people' but they are certainly not the 'townspeople': they are outsiders, as indeed is the 'doctor' himself, though his social status protects him at first from unpleasant epithets. On returning to his birthplace in 1950, García Márquez evidently saw that 'Macondo' had already been swept away by a force which the inhabitants see as fate but which he sees as history; by 1959, when he writes his great story 'Big Mama's Funeral', he will want the whole of the Colombian establishment swept away.[19]

If we return to the remarkable ambition and achievement of his technical strategies – a precise organisation of time and space; a narrative told directly, yet interwoven like a tapestry, through the consciousness of several or many characters; and the direct communication not only of thoughts and feelings but also of physical sensations – we can see that this Colombian, in his early twenties, set out to write one of the first 'modernist' novels in Latin America – indeed, the very first in Colombia – and that he had undoubtedly been reading the works of writers like Joyce, Woolf and Faulkner and had already learned almost everything he needed. Joyce and Woolf were city writers, but Faulkner had adapted modernist techniques to the rural environment and García Márquez had followed suit, triumphantly. It may be said, indeed, that he was the first member of those who would later be called the Latin American 'Boom' novelists to do so and that *Leaf Storm*, rarely viewed in this way, is the direct precursor of the first novel of the 'Boom', Carlos Fuentes's *Where the Air is Clear* (*La región más transparente*, Mexico, 1958).

And if we look at the complex and subtle social analysis – the contrast between different characters, the understanding of economic and political change and the way it may be perceived either historically or mythically – we can also see that this novel does indeed anticipate García Márquez's role as the greatest of all shapers of Latin American literary identity – and character – with his classic themes of defeat and death, certainly, but also obstinacy and courage in the face of these and, equally important, his classic tone – that of 'García Márquez' as compared with, say, 'Cervantes' – so much more attractive, so much more 'human', finally, than those of the equally brilliant Faulkner and Hemingway. (Like Cervantes, he had created a mood, a humour, indeed a sense of humour, which was instantly recognisable yet, once it came into existence, seemed to have always been there and was an integral part of the world to which it referred.) *Leaf Storm* has always been judged unfairly from the retrospective standpoint of *One Hundred Years of Solitude*, which is ironic since it so totally foreshadows it, especially in the aspect of myth. Simply on its own terms it is a fine novel (with one or two technical flaws), not to say an astonishing one for a writer of García Márquez's age in 1950–52, when it was written.

Chapter 3

The neorealist turn: *In Evil Hour, No One Writes to the Colonel* and *Big Mama's Funeral* (1956–1962)

In Evil Hour   32
No One Writes to the Colonel   36
Big Mama's Funeral (published 1962)   40

At the end of 1953, after completing *Leaf Storm*, García Márquez moved to Bogotá to work for *El Espectador*, the great newspaper of his life (with *El Heraldo* a close second and *El Universal* third). It was in that great Liberal daily that his first stories were published in 1947; there that he became one of Colombia's first cinema critics and a stellar reporter during 1954–5; and there that he would choose to publish his classic articles during the 1980–84 period.

After completing *Leaf Storm* he had written another narrative set in Macondo, 'One Day After Saturday'. A long story, it had something of the human, geographical and historical spaciousness of a novel, in clear anticipation of *One Hundred Years of Solitude* itself. Several of the characters of the eventual novel appear in it and there is a 'magical realist' plague of birds dropping dead out of the sky. It received a prize in July 1954 for the best short story published in Colombia during the previous year; but by then García Márquez, who was now doing a different kind of journalism, in a city which always made him think in terms hostile to the national establishment, was beginning to conceive of literature in a different, more political way.

For one thing, he had begun to work as a film critic. His fast-evolving political ideology at the time sharpened his sense that he had a chance to 'educate the people' and perhaps relieve them of the 'false consciousness' that made them prefer pre-packaged Hollywood products to the more aesthetically crafted works from France and, especially, those 'authentically' conceived and executed neorealist works from Italy which he particularly favoured. Italian neorealism – through the works of Vittorio de Sica and his script-writer Cesare Zavattini, Luchino Visconti and Roberto Rossellini – confirmed him in his enthusiasm for the cinema, brought about a change of direction in his fiction

(*No One Writes to the Colonel, In Evil Hour*) and sharpened his ambition to work as an investigative journalist.

This ambition was achieved in July 1954, the very month that he was anointed as that year's best story writer in Colombia thanks to 'One Day After Saturday'. His manager José Salgar had suggested that García Márquez go to Medellín to find out 'what really happened' in the 12 July landslide in Antioquia, where the hillside community out at La Media Luna, east of Medellín, had collapsed two weeks before with heavy loss of life. It would be the first of some eighty political and general-interest articles that he would write over the next year before his departure for Europe.

In this first report, as in all his future reportage, he rigorously sought out all the facts and reconstructed in minute detail how one thing led to another until the story was complete. Each account begins with a striking anecdote, before going back to the origin and reconstructing the narrative chain. This professional rigour would serve him well in his next novel, *No One Writes to the Colonel*. Now, it turned him overnight into a star reporter. This new writing, then, would have less to do with nouns and adjectives than with verbs: naming and describing – emphasised in *Leaf Storm* – now turned into telling; at last one of the twentieth century's greatest storytellers was getting his chance, in the very teeth of political censorship, and taking it with alacrity. Anyone wanting to know how a novice and dilettante turned into not only a reporter but also a world-class narrator should study the news reports García Márquez filed in 1954 and the first half of 1955.

Other important topics were the crisis in the department of the Chocó and the fate of the Colombian veterans returning from the Korean War to 'four thousand unhappy endings'. And 1955 would see the publication of García Márquez's most famous newspaper story. It was based on an immensely long interview, in fourteen sessions of four hours each, of a Colombian navy sailor called Luis Alejandro Velasco, the only survivor of eight crewmen who fell overboard from the destroyer *Caldas* when she rolled out of control in late February – supposedly during a storm – on the way back from refitting in Mobile, Alabama, to her home port of Cartagena. García Márquez made the decision to write the piece in the first person and publish it under Velasco's name, with the title 'The Truth About My Adventure'. His own name did not appear at all in the original version of the story. Many readers have found the tale as compelling as fiction like Defoe's *Robinson Crusoe* or historical narratives like the same author's *Journal of the Plague Year*. Many years later the story was re-published, after García Márquez became a world-famous writer. And he then appeared, reluctantly, as its author. It was entitled *The Story of a Shipwrecked Sailor* (*Relato de un náufrago*, 1970). Astonishingly, it became one of his most successful books, selling many millions of copies in the next forty years. No more persuasive proof could be sought for the fact that García Márquez was already a master storyteller in 1955.

In July 1955 *El Espectador* sent García Márquez to Europe. His main destination was Italy but his first assignment was to cover the negotiations between the representatives of the 'Big Four' nations – the Soviet Union, the United States, the United Kingdom and France – in Geneva. The 'Big Four' were the countries most actively engaged in the so-called Cold War. They each had negotiated control of a part of the defeated city of Berlin; they were also the countries with a veto at the United Nations Security Council and the countries which possessed or were well on the way to possessing nuclear weapons. Understanding between them was crucial if the world was to survive this unfamiliar and terrifying new era lived out under the shadow of global nuclear destruction.

García Márquez soon faced the fact that he was never, during his time in Europe, going to be able to carry out the direct investigation which had made him celebrated in Colombia nor, therefore, to achieve any spectacular scoops. He became aware, almost immediately, of the way in which, in the 'advanced' countries, the news was concocted – for example, what an advantage it was for a politician to have a lovable nickname, as the president of the United States did ('Ike'). That is why from the start his pieces were as much about him (already known as 'Gabo' to his friends), both implicitly and explicitly, as they were about the events he was meant to be reporting – as would later be the case with the 'new journalism' in the United States in the 1960s and 1970s. And from the start he showed that the news was made not by the rich and famous themselves but by the journalists who followed them around and turned them into 'stories' largely as and when they chose.

Moving to the Italy of *la dolce vita* and the *paparazzi*, he wrote a major series on the so-called Wilma Montesi scandal, about a murder mystery, which he worked on throughout August 1955, calling it, somewhat hyperbolically, 'the scandal of the century'. He wrote the whole set-piece report as a two-week series and sent the stories to Bogotá before taking part in the Venice film festival. From Venice he travelled to Czechoslovakia and Poland. However, no reports by García Márquez on those two countries would be published until his brief returns to them in the summer of 1957 when he travelled to East Germany, the USSR (VI World Youth Congress in Moscow) and Hungary. The reports on these journeys would finally appear in *Cromos*, Bogotá, in August 1959, under the title *90 Days Behind the Iron Curtain* (*De viaje por los países socialistas*). They make up a remarkable testimony of a moment, and a remarkably judicious and prescient analysis, by a friendly but critical observer, of the weaknesses of the Soviet system.

In mid December 1957, after a brief stay in London, García Márquez moved unexpectedly to Caracas, where he joined his friend Plinio Apuleyo Mendoza working for the magazine *Momento*. He would later describe his time in Venezuela as a period when he was 'happy and undocumented' (the eventual title of the book of articles he wrote in that country).

Having seen events on a world scale in Europe, he now began to witness Latin American history. The dictator Pérez Jiménez was overthrown shortly after García Márquez's arrival, and he and Mendoza produced a special number of *Momento*: they published its first ever editorial, 'Hello, Freedom' ('Buenos Días, Libertad'), written between them, and an extensive report, entitled 'The People in the Street' ('El pueblo en la calle'), with dramatic pictures taken by their staff photographers. García Márquez was in his element. He responded to the euphoria and the opportunities of the new environment as if he himself were a Venezuelan citizen and began to develop a more explicit rhetoric of human rights, justice and democracy than he had been able to express up to that time. Many readers have judged that his articles for *Momento* were among the best of his entire career. From almost the very beginning he was able to return to investigative reporting in a country living through one of the great moments of its history.

Then, quite suddenly, he and Mendoza left *Momento* following a dispute with its owner over the magazine's coverage of the controversial visit of US vice-president Richard Nixon. Mendoza managed to find García Márquez and himself another job in the Capriles group, one of Latin America's most powerful newspaper corporations. On 27 June 1958 García Márquez became editor in chief of the most frivolous of the Capriles magazines, *Venezuela Gráfica*, popularly known as 'Venezuela Pornográfica' because of the large number of scantily dressed 'vedettes' for which it was best known.

In Evil Hour

It was during this turbulent period that García Márquez's two neorealist novels were written. *In Evil Hour* is often considered García Márquez's weakest work and the author himself has often spoken disparagingly about it. *Leaf Storm* had been published just before he left for Italy in mid 1955 and he began this new novel, a Sucre-based book, set in 'the Town', under the influence of Italian neorealist cinema, towards the end of that year. He continued it after moving to Paris at the beginning of 1956 but by the end of the year had put it to one side in favour of a subplot about a retired colonel waiting for his pension: this would become *No One Writes to the Colonel*, one of his most critically admired books, which he completed, still in Paris, by early 1957.[1] When he moved to Venezuela at the end of 1957, he had become more interested in writing short stories; the earlier, still unfinished novel went with him, tied up with a necktie, and he continued to write it in a desultory fashion until he arrived in Mexico in 1961. Finally, he revised it one last time, still untitled – he wanted to call it 'This Shitty Town'[2] – to submit it for a literary prize in Colombia in 1962 and he won enough money to buy a car. Even then he was not grateful and the novel remained officially unloved.

Yet he had never thrown the manuscript away. And the truth is that *In Evil Hour*, while not giving us the satisfactions more normally associated with works by this author, has a number of important virtues, including the elementary one of usefulness. It is the pool from which most of the other works of this period – the novel *No One Writes to the Colonel* and the stories 'One of These Days', 'There Are No Thieves in This Town', 'Balthazar's Marvellous Afternoon', 'Montiel's Widow' and 'Artificial Roses' – flow and it also refers intertextually to characters from the Macondo cycles, including 'One Day After Saturday', 'Tuesday Siesta' and *One Hundred Years of Solitude* itself. Even Big Mama appears in a hallucination.

But in addition to its usefulness to those who want to fit the author's works together like a jigsaw puzzle, *In Evil Hour* is also a brilliant condensed mural of the politics of a small town lost in the river basins of northern Colombia and probably the best novel of its era about the early high tide of the nation's *Violencia* in the years after the assassination of Jorge Eliécer Gaitán.[3] During that period, from 1948 to the 1960s, perhaps 300,000 people were murdered, out of a population of between 10 and 15 million, mainly but not entirely by the Conservatives, many in the most humiliating and sadistic ways imaginable. Astonishingly, there are only two deaths in this book, one a civilian 'honour' crime which anticipates the central incident in the later *Chronicle of a Death Foretold*, and the other a more predictable political crime, which can stand for thousands of others carried out by the Conservative government – though in this novel as a result more of incompetence than of intent.

Yet even though *In Evil Hour* is a book with a political position, the word 'Conservative' does not appear in it (come to that, it doesn't need to: the politics of this book would be obvious to any Colombian reader of the era). The point, at any rate, is to show that the Conservatives do not kill people because they are evil (though they may be) or because they enjoy it (though they may do): they kill people because, in the conditions of this country, that is the only way in which they can control it. The military *alcalde* (mayor) of the town, directly appointed by the government, does all he can to keep the town 'peaceful' and 'progressive' (while feathering his own nest, naturally), but near the end of the novel he finds himself responsible for the death of one of the residents. He is 'sorry' but only in a political – a technical – sense (it has spoiled the impression of peace and progress, and now he will have to be more openly repressive again), not in any moral sense. This surprisingly dispassionate depiction of the nature of power takes the novelist far beyond the desire to moralise or engage in facile propaganda. All García Márquez's perceptions and critiques, many of them genuinely subtle, are shown through action and dialogue, as in a film: there is almost no overt commentary.

When the modernist *Leaf Storm* was published just before he left for Europe, García Márquez's socialist and communist friends had commented that although the book was, naturally, brilliant, there was too much myth and poetry, too much virtuoso 'technicism'; form had prevailed over content, the book was much too 'indirect', it didn't 'expose' or 'denounce' anything, it wasn't politically 'committed'. (This was wholly untrue, though it was true that many of his modernist precursors in the 1920s and 1930s had in fact been 'apolitical' or 'escapist'; but that was not as a result of their technique.) What was needed was some updated version, such critics thought, of nineteenth-century realism. Indeed, for most communists – and García Márquez was a sympathiser at the time, though not a militant – the cinema was the twentieth century's only truly popular medium, an art form for the masses. As it happened, García Márquez had already become an admirer of Italian neorealist cinema in Bogotá, particularly the great postwar films directed by De Sica and scripted by Zavattini, which is why he went to study cinema in Rome and began to write a novel – *In Evil Hour* – based on the neorealist aesthetic. (The films of De Sica were 'realistic' but no one could say that they were not 'artistic'.)

In Evil Hour is set in an unnamed town by a river. All attention focuses on the square and the landing boardwalk. No novel set in Macondo could have been so unremittingly grim, which is probably the main reason that most readers are not fond of this book. Even the humour is grim!

There is an astonishing number of characters for such a short work. (Some sixty or seventy appear or are referred to in a novel of only 180 pages.) There are many families but no complete or happy ones, and family life is not shown from within: this is a *social* novel. It is set, just as *No One Writes to the Colonel* will be, in October – the action takes seventeen days – and is dominated by torrential rain and asphyxiating heat. The unnamed mayor is the principal character. He is in tacit alliance with the formidable local priest, Father Angel, and the local landowning families (including the Asís family and Montiel's widow from the story of that name) and businessmen (notably the Liberal turncoat Don Sabas, who also appears in *The Colonel*). None of these alliances are spoken out but are bravely contested by the Liberal professionals, like the doctor and the dentist, almost always positive characters in this author's fiction; indeed, the priest would say that his own position was totally independent, but García Márquez's brilliant portrayal shows in minute detail just how he works to control and repress his parishioners and therefore in what ways the Church is normally a 'conservative' institution in Latin American countries.

Given the degree of repression, power over texts becomes very important. Here letters (liable to be censored, as the cinema is), political flysheets (*hojas clandestinas*) and anonymous posters (*pasquines*) dominate the scene. *Pasquines*, which play a pivotal role in this novel, are especially prevalent in the repressive conditions which have dominated life in Colombia for long periods; they usually involve malicious gossip and cause acute social tensions – including, for example, the murder that initiates the action in the novel. Thus they end the period of 'social peace' and bring the 'evil hour'. Occasionally they also have some political intention as well. (In García Márquez's works, those texts known as dreams and those other texts known as horoscopes are also always likely to appear; we cannot control our dreams and they may tell us meaningful things; and if we feel we cannot control our lives, it is tempting to resort to astrology as a way of anticipating our fate.)

So the characters live, resist and try to survive. They spend a lot of time sleeping – or trying to sleep – and tend to have dreams to relate when they wake up. They have sex, both legitimate and illicit. The weather makes them acutely aware of their bodies; but they also have lots of maladies (Sabas's diabetes), ailments (the mayor's tooth abscess) and illnesses, including hangovers and headaches: the doctor's and dentist's realm. They read books and see films; and the circus comes to town. They communicate anonymously, through the conservative medium of the *pasquín* (the priest's realm, so to speak: the realm of religious sin and 'voluntary' confession, which leads to the first death, the civilian murder of Pastor by César Montero) and the revolutionary medium of the *hoja clandestina* (the mayor's realm of interrogation and involuntary confession of political 'crimes', which leads to the second death, the military-judicial murder of Pepe Amador, who is then blamed after his death for the *pasquines*). The central character, without any doubt, is the military mayor, the man of action; but the next most important, and the one who opens and closes the novel, is the priest, Father Angel. Between them they decide who can do what, and the Church's services and censorship function in a not dissimilar way to the curfew. Between them, sometimes tacitly, sometimes explicitly, these two men run the town. Both, ironically, for all their power, are slaves to their vocation.

Although the subject matter is, to say the least, depressing, García Márquez controls his plot as tightly as the mayor controls his town. And for the first time he imposes on his novel an elementary and characteristic structure – still undetected by the critics after fifty years – of dividing the narrative into two halves. (Perhaps an outward journey and return? Or a rise to some 'high point' and fall to some 'end'? Or both these things and more?) In this novel he has not quite perfected the technique because the 'halfway' point comes at the end of the fifth chapter out of nine whereas later he would have marked the beginning of the second half at a point exactly halfway through chapter 5. (He will achieve this exactitude for the first time in *No One Writes to the Colonel*, in which the halfway point arrives by chapter, by word count and by the logic of the plot at one and the same time: one might call this a technique of *enjambement*, as in poems where a syntactic unit ends in the middle of a line.) This is the – invisible – García Márquez structural trademark.[4] Moreover, the technique frequently goes even further: not only does each book itself have a structurally decisive central moment dividing it – dramatically – in two halves; there is also a repeated tendency to divide each chapter into two halves as well. In that sense each chapter is really two chapters.

The way in which García Márquez sets about signalling the halfway mark in this novel is by thematic repetition, beginning in the first chapter with Father Angel getting up in the morning and asking, among other things, whether his servant Trinidad has managed to catch any mice in the church overnight; she tells him that she did (he is excited to hear this) and that *pasquines* were also found in the streets (he is less pleased by this news). At the beginning of chapter 6 he wakes again and makes the same inquiry; and at the end of the novel (the end of chapter 9), the action closes with, again, Father Angel, Trinidad, the mice and – expected by now – the discovery of more *pasquines* despite the reimposition of the curfew and the beginning of another brutal period of repression. This poetic use of motifs repeated at strategic moments, combined with a complex architecture built, nevertheless, on the classical symmetry and simplicity of two essential halves, gives García Márquez's novels an aesthetic underpinning which readers intuit and unconsciously appreciate but rarely consciously 'see'.

No One Writes to the Colonel

No One Writes to the Colonel was an offshoot of *In Evil Hour*. Whereas that novel was a dense yet panoramic portrayal of 'the Town' (Sucre), this one is intense and concentrated. And whereas *In Evil Hour* has some sixty characters and takes place in seventeen days, *No One Writes to the Colonel* has a mere twenty characters but takes place in a little over two months, with the central character, the colonel, appearing on every single page: this is why the novel, at less than 20,000 words, can be considered a novella or even a long short story.[5] The events take place from early October to early December 1956 (there are references to the Suez crisis). This means that *The Colonel* was written at the same time as the Colombian and Middle Eastern events it describes were taking place, and also during the period when García Márquez and a Spanish actress, Tachia Quintana, were engaged in an ill-fated affair in Paris (the novel is signed 'Paris, January 1957').

García Márquez has said that most of his novels and stories are inspired in the first instance by an image. In the case of *Leaf Storm* it was a boy – himself, of course, in his mind's eye – sitting on a chair with his legs dangling, waiting for something. *No One Writes to the Colonel* was based on the memory of an anguished-looking man García Márquez saw waiting on the dock at Barranquilla; but attached to this were other images and influences: the memory of his own grandfather waiting for his pension (although the character of the colonel in the novel is different); Vittorio de Sica's film *Umberto D.* about an old-age pensioner and his pet dog; and García Márquez's own drama with Tachia Quintana, which involved the death of their unborn baby.

A seventy-five-year-old colonel and his chronically asthmatic wife are struggling against poverty in a remote river town lost in the forests of northern Colombia.[6] He is a veteran of the Liberal army which fought in the War of the Thousand Days against the oppressive and undemocratic Conservative regime over fifty years before and for the last fifteen years he has been hoping to hear news of the pension which survivors of that conflict were promised by a recent government. ('For fifty-six years – since the end of the last civil war – the only thing the colonel had done was wait. October was one of the few things that arrived.')[7] Each day he walks to the post office to see if a letter has come but it never has: hence the title of the novel. In Spanish 'waiting' and 'hoping' are conveyed by the same word: '*esperar*'. Waiting, of course, is the fate of the powerless in Third World countries but not something, even there, which should happen to colonels. The postmaster says to him: 'The only thing that arrives for sure, colonel, is death.'[8] Now, however, as the Suez conflict takes place in the Old World and dominates the headlines, violent conflict has returned to this small, remote town, a curfew is in place and the atmosphere is heavy with menace. Violence may break out at any moment and indeed the unnamed colonel's only son Agustín, a tailor who was the old couple's only means of support but was involved in clandestine activities against the government, was killed by the military nine months before (the gestation period of a human baby: the colonel's wife remarks, 'We are the orphans of our son').[9] Since Agustín's death the economic situation of the grief-stricken colonel and his wife has gone from bad to worse, and by the time the novel begins they are going hungry but still trying desperately to keep up appearances.

If *In Evil Hour* and *No One Writes to the Colonel* are both cinematographic novels set in the same town at more or less the same moment in history, the first involves a wide-screen vision, dominated by long shots, whereas the second is, so to speak, a single case study narrated through a series of close-ups. The military mayor and Father Angel appear briefly in *The Colonel*, as do several other characters; but this novel revolves around the colonel, his wife, his ambiguous friend Don Sabas, the doctor, Agustín's three friends and of course the fighting cock. All the others are walk-on parts.[10]

The central drama of the novel revolves around Agustín's fighting cock, which the colonel has reluctantly inherited and which is thought to have championship potential. Agustín's friends,[11] also tailors and also involved in clandestine politics, are particularly interested in the future of the warrior bird, which becomes a symbol of resistance and hope not only for them but also – at first instinctively, later more consciously – for the whole of the town. The colonel tries at first to ignore this growing political reality but gradually comes to identify with the rooster, first as a way of keeping his son's memory alive and symbolically avenging him but then, slowly but surely, as a way of identifying with the political hopes and aspirations of the ordinary people of the town. At one point, outraged, the wife complains: 'They said the rooster wasn't ours but belongs to the whole town.'[12] So it proves.

At this point García Márquez's socialist ideology of the era is at its most visible. The cock symbolises hope, faith, resistance, optimism and human dignity; its survival is 'raising the consciousness' of the people through two of the very activities – sport and gambling – which usually promote 'false consciousness'. From a position of passivity and 'alienation', the colonel has moved into the 'vanguard' of political activity in the town. But so oblique are these ideological gestures and so wise and human the author's characterisation of the colonel, that the reader does not feel that the novel's truth is being unreasonably distorted; on the contrary, this is one of the great novels of political idealism.

The cock's training sessions are attended by dozens of people – who otherwise are not allowed free assembly – and the colonel looks forward to the new fighting season, months ahead, when the cock may start to earn money as it embarks on its hopefully glorious career. But in the meantime it too has to be fed – which, in due course, realising that the colonel is penniless, Agustín's friends volunteer to fund. All this brings the colonel into conflict with his own ailing wife who, despite her continuing grief over her son, believes that politics and fancy symbolism should be set aside in the interests of the struggle for survival: they have nothing to eat, and if they sell the fighting cock they can earn enough money to live with minimum decency for two or three years. For the colonel the cock is a positive way of remembering his son; for his wife it signifies male violence, which brings death, regardless of political persuasion. Despite their love and affection for each other, the old couple, after a lifetime together, find themselves at loggerheads. She says scornfully that he is now resigned to waiting and 'You can't eat illusions', to which he replies 'You can't eat them, but they can nourish you.'[13] She retorts, 'You have been waiting all of your life and now you are starving and completely alone.' He replies quietly, 'I am not alone.'[14]

Like many of García Márquez's novels, this one begins with a burial;[15] so beyond the question of the author's personal obsessions, it gives us once more the paradox of a work of art beginning with death: in other words with an ending. Structurally, there are seven brief chapters in the novel, each of about eleven pages, as if it were a week of seven days, though actually two months pass. There is much waking up and rising, much going to bed and falling asleep; also much talk of the weather; and each chapter falls naturally into two parts, possibly dictated unconsciously by the division between morning and evening – though by no means every chapter follows this pattern in practice. By contrast with this natural-mythical rhythm, the reality of the characters' waking and sleeping, their hopes and disappointments, is punctuated by intimidating church bells (moral pressure) and curfew trumpets (political pressure), in other words by historical rhythms.

It is in this novel that García Márquez definitively establishes the two-part structure mentioned in previous sections. The midpoint here occurs halfway through chapter 4 – through the technique of *enjambement* mentioned above – at the moment where both the wife's illness and the family budget fall into irremediable crisis and she and the colonel begin their bitter dispute: she wants the cock sold and the theme of politics (which killed her son) forgotten; they need to eat, and everything else should take second place in order to avoid them becoming a public spectacle and an object of other people's pity. He believes, implicitly, that politics cannot be forgotten precisely *because* it killed their son; and that dignity, finally, involves not giving in to external pressures. It is an insoluble problem, expertly conceived and expertly developed. And the moment when she shouts 'What are we going to eat?' both marks the halfway point and anticipates an even more bitter argument on exactly the same subject at the end of the novel. There, when she shrieks the same question at him, the colonel gives his famous answer: they will eat shit.[16] What he means, of course – beyond implicitly trying to shut his unfortunate wife up with this totally uncharacteristic vulgarity – is that they have been 'eating shit' for years: their entire life is a humiliation, and only by recognising this honestly is there a chance of returning to a real existence lived with the dignity that they are always feigning, in order to keep up appearances.

No One Writes to the Colonel is now almost universally acknowledged as a masterpiece of short fiction, like Hemingway's classic *The Old Man and the Sea*, with which it is frequently compared. Pefect in its self-contained intensity, its carefully punctuated plot and its brilliantly prepared conclusion, it is one of those prose works which, in spite of its undeniable 'realism', functions like a poem. It is almost impossible to separate its central themes of waiting and hoping, weather and bodily functions (not least excreting), politics and poverty, life and death, solitude and solidarity, fate and destiny. The last paragraph, one of the most perfect in all literature, seems to concentrate, focus and then release virtually all of the themes and images marshalled by the work as a whole.

Big Mama's Funeral (published 1962)

García Márquez had been writing stories interconnected with his two neorealist novels from the time he finished *No One Writes to the Colonel* in early 1957, and he worked on them with particular intensity during his stay in London at the end of that year. The stories of what would become *Big Mama's Funeral* (*Funerales de la Mamá Grande*, 1962) were written in Bogotá 1954–5, Rome, Paris and London 1955–7, Caracas 1958–9, and again Bogotá 1959–60. But the best of them are closely connected in mood and subject matter to the two novels he was writing over the same period.*

For long-time García Márquez fans, returning to the stories of this, his best-loved collection, is again like being confronted with a sort of literary puzzle. To begin with, 'One Day After Saturday' (1954) and 'Big Mama's Funeral' (1959), chronologically the first and last stories of the collection, are like two odd bookends, both strange, jumbled, emblematic works which anticipate two different classic novels lying in García Márquez's future: *One Hundred Years of Solitude* and *The Autumn of the Patriarch*. Both are supposedly set in Macondo, but the Macondo depicted in 'Big Mama's Funeral', which has a river but no railway, bears almost no relation to the Macondo depicted in any of the other works – based on Aracataca – and is actually more of an amalgam of Sucre and the even more distant river community of La Sierpe, an amalgam which has

---

* The stories of *Big Mama's Funeral* are 'Tuesday Siesta', 'One of These Days', 'There Are No Thieves in This Town' (it later became a movie), 'Balthazar's Marvellous Afternoon', 'Montiel's Widow' (became movie), 'One Day After Saturday', 'Artificial Roses' and 'Big Mama's Funeral' (1962). It is possible that all the stories except for 'One Day After Saturday' – probably written in 1953 – and the title one – 1959 – were written in December 1957 and 1958.

confused the critics for more than half a century. Readers should remember that the Macondo stories draw on the author's memories, many of them nostalgic, from his at least partially 'magical' childhood in Aracataca, whereas the stories set in 'the Town' exorcise the much more painful memories of his adolescence in Sucre. Moreover, Aracataca-Macondo was always a Liberal town, just as his grandfather was a Liberal politician; whereas Sucre, 'the Town', was always Conservative, like his father.

As mentioned, 'One Day After Saturday' was quite different from the others and should have appeared as the first story in the collection, although the plot of 'Tuesday Siesta' is foreshadowed in it. The other stories, with the sole exception of 'Tuesday Siesta' itself, are straightforward Sucre tales which, like the novel No One Writes to the Colonel, have detached themselves from In Evil Hour. In fact, the two towns themselves are interconnected in their literary design (though not in reality, except for García Márquez having lived in both of them): both have been founded within living memory; both have received visits from the legendary Colonel Aureliano Buendía; and the characters Father Angel in Leaf Storm and the unnamed Colonel in No One Writes to the Colonel are both former inhabitants of Macondo. The stories draw on different ideological and aesthetic experiences over a crucial political period of time. They are set in the brutal Colombia of the Violencia, in which Conservative and military governments ruled through terror, though García Márquez is careful not to specify the nature of the regime in any particular case. 'One of These Days', about a Liberal dentist who extracts a Conservative military mayor's tooth without anaesthetic, was a direct offshoot of In Evil Hour and much of it was eventually restored to the novel. It is, undoubtedly, a classic, though only three pages long. 'Artificial Roses', a bitter vignette about the life of a frustrated young woman living in poverty with her mother and grandmother, also includes characters from In Evil Hour.

The narrator of all these stories evidently sympathises with the people against their rulers and contrasts the resistance of the few (mainly but not exclusively middle-class professionals) with the false consciousness of the many. The stories focus not on the cold-hearted authorities who run the two towns but on the ordinary people, in close-up, and in warm colour, trying with great difficulty to live their lives with as much courage, decency, dignity and honour as their always adverse circumstances will allow. If this sounds sentimental and unlikely to be 'realistic', well, it is the genius of this writer that he manages to convince the most sceptical readers of his view of the matter. García Márquez may indeed be writing from a 'class perspective', and with an 'ideological commitment', but he is a master narrator, as much shaped by his material before the writing as he is the shaper of it in the writing itself: so not only are these ordinary people not so very ordinary but they are also people that we instinctively like; and even if there are some that we cannot like, they have our sympathy.

'Tuesday Siesta', a Macondo story, was based on a memory from García Márquez's childhood, when he heard the shout, 'Here comes the mother of that thief', and saw a poor woman go by outside the colonel's house in Aracataca. The story narrates the experience of just such a woman and her daughter arriving in Macondo by train and obliged to walk through the streets under the hostile gaze of the townsfolk in order to visit the cemetery where her son is buried, having been shot dead while attempting to carry out a robbery. Unquestionably a story in the Zavattini tradition (compare the film *Bicycle Thieves*), it masterfully tells the reader all she needs to know about these people without any unnecessary commentary. Although one of the few stories set in Aracataca-Macondo, its style is in no way magical or mythical but operates strictly within the neorealist aesthetic characteristic of this period of García Márquez's life. He has often said that he considers it his best short story and also, intriguingly, 'the most intimate' – probably because the memory from his childhood became fused, magically, with that of his own return, with his mother, in the midday heat of Aracataca in 1950, as recalled, many years later, in his memoir. Stylistically one might say that it was something like a Faulkner story written by Hemingway.

The other stories include 'There Are No Thieves in This Town', about the calamity that befalls an idle young man, living in poverty with his pregnant wife, after he steals the billiard balls from the local bar; a black stranger is blamed for the crime and punished but the thief himself soon begins to pay a heavy price. 'Balthazar's Marvellous Afternoon' tells the story of a carpenter whose speciality is making cages for captive birds; the son of Montiel, the local bigwig, orders one but Montiel has not given permission and refuses to pay for it. Balthazar lets the boy have the cage for nothing but the townsfolk believe he has secured a record price and begin to celebrate; Balthazar ends up not only without his fee but with crippling debts because he not only assumes the cost of the celebration but is finally robbed as he lies drunk in the street. 'Montiel's Widow' reveals the life of the same bigwig's widow, oppressed during her husband's lifetime and now turned insane after his death and incapable of coping with her life and his properties.[17]

The title story 'Big Mama's Funeral', however, was a different matter and could only have been written in 1959. García Márquez was still working for *Venezuela Gráfica* in Caracas when the Cuban Revolution took place on 1 January 1959. García Márquez himself had interviewed Castro's sister Emma in Caracas in 'My Brother Fidel', a report published in *Momento* on 18 April

1958, and had followed events in Cuba with mounting excitement throughout the year. He and Mendoza travelled to Havana on 19 January, three days after Castro became premier, and were plunged at once into the excitement, chaos and drama of the new revolution.

Before long the Argentinian journalist Jorge Ricardo Masetti was encouraged to found a new Cuban press agency to be called Prensa Latina. The concern to present the news from a Latin American perspective – indeed, from the perspective of the Latin American people themselves, if such a thing were possible – was already an obsession of García Márquez's. He and Mendoza returned to Bogotá in May 1958 to set up the Colombian office. Their job was to receive messages from Cuban correspondents all over Latin America and send them on to Havana.

Later, Masetti sent García Márquez to Havana for a few months to orientate himself about Prensa Latina's latest methods, help in training new journalists, and then take up some specific assignment. This turned out to be New York, where the office was located close to the Rockefeller Center. The United States had broken off relations with Cuba on 3 January so it was hardly an ideal time to be embarking on such an adventure, but it shows once again this writer's extraordinary knack of arriving at where it's at around the time that everything is just beginning to happen.

Thus García Márquez underwent the experience of contrasting the Colombian National Front government, reactionary and corrupt, with the Cuban Revolution – thereby giving his already looming 'magical realism' a political, satirical and carnivalesque edge. If the other stories exude affection for ordinary Colombians, 'Big Mama's Funeral', the product of his return to Colombia itself, not only after more than three years away but also after Europe, after Venezuela, after Cuba, expresses all the writer's accumulated frustration, scorn, and anger at a country which endlessly consumed its own children and seemed as though it would never, ever change. This story is, arguably, a unique point both of distillation and of balance, a landmark within the writer's entire literary-historical trajectory.[18] It gives García Márquez's work a new means of being 'political' without being too direct about it, one which would take him all the way through to the early 1980s.

'Big Mama's Funeral' tells the story – indeed, someone very like García Márquez tells the story – of the life and death (much more the death than the life) of an old Colombian matriarch known as 'Big Mama' whose funeral is attended by all the politicians and dignitaries of Colombia and even by distinguished visitors from abroad, such as His Holiness the Pope himself. The character of Big Mama was based in part on the legend of a self-styled 'Marquess' from La Sierpe whose story García Márquez had researched in 1949 and in part on an ignorant but pretentious would-be matriarch from Sucre who had died in November 1957 and whose ostentatious funeral had been the talk of the town. The story shows but does not say that Big Mama's entire life has been spent in the middle of absolutely nowhere, that her wealth is based on a shameless relationship of ruthless exploitation with the labouring peasant masses, and that she herself is ugly, vulgar and in every way ludicrous. Yet no one in her unnamed but unmistakable nation seems to notice these obvious facts. In other words, García Márquez is creating an allegory which shows the real moral status of the still feudal 'oligarchy' first identified by Gaitán and the hypocrisy of a *cachaco* ruling class that pretends that everything in its republic is as it should be – linguistic purity, religious fervour, sartorial elegance – and the only ones letting the side down are the poor misbegotten people that these superior beings themselves oppress. The story begins:

> This is, for all the world's unbelievers, the true account of Big Mama, absolute sovereign of the Kingdom of Macondo, who lived for ninety-two years, and died in the odour of sanctity one Tuesday last September, and whose funeral was attended by the Pope.

And fifteen pages later it ends:

> The only thing left then was for someone to lean a stool against the doorway to tell this story, lesson and example for future generations, so that not one of the world's disbelievers would be left who did not know the story of Big Mama, because tomorrow, Wednesday, the garbage men will come and will sweep up the garbage from her funeral, forever and forever.

The narrator's voice and point of view steer just shy of outright sarcasm and rest content with an almost Swiftian irony so forceful that he is able to state the very opposite of what he believes – knows – to be the case, certain that the reader is with him. The Great Storyteller has publicly and categorically announced himself. Now for his next and greatest novel!

Chapter 4

One Hundred Years of Solitude (1967): the global village

'The Sea of Lost Time'   45
One Hundred Years of Solitude   47

But the next novel would be excruciatingly difficult to write. After the battle of the Bay of Pigs, and despite the triumph of the Revolution, García Márquez left Prensa Latina following increasing difficulties with the communist hardliners. He took his family to Mexico City where the first thing he wrote, shortly after his arrival in Mexico, was a long article in homage to Hemingway. This essay, 'A man has died a natural death', was published on 9 July 1961 in the literary supplement of one of Mexico's leading newspapers. How could he or anyone else have imagined that this first article would also be almost the last serious and significant newspaper piece that he, a born journalist, would write for thirteen years?

Mexico turned out to be a difficult arena for a foreign journalist, and in the end he found himself working for a time as director of two popular magazines, *The Family* (*La Familia*), a women's-interest magazine, and *Stories for Everyone* (*Sucesos para Todos*), a very Mexican crime and scandal sheet. Within weeks García Márquez, a great professional, had improved the layout, the style and the mix of both the magazines. But they contained no serious subject matter. After that he turned to producing film scripts – a lifelong ambition and commitment – but wrote no more journalism until 1974. No novels crystallised. He did, however, write a landmark story.

'The Sea of Lost Time'

'The Sea of Lost Time' was written as early as 1961, only two years after 'Big Mama's Funeral' – itself 'ahead of its time' but in a quite different way – and four years before the start of *One Hundred Years of Solitude*. This continues the curious process whereby García Márquez anticipates, in the middle of an earlier phase, a development stylistically and conceptually quite different which will only be taken up fully when that 'earlier' phase is completed and exhausted. 'Monologue of Isabel Watching it Rain in Macondo', 'Big Mama's Funeral' and 'The Sea of Lost Time' are some of the stages of this crab-like dialectical process. Indeed, 'The Sea of Lost Time' is an especially important landmark, although – it would seem for several years – an isolated one. It has caused chaos and confusion among the literary critics because it seems to give many different messages all at once. It was one of García Márquez's first experiments – following 'The Night of the Curlews' and 'Big Mama's Funeral' – with what in Latin America and eventually elsewhere would be known as 'magical realism', a mode already developed by Guatemalan Miguel Angel Asturias (*Men of Maize*, 1949), Cuban Alejo Carpentier (*The Kingdom of this World*, 1949) and Mexican Juan Rulfo (*Pedro Páramo*, 1955), in which the story, or part of the story, is narrated through the world view of the characters themselves without any indication from the author that this world view is quaint, folkloric or superstitious. The world is as the characters believe it to be.

Or almost. Because in 'The Sea of Lost Time' there is in fact a character who knows more than the other characters do. The post-Cuban García Márquez, who had confined himself to national issues in 'Big Mama's Funeral', now – for the first time – adopts an international perspective and introduces the question of economic imperialism through the character of Mr Herbert, the *gringo* who comes as a kind of secular evangelist to the small, half-abandoned town. In the days before he appears the villagers know something transcendent is afoot because there is a smell of roses everywhere in the usually salt- and fish-filled air. Then the newcomer arrives and makes an announcement:

> 'I'm the richest man in the world', he said. 'I've got so much money I haven't got room to keep it any more. And besides, since my heart's so big that there's no room for it in my chest, I have decided to travel the world over solving the problems of mankind.'

Needless to say, Mr Herbert solves no problems; he completes the impoverishment of the town, enriches himself still further, and goes on his way. But before he does so he paints pretty pictures in the minds of the inhabitants – like a Hollywood movie maker – and leaves them with dissatisfactions they never had before and longings they can hardly even express. They were certainly not happy in the first place with the wretched conditions in which they lived, but they knew no better and they made the best of things; now they are poorer than ever and they will never be content again. Well, a personage with just this name – Mr Herbert, exactly the same character to all intents and purposes – will later bring the banana company to Macondo in *One Hundred Years of Solitude*, and to similar effect. Whereas 'Big Mama' had settled García Márquez's accounts with Colombia and attributed the country's problems to a bankrupt political system, a reactionary ruling class, and a medieval national church, 'The Sea of Lost Time' at last introduces the great Latin American staple, US imperialism – just as Castro had begun by attacking Batista and the Cuban ruling class and only then moved on to confront the United States imperialists who had backed and funded them. (Despite this change of tack it is noteworthy that in these stories 'the people' are no longer without faults or nasty instincts and feelings.)

For the longer term, this story had another significance. It was a pointer to the future, away from Macondo-Aracataca and 'the Town'-Sucre, that is, away from Colombia and towards not only Latin America but literary universality. 'Big Mama' had finally fused the two small towns and in a sense had ironised both of them, preparing them for liquidation as the writer searched for a way to paint on a larger canvas. *One Hundred Years of Solitude* would still be set in Macondo but it would be obvious to the informed reader from the first page – whose themes are discovery, identity and violence – that this was an allegory of Latin America as a whole: Macondo had made the great leap from national to continental symbol. And *The Autumn of the Patriarch* would be about a military dictator, that archetypal Latin American figure, who would stand for all the dictators of the continent and whose country of origin would be a composite of several Latin American republics. *One Hundred Years of Solitude* would draw on the magical Macondo side of his previous oeuvre, *The Autumn of the Patriarch* on the sinister Sucre side. 'The Sea of Lost Time', by contrast, is set in a new venue which, if we were forced to place it, would be those fishing villages either side of Barranquilla where the Barranquilla Group used to spend their 'lost weekends', and where they filmed a legendary movie, *The Blue Lobster*. (Other similar stories would follow but not for another decade, and they would form part of the *Eréndira* anthology.)

One Hundred Years of Solitude

By 1962 García Márquez's life was settled, though not to his entire satisfaction. He was resident in Mexico, perhaps Latin America's most exciting and influential country, after seven turbulent years living in Rome, Paris, Caracas, Bogotá, Havana and New York. He was married with two sons. He had given up investigative journalism, after the two difficult years with Cuba's Prensa Latina, but had a range of prospects in Mexico, including public relations and, especially, writing scripts for movies. And he had finally managed to publish his three short but dense neorealist books, *No One Writes to the Colonel*, *In Evil Hour* and *Big Mama's Funeral*. None of them had come out with major publishing houses, nor had they attracted wide attention, but it was progress: he was up to date. Perhaps now he could write the books he felt he really had inside him.

He went back to 'The House', his first love, about the Aracataca of his childhood and his grandfather's old house, but once again he got nowhere. He started a book called *Autumn of the Patriarch* about an old Latin American dictator; the idea had occurred to him in Venezuela but although he wrote a couple of hundred pages he could not give adequate expression to the feelings he had about it. He became anxious. His friends began talking about writer's block: in those early 1960s, at a time when the Latin American novel was beginning to explode on the international scene –partially as a result, no doubt, of the Cuban Revolution – with the appearance of a series of extraordinary novels by Carlos Fuentes, Julio Cortázar, Mario Vargas Llosa and others, it seemed that García Márquez might be finished.

And then one day in 1965, as he drove his family down to Acapulco for a brief vacation, the first sentence of a novel appeared in his head and behind it, floating, the entire book. It was 'The House' again, after all, but in a form he had never imagined: something extraordinary. He turned the car around, drove back to Mexico City and locked himself away for a year. By the middle of 1966 he had written probably the most important and certainly the most famous novel in the history of Latin America, and one of the universal masterworks of the second half of the twentieth century: *One Hundred Years of Solitude*. His first novel, *Leaf Storm*, had been a 'modernist' work, inspired by the European and North American writers of the 1920s and 1930s; but it was also, given the cultural time lag in those days between Europe and Latin America, a precursor of the 'Boom' novels being written by his Latin American contemporaries. *No One Writes to the Colonel* and *In Evil Hour*, by contrast, had been neorealist works, written under the influence of socialist realism as well as the cinema. And the stories of *Big Mama's Funeral* were also mainly neorealist and closely connected, not only in technique but also in subject matter, to those two most recent novels. But we can see in retrospect that the stories 'One Day After Saturday' and 'Big Mama's Funeral' itself, as well as that more recent, isolated story, 'The Sea of Lost Time', provide between them a series of steps, or advances, on the way to the new novel. The two former works are set in different versions of a small town called Macondo: the first, closely based on Aracataca itself, gives a sense of the eccentricity and fanaticism of small communities lost in a huge continent; the second incorporates a new note of satire and a taste for hyperbole; and in the third a new theme, imperialism, is unveiled and a different literary conception, a different way of looking at Latin America, what would be widely known as 'magic' or 'magical' realism, is applied.

One might suggest, simplifying for effect, that *Leaf Storm* had applied the modernist (avant-garde) techniques from what would later be called the First World to the realities of Latin America (part of what what would later be called the Third World); and that *In Evil Hour* and *No One Writes to the Colonel* had followed the nineteenth-century doctrine of realism, updated by twentieth-century cinematographic techniques (above all montage and objectification), as prescribed by the socialist ideologues of the Second (or communist) World to those same Latin American realities, from a more consciously political and supposedly progressive standpoint. Finally, with *One Hundred Years of Solitude*, García Márquez made the leap to a new way of writing, one which he had not invented (Asturias and Carpentier had done that between the 1920s and the 1940s) but to which he gave the paradigmatic form. And if his first works were 'modernist', based on aesthetic conceptions originating in pre-Second World War Europe, *One Hundred Years of Solitude*, a truly revolutionary work, would be the paradigm of another literary conception, the 'postmodernist' novel, which in this case was also a 'postcolonial' or 'Third Word' novel, not to mention, in the minds of most readers, *the* archetypal Latin American novel and the very heart and soul of the 1960s 'Boom'.

García Márquez would be considered one of the greatest Latin American novelists even if he had not written *One Hundred Years of Solitude*. But we can be certain that he would not be considered as great a novelist as if he had *only* written *One Hundred Years of Solitude*. In other words, he would be immortal thanks to this book even had he written no other: it is because of *One Hundred Years of Solitude* that people have become obsessed with him and with the now familiar cluster of García Márquez motifs: Macondo, Colonel Aureliano Buendía, Ursula Iguarán, the Duke of Marlborough, Francisco the Man, the banana massacre, yellow butterflies, magical realism, power, solitude, love, etc. It is a book which has imposed its own style and content on the world.

It is also a book which brought the entire world to the tiny Latin American town of Macondo: readers can see, inside its magic screen, such diverse influences as the Bible, the Arabian Nights, Rabelais, Cervantes, the chronicles of the Spanish conquest and the European novels of chivalry, the works of Daniel Defoe, Virginia Woolf, William Faulkner and Ernest Hemingway from outside Latin America, and Asturias, Carpentier, Juan Rulfo and the 'Boom' novelists from within. On the very first page of the novel there are coded references to the beginning of the world and the discovery of Latin America, mixed in with memories of García Márquez's childhood and the history of Colombia. Indeed, García Márquez's own family and friends are in the first chapter, not to mention the writer himself, fused with the alchemist Nostradamus and the immortal Argentinian Jorge Luis Borges within the figure of the great writer-creator Melquíades, another genius who locks himself away in a small room to encapsulate the entire cosmos in that enchanted space, both timeless and time-bound, which we call literature. By this means a novel was produced in which, more than in any other, Latin America at last recognised itself and was recognised at last, in turn, by the rest of the word. Rarely has the importance of literature in reflecting or creating national – or in this case continental – identity been so clearly and resoundingly exemplified.

One Hundred Years of Solitude is a family saga, or indeed, if one prefers, a postmodernist parody of a family saga. Although based very directly on García Márquez's own family, the book is also a symbolic representation of the history of Colombia and indeed of Latin America as a whole, as well as particularly appealing to readers in other Third World countries and of course to audiences for 'universal' literature all over the planet. Not many novels have spoken so directly to such a range of readerships.

The Buendía family in the novel originates in the Colombian Guajira during the colonial period (as García Márquez's own maternal family had done). Then the patriarch of the umpteenth generation, José Arcadio Buendía, moves the family over the mountains to a place very like Aracataca some time in the nineteenth century. Although his whole name ('Joseph', 'arcadia', 'good day') suggests the idea of utopia, he is the author of the family's original sins: incest – a symbol of solitude or self-obsession – and violence. He begins by marrying his first cousin, Ursula Iguarán, giving rise to the danger, according to local superstition, of engendering a child with a pig's tail and thereby ending the family line; and then, when his best friend Prudencio Aguilar taunts him about this, he kills him out of a combination of honour and *machismo* (concepts difficult to separate in the Hispanic world), and is haunted by the man's ghost, whereupon the family is forced to flee the Guajira and found a new community, Macondo, beyond the mountains. (The duel is a literary version of a gunfight García Márquez's grandfather had fought with a military comrade in a town called Barrancas, which did indeed lead to the family having to move; in *Leaf Storm* the reason for the migration was attributed, less pointedly, to the ravages of the civil war.) There José Arcadio and the unexpectedly resilient Ursula build a house and become the unofficial leaders of the new community.

The pioneer couple have three children, Arcadio, Aureliano and Amaranta, none of whom is born with a pig's tail, and over time they take in a number of other children. One of the household servants, the unmarried Pilar Ternera, has babies following relationships with several members of the family down the years, thereby compounding the fear that eventually there will be an incestuous coupling, unknown to the participants, which will indeed produce the dreaded pig's tail and put an end to the Buendías.

Macondo's arcadian innocence cannot endure; the outside world soon begins to impinge. First it is discovered by gypsies, frequent visitors who bring trade and scientific discoveries, led by the brilliant, worldly-wise Melquíades, who eventually stays on in Macondo and is given a room in the Buendía family house. Later less welcome visitors arrive, representatives of the central government which wishes to tax the community and control it by installing political, military and bureaucratic officials. This development leads to a series of civil wars in which the sombre Aureliano, once grown up, becomes a fanatical participant on the side of the Liberal Party until eventually he is known throughout the country as the legendary warrior Colonel Aureliano Buendía. Finally, even more menacing outsiders appear, traders like the gypsies but far more systematic and far more difficult to say no to: the North Americans. They arrive in the shape of the multinational Fruit Company whose business is to monopolise the trade in bananas and ship them to the other side of the world. In no time at all they bring their ocean steamers and their railways, transform the economy and the culture of Macondo and eventually provoke a strike of plantation workers which prods the central government into action – in support of the ruthless *gringos*, naturally. The national army arrives in the town and more than three thousand workers with their families are machine-gunned and their bodies dumped in the Caribbean Sea.

After this sombre episode – the novel's imperialist heart of darkness – Macondo goes into steep decline, a decline confirmed in the novel by the death of Ursula, the matriarch who is its backbone. (Her son, the warrior Aureliano, has died several chapters before.) Following her disappearance the younger generation, no longer creators of myths but victims of them, find themselves plunging back into some form of primordial darkness and sinfulness. Eventually the last member of the family, the illegitimate Aureliano Babilonia, has a torrid affair with his aunt and, as has so long been predicted, a child with a pig's tail is born and very quickly dies of neglect following his mother's death in giving birth to him. Then the heartbroken Aureliano Babilonia himself is swept away in an apocalyptic hurricane wind at the very moment that he unravels his own story as he reads the family history written down and encrypted by Melquíades a hundred years before.

In terms of the overall structure – and much else, not least the meaning of this melodramatic conclusion – *One Hundred Years of Solitude* is a very difficult novel to decipher. The book is highly repetitive (though always amusingly, not tediously so): each generation names its children after those of previous generations, and it is extremely difficult to follow who is who and where we are, not least because the author constantly gives us ostensibly reassuring times of the day, days of the week and months of the year without ever also giving

us the extra information we need to make sense of them. This is clearly intentional: at a first reading the novel appears completely radiant and diaphanous
line by line and yet, in many respects, its direction is almost totally obscure.
And this too is intentional and clearly part of the book's meaning. We don't
know where we are because the characters never know where they are or, if
they think they do, they are invariably mistaken. And the structure of the book
adds to our problems. There are twenty chapters of almost equal length but
they have neither titles nor numbers: the novel seems just to roll on as if it
might go on for ever or until it reaches some natural conclusion. Eventually
we learn that what it has reached is an inevitable conclusion, which leads us
to wonder what 'natural', or 'inevitable', or other such words – like 'logical',
say – might actually mean when applied to history and other human affairs,
like family life. Do they all mean the same thing or different things, and, if the
latter, which of them is 'true'?

Nevertheless, despite the absence of numbering and, at first sight, of direction, a careful reading reveals that this novel's structure conforms to the two-
part overall design we have identified in our analyses of earlier novels. In the
case of *Leaf Storm*, the reader will recall, the two-part structure was vertical, not
horizontal: that is, based on a dual time-frame, present and past, not on a division in two chronological halves. (Later, in *The General in His Labyrinth*, García
Márquez will combine both vertical and horizontal methods.) In the present
case, the novel is divided into two exactly equal sections, chapters 1–9 (our numbering, of course) and 10–18, followed by an epilogue of two chapters, 19 and
20. This small variation is determined by the fact that the novel is a family saga
based upon the cycle of generations, and the two extra chapters give not only a
sense of onward dynamism – with a third generation beginning its adult adventure – but also, at its very end, a reversal of expectations when the book and the
family history both come to a shuddering halt. The world of García Márquez is a
world of twos, not threes. Indeed, by the time of *One Hundred Years of Solitude*
the tendency is not only for the book to fall into two equal halves but for each
chapter, internally, also to fall into two more or less equal sections; and this novel
also opts decisively for a phenomenon which follows logically and directly from
this, namely that all the chapters, throughout the book, shall have, as far as possible, approximately the same number of pages and words.

These symmetrical phenomena are so evident – so obsessive, one might
almost say – that it is astonishing that readers and critics seem never to have
noticed them. One might fear, when the practice is stated in this bald way
(García Márquez sometimes calls his techniques his literary 'carpentry'),
that the books would end up too planned, too structured, too mechanical
and 'just-so' as a result. On the contrary, such is García Márquez's mastery,

so extraordinary his particular combination of self-awareness and intuition, that the result is almost certainly to contribute, in this 'tropical', 'baroque' and 'magical realist' creator, a contrary and balancing, an almost classical sense of underlying equilibrium – achieved through counterpoint – which is instrumental in the 'García Márquez' effect: a kind of order out of chaos, a radiancy and transparency out of obscurity and profundity.

Chapter 1 is one of the best-known first chapters in twentieth-century literary history, and its first sentence – 'Many years later, as he faced the firing squad,' etc. – is probably the best-known first sentence in Hispanic literature since the publication of *Don Quixote* over 350 years before. Later, chapter 10, which begins the story of a new generation – novels impose these neat divisions, though life itself is much messier – quite consciously inaugurates the second half. The phrase 'years later' is repeated at the very beginning, followed by 'on his deathbed' instead of 'as he faced the firing squad'; and whereas in the first chapter a José Arcadio was the father figure and an Aureliano was one of his sons ('the first human being to be born in Macondo'), now the first-named protagonist is an Aureliano (Aureliano Segundo) and his first-named son is a José Arcadio. The mother of this José Arcadio, Fernanda del Carpio, is an outsider, from the oppressive highland capital of the country (which is Bogotá, of course, though never named in this novel). In chapter 18, at the end of the second half, Ursula dies, and with her the family history as we have come to understand it. And finally the truncated third part, which is also, contradictorily, an epilogue, begins with chapter 19 and the arrival of another woman from outside Macondo, though not from the highlands: Amaranta Ursula has been living abroad and returns married to a foreigner but soon embarks on the calamitous incestuous affair with her nephew Aureliano Babilonia which, with the arrival of the last child ever to be born in Macondo, brings the disaster feared by the family and predicted by Melquíades. This overall design has not previously been identified by critics.

The meaning of the ending has divided readers from the moment the novel was published: in particular, is it optimistic or pessimistic? The great majority have concluded that, surprisingly for a book written by a socialist – not least the socialist who had written *No One Writes to the Colonel* – the conclusion was pessimistic: the archetypal Latin American family has been destroyed by its own internal and external contradictions, that is, by lust, incest, greed, stupidity and an addiction to selfishness, self-centredness and solitude, as well as by an inability to read the signs of history.

The novel certainly allows this reading. And indeed Latin American history allows this reading. The continent has never managed to establish itself in the world in the way that Europe, Asia and, more recently, the United States, have done. Even the continent of Africa, for all its tragedies, has a clearer identity in the marketplace of global cultures than 'Latin' or 'South' or 'Hispanic' or 'Iberian' America. But my own reading suggests to me that García Márquez wishes to allow this reading not because he believes it himself – though whether he would come increasingly to believe it in later decades is another matter – but because, on the one hand, his characters (representatives of a majority of Latin American intellectuals) believe it and, much more importantly, he knows full well that his target audience of international readers believes it. (In *No One Writes to the Colonel*, set in a remote Latin American town undergoing dramas the rest of the world knows nothing about during the 1956 Suez crisis, which that same world deems the most important event of the moment, one character says to another: 'For the Europeans South America is a man with a moustache, a guitar and a revolver ... They don't understand the problem.') Nevertheless, García Márquez hopes that his more sophisticated readers will understand Latin America's problem – its historic solitude – and that they will be able to *deconstruct* the end of the novel and therefore, retrospectively, the rest of the book.

The theme that should allow them to do so is memory. It has often been said that those who do not remember their history are condemned to repeat it, and this is certainly one of the vertebral themes of *One Hundred Years of Solitude*. And the central historical event in the entire novel is unquestionably the massacre of the banana workers of Macondo, by the army of the Colombian government, on behalf of the shareholders of the North American company: a story of class struggle, capitalism and imperialism, to convert those events into abstract language. It is therefore the theme of proletarian struggle which can guide the reader out into the light at the end of the labyrinth. (Fifteen years later García Márquez's Nobel Prize address, 'The Solitude of Latin America', would seem to support this interpretation.)

The historic massacre on which the literary one was based took place in the town of Ciénaga in 1928, which for many years García Márquez seems to have believed to be the year in which he was born (or did he just like to think so?).[1] It is at about this time that Meme Buendía's son, the illegitimate Aureliano, is born in the novel. His mother had been forbidden to see Mauricio, his father, because, as an apprentice mechanic in the company workshop and one-time employee of the entrepreneur Aureliano Triste, he was from an inferior class. Mauricio's surname is Babilonia, conceivably because the proletariat, which he represents, will bring about the historical destruction of Macondo. Interestingly, Mauricio looks like a gypsy,[2] which suggests that as a migrant manual worker, a member of the 'leaf trash' so despised by García Márquez's own family, when he was a child, he is a vehicle of the same kind of internationalist consciousness and impact as the real gypsies led by Melquíades in the earlier sections of the novel. Mauricio is permanently crippled in an accident at the end of chapter 14, shortly after Meme becomes pregnant, and appears no more. But, at the beginning of chapter 15, the arrival of his illegitimate son is made to coincide explicitly with the author's own prophecy of doom for Macondo: 'The events which were to deal Macondo its mortal blow were already on the horizon when they brought Meme Buendía's son home'.

These apocalyptic 'events', then, are evidently historical ones, even if the characters – and many readers – insist on interpreting them in mythical terms (fate, destiny, and so on). It is in fact Aureliano Babilonia himself who will eventually decipher Melquíades's parchments – the history of the family and of Macondo – on the final page of the novel. All the disasters revealed then and before had in fact already been presaged by a previous textual moment, at the end of chapter 11, through a familiar image of progress: 'the innocent yellow train that was to bring so many insecurities and uncertainties, so many joys and misfortunes, so many changes, calamities and nostalgias to Macondo'. The decision to bring the yellow train, inaugurating the final stage in the penetration of Macondo's introversion and self-centredness, was taken by Aureliano Triste, the man who turned the magical ice into a commodity, representative of the impact of the embryonic local bourgeoisie: 'they remembered him well because in a matter of hours he had managed to destroy every breakable object that passed through his hands'.[3] The little yellow train in its turn brings the multinational banana company, United States imperialism, and eventual disaster, a perfectly logical sequence of events carefully detailed by the author himself, and which has little to do with pigs' tails.

The banana company brings temporary prosperity around the time of the First World War, but as profits are threatened in the late 1920s the workers begin strike action. José Arcadio Segundo, great-uncle of the baby Aureliano Babilonia, and at first a foreman in the company, becomes a trade union leader and plays a leading role in the conflict. He is one of the few survivors of the massacre and insists on repeating his eye-witness account of the death of more than three thousand demonstrators until the day he dies. Indeed, his last words – to none other than Aureliano Babilonia, in Melquíades's old but ageless room – are: 'Always remember that there were more than three thousand and that they threw them in the sea.'[4] At which the narrator comments: 'Then he collapsed over the parchments and died with his eyes open.' The massacre had been denied by the authorities: 'In Macondo nothing has happened, nor is anything happening now, nor will it ever.' Then all history and all memory were comprehensively blotted out by the rain which lasted four years, eleven months and two days, and which recalls the previous 'plague of insomnia' in chapter 3, significantly provoked on that occasion by the suppression of

Colombian Indian history, another scandal the authorities preferred to erase. Now proletarian history was to be buried. After the interminable rain, Ursula's own 'one hundred torrential years' come to an end, and with it her morality and her view of the world, the cement that has held the family together until these final chapters. When she dies, Macondo's decline accelerates and the doom of the entire Buendía family rapidly approaches. Nevertheless, as García Márquez shows, all is not forgotten. First José Arcadio Segundo, then Aureliano Babilonia, keep the memory of the workers' struggles and their suppression alive, at the same time that they themselves strive to decipher the broader historical panorama encoded in the parchments in Melquíades's room:

> In reality, although everyone took him for a madman, José Arcadio Segundo was at this time the most lucid member of the household. He taught little Aureliano to read and write, initiated him in the study of the parchments, and instilled in him so personal an interpretation of the meaning of the Banana Company for Macondo, that many years later, when Aureliano finally went out into the world, people would think that he was telling some hallucinatory story, because it was so radically opposed to the false version accepted by the historians and confirmed in the school textbooks.[5]

Nothing, surely, could be clearer. After José Arcadio Segundo's death, Aureliano Babilonia remains in Melquíades's room, continuing his own education and the deciphering of the parchments, sometimes aided by the ghost of Melquíades himself. The room, needless to say, is that timeless space of memory, domain of history and literature (García Márquez in his writer's solitude), marked by the 'diaphanous purity of its air, its immunity against dust and destruction',[6] until, that is, Melquíades himself dies and time pursues its work in his room also.

Eventually Aureliano makes a new friend, Gabriel, who is none other than the author, and his fiancée, Mercedes, none other than the author's wife. Gabriel leaves for Europe to become a writer after winning a competition. This would be in 1955, in the midst of the *Violencia*, when Colombia as a whole was indeed, like Macondo, in an advanced stage of social decomposition. It was to Gabriel that Aureliano, now left behind, had felt closest, for a very important reason. Both knew the story of the strike: 'Aureliano and Gabriel were linked by a sort of complicity, founded on real events in which no one else believed and which had so affected their lives that both were adrift in the wake of a world that was gone, and of which only their own nostalgic longings remained'.[7] Once again, could anything be clearer? García Márquez leaves the novel for Paris, but he also remains through the medium of Aureliano, who is so closely linked to him and to José Arcadio Segundo through their shared interpretation of the history of Macondo and of the Buendía family. Moreover, Aureliano is the character who eventually deciphers the parchments (the novel, his own life, Latin American history) on the very last page.

In other words, it is the apparently decadent younger generation, that of García Márquez himself (Aureliano Babilonia and Gabriel), representatives of the 'Boom' generation in narrative fiction, who finally come to read and write the real history of the continent. They do so precisely by deciphering the magical reality and labyrinthine fantasies of the previous one hundred years of solitude, this very novel, which is their world, and in which so many other characters have been bewitched and bewildered. Hence the mirror/mirage ambiguity on the very last page. There we find Aureliano Babilonia – and the author reminds us of his surname – 'deciphering the instant he was living, deciphering it as he lived it'. His reading literally puts an end to one hundred years of solitude, to *One Hundred Years of Solitude*, and turns the reader who is reading about him back out into the history outside the text. The apocalypse of the Buendías is not – how could it be? – the end of Latin America but the end of primitive neocolonialism, its conscious or unconscious collaborators, and an epoch of illusions.

The book has been such a joy to read, so absorbing and unforgettable – so magical, in short – that many readers, quite understandably, are reluctant to emerge from myth into reality, from the radiance of childish enchantments into the darker world of adult preoccupations and responsibilities. To those who complain that the novel does not actually say all this, one can only respond: What other significance is there in the chain of memory from the banana massacre through José Arcadio Segundo, Aureliano Babilonia, the fictional and the real Gabriel García Márquez and the reader himself? And if others complain that Latin American history itself did not turn out as García Márquez was hoping – the 1970s and 1980s were an age of horror, not revolutionary transformation – one can only sympathise and agree. Nevertheless, the continent has known itself better and has been better known by others since that time.

To this extent one should perhaps revise the impression of a novel whose two levels, magical and realist, mythical and historical, are entirely inseparable, since after the massacre and death of Ursula they slowly but surely begin to come apart. The opening of the novel – 'recent', 'diaphanous', bathed in light – is an evocation not only of Latin America's mythical innocence after Independence but of the magical childhood world which García Márquez inhabited in Aracataca with his grandfather the colonel. The endless civil wars in the novel between Liberals and Conservatives bring little enlightenment, only disillusionment and despair, but still the sense of an almost innocent world only just beginning persists. Nevertheless, as the novel wears on and García Márquez himself as narrator gradually metamorphoses from child into adult, finally becoming himself only on the last page of the book, the characters slowly, reluctantly come to understand, among other things, what it is that Latin American colonels are generally paid to do, and innocence comes to an end. Whereas at the start of the novel the characters are mainly innocent, optimistic and forward-looking, by the time the narrative is halfway through they begin to hear the music not of hope and destiny, but of nostalgia for the past and for innocence itself. Once Ursula loses her residual faith in the purpose and coherence of the present, she dies, and once she has died the solid unity – or mystification – of myth and history is broken.

The rest of the novel condenses the decipherment of Colombian history which García Márquez and his generation – especially the Barranquilla Group – carried out in the wake of the 1948 *Bogotazo* (he was twenty years old at the time), when the workers' movement was again denied its place in national life, and on through the dark years of the *Violencia*. It seems clear that he was able to do this precisely by having distanced himself from these realities, by escaping at last from Colombia, Aracataca and his family 'demons' (to quote Vargas Llosa's book on García Márquez). This is one more illustration of the truth that Latin American authors can best achieve greatness not through a national, still less a cosmopolitan perspective but from a continental standpoint: by conceiving of themselves as Latin Americans. Seen in this multiple light, *One Hundred Years of Solitude* is clearly a demystification, though apparently one so scrupulously labyrinthine in itself that most readers have managed to get themselves as lost in its winding corridors and spiralling stairways as most Latin Americans, including the Buendías, in the phantasmagorical history which it reconstructs.

So much for the labyrinths of history. What about the labyrinths of literary technique and especially narrative point of view in this most Latin American of novels? This brings us inevitably to the question of magical realism – or perhaps one should say of 'so-called magical realism'. This, after all, is the novel which, more than any other, was taken to confirm the historical demise, not only of social realism, but of the kinds of modernist works which, despite their experimental aspects, nevertheless sought to produce 'cultural knowledge', and therefore to herald the arrival of the linguistically inclined, experimental or postmodernist novel. But this is surely a complete – and sometimes, one suspects, wilful – misreading of *One Hundred Years of Solitude*, which contains a greater variety of carefully encoded material relating to the positivistic orders of social psychology, political economy and the history of ideas than almost any other Latin American novel that comes to mind.

The main reason why so many readers have missed these otherwise obvious facts is the elementary one that García Márquez, like most modernist writers, presents most aspects of reality from the standpoint of his characters. Magical realism is a complex and maddeningly shifting label which has given rise to more heat – tropical heat, naturally – than light and has allowed readers to interpret it as they will. It has often been discredited by the fact that to exoticise Third World peoples by emphasising their 'difference' – of colour, culture and creed – may lead at best to a patronising view that sees them as childlike or as noble savages and at worst to a view that they are racially and culturally inferior and in need of 'help' or correction from other, superior – usually Western – societies. In other words, readers from Europe and the United States may be 'enjoying' books like *One Hundred Years of Solitude* for the wrong reasons; whereas the originators of magical realism, Asturias and Carpentier, were more than aware of such dangers. They consciously set out to juxtapose a Western world view whose 'rationalism' is nearly always cynical and self-serving, with an anthropological understanding of the world view of native peoples which takes their belief systems seriously and presents them, as far as is possible in that Western form known as the novel, on equal terms. This is why priests levitate, beautiful young women ascend into heaven and incestuous sex produces babies with pigs' tails: to 'us' it may be colourful and either lovable or contemptible; but to many of the characters of *One Hundred Years of Solitude*, it is real. In short, although history is sometimes devoured by myth, every myth has its history. This novel is not about some undifferentiated fusing of 'history-and-myth', but about the myths of history and their demystification.

In the decades since Carpentier and Asturias inaugurated this literary mode, the same term has often been used, consciously or unconsciously, as an ideological stratagem to collapse many different kinds of writing, and many different political perspectives, into one, usually escapist, concept: a kind of 'magical realism lite' produced by people with none of the ethnological insight necessary to make it historically meaningful. Like the surrealist movement from which it ultimately derives, magical realism can sometimes be seen as an unconscious – irony of ironies! – conspiracy between critics eager to get away, in their imagination, to the colourful world of Latin America, and certain Latin American writers desperate to take refuge, in their writing, from the injustice and brutality of their continent's unpalatable reality.

García Márquez is such a master of magic and mystery, his writing in this novel is so consistently and uniquely enjoyable, that one is tempted to forget that to believe, even temporarily, in illusions is to settle for a world that is undecipherable and unknowable. But this is surely not the job of criticism. In *One Hundred Years of Solitude* he found a way at last of relativising and universalising his childhood experience and perception of his family, his region and his nation. This – to the great disappointment of millions of readers – would mean the end of 'Macondo' and a turn to other topics.

Chapter 5

The Autumn of the Patriarch (1975): the love of power

Innocent Eréndira and Other Stories (1972)   61
The Autumn of the Patriarch   63

After the astonishing success of *One Hundred Years of Solitude* when it was published in Buenos Aires in 1967, García Márquez and his family moved to Spain and took up residence, like other members of the 'Boom', in Barcelona. Although the whole literary world was begging for more Macondo, and he could probably have written profitable sequels to *One Hundred Years of Solitude* for years, García Márquez adopted Hemingway's motto that every completed novel was a 'dead lion' and that you had to move on to something new. Nevertheless, in his case the new project was in fact an old one: the novel he had begun in Mexico and then abandoned, about an old Latin American dictator. Unlike his other novels at this stage of production, it already had a name: *The Autumn of the Patriarch*. It would be his most difficult work, both for him to write and for his audience to read. It took him almost seven years to complete and it would never be his most popular book.

Innocent Eréndira and Other Stories (1972)

During his first two or three years in Spain, when the new novel was proving difficult to write and, indeed, in order to make sure that it would be different from the books he had written before, García Márquez undertook a new sort of writing by producing a new short story collection, his third, with a different style. The collection, to be entitled *Innocent Eréndira and Other Stories*, was begun in Mexico in the early 1960s but mainly written in Barcelona in the late 1960s and early 1970s.* García Márquez has left Macondo and 'the Town' (indeed all towns)

---

* The stories of *Eréndira* are 'A Very Old Man with Enormous Wings' (1968, 'A Tale for Children'; became movie), 'The Sea of Lost Time' (1961; became movie), 'The Handsomest Drowned Man in the World' (1968, 'A Tale for Children'),

far behind for a world which is primitive, elemental and mythical. Most of these stories are set by the sea in places largely devoid of topographical or cultural characteristics, though the writer seems to be remembering the coastal villages between Cartagena and Santa Marta or imagining the Guajira he hardly knows, that desert zone between northeastern Colombia and Venezuela that his maternal ancestors were from. Sea, sky, desert, frontier: he seems to be like a painter who has radically altered his palette; the default colours seem to be white, blue and grey. One might say that the atmosphere is no longer the black and white world of De Sica and Zavattini's neorealism – as in the stories of *Big Mama's Funeral* – but the dreamy magical realist world of Fellini and Antonioni.[1]

They are reminiscent of García Márquez's magical realist predecessor, Miguel Angel Asturias (*Leyendas de Guatemala, El espejo de Lida Sal*). They are also somehow feminised – his critics would say sanitised – and thus also reminiscent of his brilliant imitator, Isabel Allende (as well as others such as Laura Esquivel). The great exception – his story collections always seem to need an odd man out – is 'Blacamán the Good, Vendor of Miracles', which has a crafty satirical edge like 'Big Mama's Funeral' and really belongs, spiritually and stylistically, in the previous collection.[2]

'A Very Old Man with Enormous Wings' is about a decrepit angel who turns up at a coastal community, is mistreated by almost everyone and eventually manages to fly away. García Márquez gave the story the subtitle 'A Tale for Children', though it is hard to see what separates this story's theme and treatment from any of the others. 'The Handsomest Drowned Man in the World' is similarly subtitled and similarly perplexing: why a story about a beautiful corpse which transforms a village's self-image for the better and is then returned to the ocean would be especially suitable for children is equally difficult to understand. What is certainly true is that all of these works have a curious childlike quality, like fairy tales or dreams – yet the stories they tell involve murder, rape, incest, prostitution and almost every other adult theme one could imagine. 'Death Constant Beyond Love' is about the crazy infatuation of a corrupt senator who has only six months to live for the daughter – the 'most beautiful woman in the world' – of a wife-murderer who offers to sell him the girl in exchange for a new passport. It is perhaps a measure of García Márquez's skill that the story does not seem so bizarre in the reading as it does in the summary. 'The Last Voyage of the Ghost Ship' is about an embittered young man who manages to lead a colossal ghost liner away from the nearby city to which it is heading to come

'Death Constant Beyond Love' (1970), 'The Last Voyage of the Ghost Ship' (1968), 'Blacamán the Good, Vendor of Miracles' (1968) and 'The Incredible and Sad Tale of Innocent Eréndira and Her Heartless Grandmother' (1972; became movie).

aground on the shores of his impoverished village. In the oedipal 'Blacamán the Good, Vendor of Miracles', a younger magician and quack doctor called Blacamán the Good overcomes his master and eventual rival Blacamán the Bad and subjects him to eternal punishment and torment.

The title story of *Eréndira* is one of his longest tales – more a novella than a story – and one of the most important. It is based on an adolescent girl he met as a young man, who had been prostituted by her grandmother and hawked around the Colombian Costa for queues of men to have sex with. One of the early episodes of *One Hundred Years of Solitude* is inspired by the story and *Eréndira* provides a much longer, more romantic and more magical version. In this one Eréndira, already treated as a full-time servant by her hugely fat grandmother, accidentally sets fire to her house and the old woman turns her into a prostitute until the fees have paid all of the lost money back. Eventually a handsome young man called Ulysses, whom Eréndira loves, but not as much as he loves her, kills the grandmother; but instead of escaping with him, Eréndira takes off alone, 'running into the wind, swifter than a deer, and no voice of this world could stop her'. Evidently she is not prepared to exchange subservience to a woman for subservience to a man. Many of García Márquez's stories have what could be called a feminist slant, but this one is much more unambiguous than most. García Márquez himself appears briefly in the narrative, as do several of the characters from the other stories in this collection.

With these strange, phantasmatic, painful yet curiously whimsical stories – one thinks again, inevitably, of Fellini – García Márquez approached one of the distant frontiers of his trademark magical realism. *The Autumn of the Patriarch*, which he was writing at the same time, would reach towards another of those frontiers. It would be presented as a kind of grotesque political farce, but its magical realism would take on a truly nightmarish form.

The Autumn of the Patriarch

Once the short stories were completed to his satisfaction, García Márquez concentrated full time on his new novel. From a purely literary point of view, it would be one of his most important books. It became, instantly, one of Latin America's best-known novels about dictatorship, a profound meditation on power, fame and solitude – meaning, inevitably, and as the author himself has stated, a radically autobiographical work. But where *One Hundred Years of Solitude* was limpid, diaphanous and apparently simple, a grown-up book that was almost like a children's story, *The Autumn of the Patriarch* was baroque, contorted and intimidatingly dense, with subject matter that was often sordid and even repulsive. Where the former was endlessly narrative, a masterclass in the art of storytelling that simply sailed onwards like novels from a pre-twentieth century era, the latter was impenetrable and even incomprehensible, with a plot that was hard to grasp, a historical timeline that was difficult to establish, and a repetitiveness and obsessiveness that made some readers shrug their shoulders and ask, 'What is the point of this?' and 'Is it really worth it?'

If many of them persisted, the main reason was that the new novel was superbly well written in a purely literary sense; despite its disagreeable subject matter, it achieved heights of poetic grandeur rarely seen in the second half of the twentieth century. Yet there was a feeling that García Márquez was rather obviously, not to say perversely, doing his own thing, and that his ordinary readers were not necessarily his first consideration this time. Although *One Hundred Years of Solitude* had caused an unparalleled sensation, there was a sense in which it had been set aside from other novels of the 'Boom', as if, in its very transparence and accessibility, it were an ingenuous, primitivist work by some Henri Rousseau of fiction. (Critics talked of the book's 'happy anachronism' and its mastery of 'the forgotten art of storytelling'.)[3] Well, now García Márquez was going to show them that although he had written the most original novel seen in Latin America for a generation, he could quite easily 'go back' and write the kind of 'modernist' work with which Cortázar, Fuentes and Vargas Llosa had made their names – works which, ironically enough, in saluting precursors like Joyce and Woolf from the 1920s, were in a technical sense decades behind the sort of postmodernist revelation that *One Hundred Years of Solitude* had provided.

The new novel also had two very precise points of departure. One was an event in Caracas after the overthrow of Pérez Jiménez in 1958 when García Márquez witnessed a soldier holding an automatic weapon backing nervously out of the presidential palace; evidently he had come second best in the power struggle. The other came even earlier, when in a small tropical hotel García Márquez read the following lines from the early pages of Virginia Woolf's *Mrs Dalloway* about a hand, which may be that of the king of England, waving mysteriously – mythologically – from a black limousine:

> the enduring symbol of the state which will be known to curious antiquaries, sifting the ruins of time, when London is a grass-grown path and all those hurrying along the pavement this Wednesday morning are but bones with a few wedding rings mixed up in their dust and the gold stoppings of innumerable decayed teeth. The face in the motor car will then be known.

Thus the new book would be linguistically and technically 'experimental'. The reader would find herself lost in a series of labyrinths, often unsure of who was talking and when, with a constant sense of déjà vu and a frustration that the book, while advancing, never seemed to get anywhere. She would certainly notice the absence of full stops, the endless sentences – there appear to be only 100 in the entire novel – which grow longer and longer until in the last of the book's six parts there is only one full stop, which, naturally, follows the last word (which is, naturally, 'end').[4] There are constant switches of narrative person from first ('I', 'we') to second ('you', 'General sir', 'mother of mine') to third ('he', 'she', 'they'), although the latter is nearly always inside another first-person voice. García Márquez himself, the 'writer' as conventional third-person narrator, is almost entirely absent, yet none of his novels is more dominated by his familiar literary voice and style.

The Autumn of the Patriarch is the story of an unnamed and uneducated Latin American soldier, a tinpot general – García Márquez has risen from colonels to generals! – from an unnamed but evidently tropical Latin American republic which is equally evidently an aggregate of different countries. He seizes power early in the nineteenth century, not long after independence, despite his lack of qualifications and experience, and manages to rule as dictator for over two hundred years. (This brief summary alone confirms that this is not likely to be a 'realist' novel.) To create his literary monster, García Márquez drew on the biographies of numerous Latin American dictators: Porfirio Díaz of Mexico (1884–1911), Manuel Estrada Cabrera of Guatemala (1898–1920), the Venezuelans Juan Vicente Gómez (1908–35) and Marcos Pérez Jiménez (1952–8), who was still in power when García Márquez arrived in Caracas late in 1957, Rafael Trujillo of the Dominican Republic (1930–61), the Somozas of Nicaragua (Anastasio, Luis and Anastasio Jr, 1936–79), and also, of course, Francisco Franco, who had been in power in Spain since 1939 and who would die a few months after García Márquez's novel was published.[5]

Dictators and Latin America go together in the popular mind. Indeed, precisely because the continent created so many constitutional and theoretically democratic republics after independence from Spain in the early nineteenth century, republics that usually failed to live up to their own democratic aspirations, it is probable that no other part of the world – before the recent history of Africa – had produced so many examples of the phenomenon of the dictator since the times of the Roman empire. And this is reflected inevitably in Latin American literature: Domingo Faustino Sarmiento's *Facundo: Civilization and Barbarism* (1845) on the Argentinian dictator Rosas; the Spaniard Ramón María del Valle-Inclán's *Tirano Banderas* (1926); Miguel Angel Asturias's *The President* (*El Señor Presidente*, completed 1933; published 1946) on Guatemala's Estrada Cabrera; Juan Rulfo's *Pedro Páramo* (1955) on a Mexican landowner and caudillo who, though not a president, has all the instincts and methods of the species; Alejo Carpentier's *Reasons of State* (1974) on Cuba's Machado; Augusto Roa Bastos's *I the Supreme* (1974) on Paraguay's Francia; and Mario Vargas Llosa's *Conversation in the Cathedral* on Peru's Manuel Odría (1969) and *The Feast of the Goat* (2000) on the Dominican Republic's Trujillo.

As can be seen, García Márquez's novel arrived in the midst of a sudden flurry of dictator novels in the mid 1970s, inspired by the unexpected shock of dictatorial governments reappearing all over the continent from the mid 1960s, and in some of the largest and most developed nations: first in Brazil (1964) and then most notably in Chile (1973), Uruguay (1973) and Argentina (1976). This caused a number of misunderstandings because readers naturally expected the new novels on the subject to reflect current events, whereas Roa Bastos was looking at the first half of the nineteenth century, Carpentier at the 1920s and García Márquez at a vast period of time that seemed to go from the post-Independence period until – possibly – the late 1950s or early 1960s. Of course these writers were trying to diagnose the historical reasons for the phenomenon; but this did not appease the activists, some of whom accused the novelists of 'escapism' and other moral crimes. García Márquez only made matters worse when he declared that he had deliberately written a sympathetic portrait of the dictator because 'all dictators, from Creon onwards, are victims'.[6] The unfortunate truth was, he insisted, that Latin American history was not as intellectuals would have it: most dictators were from the popular classes and were rarely overthrown by the people they oppressed. Many dictators were even loved by large sections of the population for long periods of time.[7] It was not that myth had triumphed over history but rather that history itself always becomes mythologised. It is an essential function of literature to exemplify this process.

García Márquez's novel is set in a fictitious but apparently Caribbean republic (the sea is crucial both as material reality and as metaphor), which seems to have Colombia – or, more specifically, Bogotá – as its neighbour, so it may be thought of as either a country something like Venezuela or as the Colombian Costa itself, divided off notionally from the Andean highlands. (Colombia, one of the most regionally complex territories in Latin America, is many countries but it is certainly at least two: the Costa and the highlands. It is repeatedly rumoured in the novel that the Patriarch must be a highlander.) In that sense, as a nameless state, it bears comparison to the fictitious countries invented – and given fictitious names – by two non-Latin Americans in the early decades of the twentieth century: Joseph Conrad's Sulaco in *Nostromo* (1904) and Valle-Inclán's Santa Fe de Tierra Firme in *Tirano Banderas* (1926). At one point, indeed, uniting past and present, the dictator has a vision of the bay with 'the familiar battleship the marines had left behind at the dock, and beyond the battleship, anchored in the darkening sea, he saw the three caravels'.[8] These are presumably the three ships with which Columbus arrived in the Caribbean in 1492 to discover what would later be called Latin America, and one senses that, as García Márquez would underline in his Nobel speech, Latin America has still not finished being discovered.

García Márquez had always spoken deprecatingly of Miguel Angel Asturias, who won the Nobel Prize in Literature in 1967, the year in which *One Hundred Years of Solitude* appeared. But Asturias's *The President* is undoubtedly the most direct and significant precursor to García Márquez's novel, not only in its seeking after maximum impact through hyperbole and literary shock tactics (what Spanish critics sometimes call '*tremendismo*') but also through the disconcerting strategy of describing the most morally and physically repulsive phenomena through the most aesthetically beautiful avant-garde language: a poetry of the putrid.[9] Both novels seek to communicate the effect of the dictatorship on the consciousness of ordinary people, though García Márquez is more concerned with the consciousness and motives of the dictator himself while Asturias concentrates especially on the system, conceived as a grotesque web with the remote dictator as giant spider pulling the strings from its centre.

Known to the reader only as the 'Patriarch', or the 'General',[10] the book's monstrous protagonist is all-powerful yet solitary, vulgar and barbaric yet sentimental. Insensitive almost to the point of stupidity, he nevertheless has an uncanny instinct for power and a uniquely intuitive insight into other men's motives ('he saw others just as they were while the others were never able to glimpse [his] hidden thoughts'.)[11] Women, however, remain a mystery to him. García Márquez has told interviewers that his patriarch was what Colonel Aureliano Buendía would have turned into had he won his federalist war against the Conservatives, whereas in fact Colombia has remained a conservative country and Venezuela an essentially liberal one. The Patriarch is gross and ugly, with an elephant's feet and a huge herniated testicle for which special arrangements have to be made; no woman working in the palace is safe because he is liable to launch himself upon her like a dog in heat at the least expected moment.

The book unfolds in an impossible historical time – impossible in the sense that no one man could live through it – which stretches over more than two hundred years, probably from the late eighteenth century, when the protagonist's mother has her youth, until the post-Second World War era. Most of it is narrated through intricately embedded flashbacks and follows the general outlines of Latin American history (colonial period; independence; anarchy and dictatorship; twentieth-century neocolonialism) until the sea is expropriated by the hated *gringos* in the 'twilight' of the Patriarch's 'autumn' – nothing, finally, can be done about the *gringos* ('the English sat you there and the gringos kept you there …') – followed by his death and the consequent end of his regime. The dictator inhabits a world in which the military, the Church and the *gringos* are constantly jockeying for power – *his* power. 'The People' themselves are virtually passive; there is no genuine progress in the novel because there is no real history – they are almost completely marginalised and excluded from politics – and so for them there is no real passage of human time, only natural time.Yet the relationship between the dictator and the people is perhaps the central focus of the novel and García Márquez's gesture at the end of the novel, when the people celebrate the Patriarch's demise, is to hand the book over, symbolically, from the dictator to his previously powerless subjects.

Speaking in more individual terms, the Patriarch's closest relationship on earth is with his mother, Bendición Alvarado. (He has never known his father and claims he never had one: 'he considered no one the son of anyone but his mother ... he knew that he was a man without a father like the most illustrious despots of history ...') His wife is the ex-nun Leticia Nazareno, whom he kidnaps as an adolescent and later almost certainly murders when she too begins to impinge on his power; the lover he pursues but never wins – even dictators can't have everything, it seems – is the beauty queen Manuela Sánchez; and his only successful erotic relationship, bizarre and disturbing, is with a twelve-year-old schoolgirl when he is already senile. On the male side he has a double, or public face, Patricio Aragonés; just one good friend, Rodrigo de Aguilar; and, late in the novel, an evil genius, the glamorous Security Minister José Ignacio Sáenz de la Barra, a political fixer similar to the sinister advisers of the military regimes terrorising Chile and Argentina while García Márquez was writing the novel.

As it happens, this structure of relationships conforms exactly to the classic pattern of Western myth as analysed by Northrop Frye in *Anatomy of Criticism* (1957), which correlates archetypal characters with symbolic seasons or phases – though we can be sure that García Márquez, who has a strong aversion to literary criticism, had never read Frye. The very title of the novel suggests a concentration on a particular moment in the human person's procession through the seasons from spring (birth and childhood) to winter (dissolution and death).[12] The reader finds herself asking what and when exactly the Patriarch's 'autumn' really is and how it relates to the book's other repeated yet confusing concept: what it means for him to have 'all of his power'. The basic thematic oscillation of the entire novel is between the Patriarch's desire for absolute individual power and the reality that he needs others to do his work for him; whenever he hands over any of his power it begins to be expropriated and redistributed and he has to make a violent and ruthless effort to regain it and to 'become master of all his power' all over again. The search for the meaning of these two concepts, 'autumn' and 'power' – when we reach our autumn our powers are waning – eventually does much of the work required to understand the book.

As usual the book is in two halves, though this novel's structure is so extraordinarily complex and labyrinthine – it is a constantly self-deconstructing rather than a self-structuring work – that this phenomenon is perhaps not as decisive as in some other books.[13] Here the play between the events as they would unfold in reality in chronological order (what the Russian formalists and French structuralists called *fable*) and the events as García Márquez chooses to narrate them (*sujet*) is much more complicated than in almost any other novel – of his or anyone else's – but still the two-part structure imposes its own meaning on the book. And that meaning relates, unmistakably, to the onset of his autumn.

By extrapolating, we can establish the main things that happen over the approximately two hundred years covered by the novel and organised into its six chapters. Given the general impenetrability of the book, this may be helpful. Chapters 1 to 3 (our notation; the author, as usual, gives no numbers at all), in other words the first half of the novel, include the following phases and/or events: (1) The early years of poverty and humiliation endured by the general's mother Bendición Alvarado in the uplands, probably in the late colonial period; (2) his own childhood, possibly in the early emancipation period; (3) the anarchy of the federalist war, some time in the mid nineteenth century after the era of the conservative regimes; (4) his arrival in the capital down on the coast and his assumption of power some time after the mid nineteenth century, when he is installed by the British; (5) his messianic early days as president when he was an amazing force of nature but didn't yet believe that he was and therefore did not yet understand his power; (6) the occupation by the US marines that reduced him to impotence and showed him the limits of his power – his first defeat, in the early twentieth century; (7) the time of constant danger to his person when his double Patricio Aragonés and his trusted comrade Rodrigo de Aguilar together protected him, before and behind the scenes, on the the 'eve of his autumn'; (8) the unrecognised hegemony of Rodrigo de Aguilar in the general's 'times of glory' near the beginning of his autumn; (9) his infatuation with beauty queen Manuela Sánchez and her escape and disappearance – his second defeat; (10) his continuing struggle against the army and the entrapment and horrific death of Rodrigo de Aguilar, his only friend, who he decides has betrayed him.

We see, then, that the first half ends on the eve of the dictator's 'autumn', when he has definitively established his control of the army, symbolised by the most grotesque and hyperbolic event of the entire novel, the moment when 'the eminent general Rodrigo de Aguilar came in on a silver tray ... ready

to be served up at a banquet of comrades by the official carvers to the petri-
fied horror of the guests.[14] We never know whether he was 'guilty' of trea-
son: if so, it would have been more than justified. Chapters 4 to 6, the second
half, then narrate: (11) the death of the general's mother Bendición Alvarado
and his struggle with the Church over her legacy – he has now lost both the
most important person in his life and the man who was his only true friend:
his 'autumn' will be a long and difficult period in which what will eventually
defeat him is a combination of ever increasing solitude and the ravages of old
age, including memory loss; (12) the moment when, following the death of his
mother, he briefly reaches out and finds his only wife Leticia Nazareno, whose
hegemony then begins, followed by her inevitable death and that of their son,
the Patriarch's only heir; (13) the hegemony of Sáenz de la Barra, during the
TV era, that is, in the second half of the twentieth century, when the Patriarch
celebrates his first century in power, and Sáenz's assassination; (14) the expro-
priation of the sea by the *gringos* at the 'twilight' of his autumn, which seems
to lead, if only symbolically, to his winter and the end of his regime; (15) the
Patriarch's old age, memory loss and death, celebrated by euphoric multitudes
on the last page of the book.[15]

This novel radically altered and deepened García Márquez's approach to
the twin problematics of power and love, his two central themes, entwined
in his work in so many ways, with their associated motifs of memory, nostalgia, solitude and death. Power and love, the love of power, the power of love,
are central aspects of human experience, with a particularly strong momentum in Latin American history, society and literature such as has not been felt
in British society (for example) since the times of Shakespeare and Milton.
Still, what is eternal in the novel is not dictatorship, nor the condition of Latin
America (though it *is* painfully slow to change) but power itself: its inevitability, its impact upon the relation of history to myth, the human desire for it, and
its effect upon the individuals who hold it and the individuals and groups who
are outside it but subject to it.

Simplifying to some degree, one might say that 'power' is the theme that
governs the relationships between men and other men; and that 'love' is the
theme that governs the relationships between men and women (though García
Márquez would certainly not deny that men have almost always, over time,
had power over women). In this surprisingly ruthless writer's perspective –
and indeed, language – the word 'love', *amor*, usually means, or at least is
inseparable from, sex. (But then, even in English, 'making love' is inseparable
from 'having sex'.) This is the essence, or rather the basis, of García Márquez's
view of human relations, and given that this is so, it is extraordinary that when

readers speak of his works they so often give an indulgent and almost sentimental smile. Evidently he is a writer who has found a way to make reality
bearable to millions of readers even though he is, to repeat the adverb, ruthlessly realistic. This suggests that perhaps we should not repeat another word
previously used in this chapter: 'cynical'. And perhaps the secret, finally, is that
his view of the world is indeed ruthlessly realistic but not cynical. He reveals
the terrible beauty of life, with all its tragedies and injustices, but he never
leaves the reader feeling that it is not worth living.

Each chapter of the novel begins with García Márquez's usual obsession,
the motif of burial, though the reader cannot be sure whether the body
repeatedly found is that of the tyrant or, indeed, if he is really dead. Thus
the narrative 'we' of these sections – we the people who found the corpse –
proves to be conjuring up a world in retrospect through a few short sentences
on the first page of each chapter with variable details about the discovery of
the body, after which the narrative plunges into the labyrinth or whirlpool of
flashbacks relating the life of 'him', 'the General', which dissolves gradually
into an autobiographical 'I', the Man of Power. The labyrinth, as in all modernist works, is both topic (life) and technique (the way through it). Thus
the reader's overwhelming experience is one of uncertainty and confusion
(in part the uncertainty and confusion of the people, who can only speculate
about the character and motivations of the mysterious man who governs their
destinies). The entire point of view, structure and even chronology of the
novel are determined by the confusion of a succession of narrators who are
never sure of anything but spend their time exploring the endless dilemma
as to whether the dictator does or does not control 'all of his power', which is
perhaps the most reiterated and the most disorienting concept of the whole
novel – magnified enormously by the fact that it is considered above all from
his own point of view, which is at once stupid and unreflective, hypocritical
and self-serving, but also, as we have noted, demonically intuitive and shrewd
where power itself is concerned.

All modernist works really need to be read at least twice, but this one more than
most. A reader too busy to do this should at least reread the first six pages because
these not only inaugurate almost all the major themes of the novel, including the
general's deaths, the matter of his power and the phases of his regime, but also
introduce many of the refrains which will be repeated throughout. By then the
reader is already aware that this is a shifting, unstable world and that the line
between history and myth is going to be especially difficult to draw.

Near the very end of the novel, the painfully senile Patriarch remembers
what his whole life he has tried desperately to forget, 'a remote childhood

that for the first time was his own image shivering in the icy highlands and the image of his mother Bendición Alvarado who stole the innards of a sheep away from the buzzards on the garbage-dump for his lunch.[16] This sudden insertion mitigates the general's crimes but does not absolve him of the judgement made only two pages later, namely that he ruled through lies and those lies deceived him as they deceived everyone else, except he was deceived about everything but power itself; but this obsession with power denied him the knowledge to which even the most ignorant of his people instinctively held on, namely that life was in the living, 'that it was arduous and ephemeral but there wasn't any other, general, because we knew who we were while he was left never knowing it forever'; and so at last he dies, condemned by his author despite all the indulgence shown to him, 'alien to the clamour of the frantic crowds ... the bells of glory that announced to the world the good news that the uncountable time of eternity had come to an end'. The lesson learned by the reader through this moral fable is that life is almost impossible to understand, and we all have excuses for our crimes and misdemeanours, but there are certain 'moral' truths despite all our illusions which cannot be denied and there are no excuses for ignoring them. These moral truths are roughly those of Christianity (without the transcendence) and Socialism (without the totalitarian temptation) combined: human solidarity and love, putting others before oneself, turning the other cheek when it is a question of defending oneself but doing whatever is necessary to protect the weak and defenceless, etc.

This conclusion is mainly implicit. (García Márquez's interviews from this time are clearer on these matters.) And all this is in the realm of what should be. In the realm of what is and has been, few works of literature are more balefully realistic; few have fewer illusions. García Márquez's view of history and human motivation is very close to that bleak vision which Machiavelli first theorised and Shakespeare best exemplified. Power is a social, not an individual phenomenon; power abhors a vacuum; power has to be used: 'someone has to do it'. The only question, then, is to find the best way of organising power for the best – at once most ordered and most equitable – interests of society in a world where most people are serving their own best interests. No one emerging from this novel could deceive themselves that creating a just society in a difficult world is ever going to be easy.

But García Márquez had not finished shocking people with the subject matter and point of view of his book. He announced that it was a sort of autobiography! Yet his dictator, although in some ways treated indulgently by his author, is one of the most repugnant characters ever created, which, if García Márquez was not just trying to scandalise the international bourgeoisie, might make this one of the most startlingly self-critical works of world literature since Rousseau's *Confessions*. If the assertion is to be taken seriously, is he merely using himself as an example of a world more brutal than most of us ever wish to imagine, or is this an exclusively personal and thus uniquely devastating self-analysis? My answer is that it is mainly the former but also, and to a significant degree, a certain portion of the latter. García Márquez thinks he has been over-weeningly egocentric, selfish and ambitious, and the book is in part an act of self-recognition and a promise to himself that he will mend his ways. His enemies would never accept it, but if this interpretation is correct then *The Autumn of the Patriarch* must be counted not only a remarkable novel but an extraordinary act of moral introspection.

Where does this book stand in the García Márquez trajectory? Clearly it is the climax of his literary meditations on power. Clearly also, as mentioned, it is intended as a tour de force, a 'take that' sort of work which shows that he too could have written a 'modernist', typically 'Boomish' sort of work if with *One Hundred Years of Solitude* he had not vaulted over the 'Boom' into the white light of postmodernity. Stepping back a little further, however, it may be said that if *One Hundred Years of Solitude* is the literary centre of his *life* – his past, his family, Aracataca, that house, the colonel, the history of his country, all finally recuperated and distanced, all literarily encompassed and achieved, all his earlier works assimilated and incorporated – if *One Hundred Years of Solitude* is all that, *The Autumn of the Patriarch* is the centre – better, the axis – of his *work*. That this is so can easily be demonstrated by playing with the titles of other works, past and future, and adapting them as alternative titles for this book: 'Two Hundred Years of Solitude', 'Big Daddy's Funeral', 'No One Speaks to the General', 'Chronicle of a Death Foretold' (no need for a change), 'The General in His Labyrinth' (ditto), 'In Evil Hour' (ditto), 'Love and Power in the Time of Cholera', 'Of Love and Power and Other Demons'.

Although he was confronted with the challenge of producing another grand success after *One Hundred Years of Solitude*, there was no dilemma about what to write: it was always going to be *The Autumn of the Patriarch*. The problem was not *what* but *how*. *The Autumn of the Patriarch* was not, in short, the first book of the second half of his career, as most critics and historians have concluded, but the last book of the first half. The first half is devoted almost entirely to matters of power and we discover that power, though it has everything to do with desire, has very little to do with love. All the works up to and including *The Autumn of the Patriarch* (with the – only partial – exception of *No One Writes to the Colonel*) are about an absence of love, not the active pursuit of it.

At this moment in his life, García Márquez did not yet know that he would be devoting most of the second half of his career to love; but he did know that he could go no further with the theme of power (*The General in His Labyrinth*, about Bolívar, though a wonderful novel, is really a rewrite, an exercise, an addition, not a further exploration) – and this even though, in his own life, paradoxically, he was just about to pursue the friendship of Fidel Castro.[17] So he gave up writing novels for a while and turned to that exercise in power and on power called literary journalism. Once again, the devotees of his fiction would have to wait.[18]

Chapter 6

Chronicle of a Death Foretold (1981): postmodernism and Hispanic literature

Militant journalism: *Alternativa*, Bogotá (1974–1980)   75
A return to the newspaper 'chronicle' (1980)   77
Chronicle of a Death Foretold (1981)   78

The Autumn of the Patriarch was published in 1975, to mixed reviews, though García Márquez claimed to be confident that it was his most important work, even if the critics were slow to appreciate it. Now he was not sure what to do. After the publication of *One Hundred Years of Solitude* he had known that *The Autumn of the Patriarch* was his next project even if, in the event, it took him much longer to write and caused him much anguish in the writing. But now his natural trajectory seemed to have been completed and he was not at all sure what to do next.

Militant journalism: *Alternativa*, Bogotá (1974–1980)

What he did know was that he had sorely missed journalism since writing his last articles in 1960–61, and now that he was a widely known Latin American celebrity he wanted to 'use his fame' to intervene in the debates about Latin American politics. He was still an admirer of the Cuban Revolution of Fidel Castro – whom he would soon befriend – but he was horrified by what was happening in the rest of Latin America in the early 1970s. He confessed that the military overthrow of Salvador Allende's democratic socialist regime in Chile in September 1973 was a 'personal catastrophe' for him and he declared, somewhat recklessly, that he would not publish another novel until the military junta now ruling Chile had been overthrown. In order to return to journalism and influence events, he helped to found a left-wing magazine called *Alternativa* (1974–80) in Bogotá and, while spending most of his time in Europe and, in particular, in his new home in Mexico City, he devoted himself conscientiously to campaigning journalism and other political activities over the next six years.

His enemies might suppose that García Márquez only turned to journalism when he needed money, but this is not true. The journalistic impulse was with him all his life, evident even in his early writings in the Colegio San José in Barranquilla (or even earlier, when his grandfather made him turn his experience of seeing movies into telling stories about them). Literature tends more to an expression of the self; journalism involves thinking more about your audience.

What is true is that both in 1948 (the *Bogotazo*) and 1959 (the Cuban Revolution), politics decided his destiny as a journalist. And the same thing happened again in 1973. He had almost completed *The Autumn of the Patriarch*, about a monstrous Latin American dictator, when the government of Salvador Allende was overthrown on 11 September 1973 and a real-life monstrous dictatorship was established. García Márquez decided to act, and the first action he took was to return to journalism in a dramatic way. After discussions with young Colombian intellectuals, he decided to create a political magazine to be called *Alternativa*, whose first number would appear in February 1974. The magazine would last an astonishing six years and García Márquez, who would spend relatively little time in Colombia despite his best intentions, would nevertheless be a regular contributor and would make himself permanently available for consultations and advice.

The magazine included the first of two articles by García Márquez under the headline 'Chile, the Coup and the Gringos'. It was his first ever incursion into openly political journalism using his own voice and achieved worldwide distribution (published in the US and UK in March) and immediate classic status. Over the next six years García Márquez would interview leading politicians, activists and intellectuals such as CIA renegade Philip Agee, leaders of the 1974 Portuguese Revolution, Régis Debray, General Omar Torrijos of Panama and Spanish Socialist Party leader Felipe González – all this at a time when he was a member of the famous Russell Tribunals and administering his own human rights organisation Habeas.

In July 1975 he finally returned to Cuba. The revolutionary authorities gave him all the facilities necessary to travel the length and breadth of the island, going where he pleased and talking to whomsoever he wished. The idea was to write about 'how the Cubans broke the blockade inside their own homes; not the work of the Government or the State but how the people themselves solved the problem of cooking, washing and sewing their clothes, in short, all those everyday problems'. In September he published three memorable reportages, under the general heading 'From One End of Cuba to the Other'.

In March and April 1976 he returned to Cuba to prepare to write about the epic story of 'Operation Carlota', the Cuban expedition to Africa, the first time a Third World country had ever intervened in a conflict between the two superpowers from the First and Second worlds. At the end of 1976 Prensa Latina announced the imminent publication of his articles on the Cuban campaign: the Spanish version appeared in *El Espectador* in Bogotá between 9 and 11 January, and the English version appeared in the *Washington Post* between 10 and 12 January.

Meanwhile, Central America continued its convulsive revolutionary process. In Nicaragua the Sandinista rebels had been intensifying pressure on the Somoza dictatorship throughout 1977 and 1978. On 22 August 1978 a group of FSLN commandos led by Edén Pastora took the National Palace in Managua, kidnapped twenty-five parliamentarians, held them for two days and flew four of them to Panama with sixty freed political prisoners. García Márquez spent three days talking to the exhausted leaders of the spectacular assault and published the report in *Alternativa* in early September. Less than a year later the Sandinistas took power and García Márquez became one of their most important advisers.

By the end of 1979 *Alternativa*'s inherent economic problems had grown critical. The last issue, number 257, appeared on 27 March 1980. García Márquez again returned to literature, preparing *Crónica de una muerte anunciada* (*Chronicle of a Death Foretold*) after his six-year strike. But he was also working in committee – in Paris – on the final version of the report of the International Commission for the Study of Communication Problems (MacBride Report) which had been set up by UN director-general M'Bow in 1976. García Márquez would later say that he had never been so bored nor, as a 'solitary hunter of words', felt so useless, but equally he had never learned so much – above all, that information flows from the strong to the weak and is a crucial means of domination of the rich over the poor.

A return to the newspaper 'chronicle' (1980)

After the demise of *Alternativa* García Márquez never wrote such politically committed articles again. Even before the award of the Nobel Prize in 1982 his growing awareness of his extraordinary celebrity both liberated him and gave him a different sense of political responsibility: while still broadly committed to the Left, he realised that he would now have much more influence with the lords of the earth, as well as the common people, and that he should use it wisely and responsibly. The articles he wrote from this moment reflect this change.[1] Just a few months after the death of *Alternativa*, and anticipating a return to Colombia, he negotiated with his friends in *El Espectador* (Bogotá) and *El País* (Madrid) in order to embark upon a quite different kind of journalism. His new articles were mainly 'chronicles', the kind of thing he had written in the 1940s and 1950s in Cartagena and Barranquilla: in other words, no longer just political and cultural commentaries, but also memoirs, a kind of public diary, a fragmentary autobiography, a weekly letter to his friends and a circular to his fans. The articles began to appear in September 1980 and would continue virtually without interruption until March 1984, an astonishing total of 173 weekly articles during one of the busiest periods of the writer's entire life. They included, in 1982, less than a month before the Nobel award was to be announced, a withering attack on Israeli leader Menachem Begin – and, by implication, the Nobel Foundation which had awarded Begin the Nobel Peace Prize in 1978. Sharon and Begin should get a Nobel Death Prize, he declared. In general, however, these articles were very much less political than his previous journalism and are too diverse to be studied here. Nevertheless, they offer an invaluable resource for anyone wishing to get to know 'García Márquez the man'.

We should also note that García Márquez has written several works of 'documentary narrative', as by-products of his journalism, which are among his most successful publications: *Story of a Shipwrecked Sailor* (1955); *Miguel Littín Clandestine in Chile* (1986) and *News of a Kidnapping* (1996) are the best known of these. All are at least as close to journalism as they are to those literary narratives we call the novel or the short story. Moreover his best-selling novel *Chronicle of a Death Foretold* is narrated as if it were the product of a somewhat mediocre, or at least unsuccessful, journalist – as well as including the world 'chronicle' in its title. And his last novel, *Memories of My Melancholy Whores* (2002), is narrated by a man in his nineties who has indeed spent his life as a second-rate journalist in the city of Barranquilla.

Chronicle of a Death Foretold (1981)

After six long years, as it became clear that the regime of General Pinochet was not going to fall any time soon, and as *Alternativa* began to encounter financial difficulties, García Márquez declared that he was 'more dangerous as a writer than as a politician' and began work on a new novel. It was something he had had at the back of his mind for thirty years, the story of an honour killing: the brutal murder, in Sucre, of a friend accused of having seduced and deflowered a young woman returned to her family by an outraged and disillusioned husband after discovering she was not a virgin on her wedding night. García Márquez had promised his mother that he would not write the novel until certain protagonists who were her friends had passed away. By 1980 this was finally the case. Once again, then, the subject matter had been sleeping and growing in his unconscious for many years. But once again the trigger was an image: the sight, on one of his many journeys at this time, of an Arab prince carrying a falcon through an international airport. This gave him an 'angle' on the story which would begin to shape his vision of the long-delayed novel before he had even written the opening words. First, the protagonist would be, to some extent, an outsider, the son of an Arab (whereas the historical protagonist, Cayetano Gentile, had been of partly Italian stock); second, although in most respects a regular guy, he would be a seducer, a falcon who went hunting for smaller and effectively helpless birds: impressionable young women. Hence the epigraph to the novel from Gil Vicente: 'the hunt for love is high-flown falconry'.

This would be one of García Márquez's most successful novels, brilliantly conceived and executed and almost unanimously greeted by critics as a tour de force. As with *One Hundred Years of Solitude*, a great writer had found a way of making sophisticated narrative techniques pioneered by Woolf and Faulkner totally accessible to the so-called general reader. As a matter of fact, many of these techniques had been used in *The Autumn of the Patriarch* but what was deliberately difficult and opaque in that novel became more obviously functional and transparent in the new one. It also introduced the overtly self-referential and autobiographical frame that would characterise much of his fiction from this moment onwards.

Yet the book marked a radical and even disconcerting shift after a decade of political commitment and activism. It dealt with the time-honoured 'Hispanic' themes of honour and shame and seemed to suggest, contrary to the optimistic implications of García Márquez's socialist credo, that society – especially, perhaps, Colombian society – might be much more inherently conservative and therefore much more immune to change than he had previously hoped and believed.

Like *No One Writes to the Colonel* and *In Evil Hour*, this novel is set in an unnamed small town based on Sucre, where the García Márquez family lived from 1940 to 1951.[2] In fact it was in large measure the murder re-enacted in the novel, typical of the violence sweeping the region at the time, that had led the family to flee Sucre and migrate to the city of Cartagena. And yet, despite all the topographical similarities, this does not seem to be the same town. For one thing, none of the previous characters appears in this novel and, for another, the political dimension is almost completely absent and, when it does appear (reference to the Mayor having been involved in 'massacres', for example), it seems to be incidental (unless we are meant to critique and even disbelieve the narrator, and the signs of this are few and at best ambiguous). For that very reason, perhaps, centred on violence though it is, this is not a novel of the Colombian *Violencia* – its emphasis is straightforwardly social and moral, not political and ideological – even though the event which inspired it took place in January 1951 at the very height of the undeclared civil war. For this reason, presumably, García Márquez sets it back in the 1940s. (It appears to take place over three days in February 1944.)

Another reason for this temporal displacement may be to give himself, as author, narrator and character, some historical-imaginative space: he prefers to be an adolescent high-school student of seventeen rather than the twenty-four-year-old he actually was when the murder of his friend Cayetano Gentile (aka Santiago Nasar) took place – just as in *Leaf Storm* he had portrayed the character based upon himself as a ten-year-old boy in 1928, rather than 1938, as would have been the case in reality. At any rate the Sucre described here, twenty-five years after the writing of *No One Writes to the Colonel* and *In Evil Hour*, is, disconcertingly, a Sucre prior to either of them and yet the horrific event at its core is described with a vivacity – and, at times, a levity, or post-modern irony – which gives it a completely different atmosphere and makes its events appear more recent than those of the earlier works. Added to which, this is a supreme narrator at the very height of his powers whose resources are infinitely more varied and subtle than those of the writer of those early novels.

The story is quickly told, though its twists and turns are constantly surprising. When Bayardo San Román, until recently a stranger to the small river town with no name, returns his wife Angela Vicario to her family on their wedding night after discovering that she is not a virgin, her outraged family, humiliated – like the newly wed husband – in front of the whole community, sets out to bully her into revealing who the seducer had been. Eventually she declares that the guilty man was Santiago Nasar, the son of a local Arab land-owner (though the Nasar family is Christian). Nasar, a popular young man, is betrothed to another young woman and shows every sign of being unaware that he is in danger. This suggests that he is either innocent of the seduction or confident that his class position will keep him from danger.[3] In accordance with the local code of honour – and indeed with the code of honour of many, perhaps most rural societies all over the world – Angela's twin brothers Pedro and Pablo are obliged to restore the family's good name by taking revenge on Nasar, and they announce to all and sundry that they are going to do so. Nasar is the last to know – this is the irony underpinning all the other ironies in the book – and dies a horrific death when he is almost literally cut to pieces in the town square, as if in a bullring, in front of scores of spectators. The novel is full of tension even though García Márquez announces the death on the very first page: the suspense therefore resides in the telling and in the reader's anxiety to know why no one managed to warn the unfortunate protagonist, and what were the fatal steps that took him to the atrocious end that has him trying to return to his house and to his mother with his intestines in his hands like a bunch of roses.

And there is a second dimension. Someone very like García Márquez himself has attempted to reconstruct this terrible story. However, unlike the book's author, a world-famous novelist little more than a year away from winning the Nobel Prize in Literature, the narrator is an unsuccessful and world-weary journalist who has decided to go back to the small town where he was born, twenty-seven years after the original events (which would make the narrator of the novel a man of forty-four), and try to solve the mystery of whether Santiago Nasar was 'guilty' as alleged and how it came about that no one was able to warn him of the fate that awaited him in the town square.[4] Thus to the primary level of suspense – will Santiago Nasar be murdered, as the book predicts from the first page? – there is a secondary level of suspense: will the journalist as detective discover what 'really' happened all those years before? García Márquez said at the time that the book was 'a sort of false novel and a false reportage': as an investigator the narrator is journalist, autobiographer, historian, detective and judge.

In other words, when García Márquez refers in his title to 'a death foretold' he is referring both to the nature of the story he is telling – the brothers proclaimed what they were intending to do (almost certainly hoping that in this way they would be prevented from doing it) – and the way he himself has chosen to tell it: by announcing the death in the first line of the first chapter, repeating it several times more in the following chapters – Nasar dies many times in the novel – and then finally having the wretched protagonist announce it in the last lines of the drama: 'They've killed me, Missy Wenefrida.' It is as if, like some literary conjuror, García Márquez is proclaiming: 'This is the trick I'm going to perform, before your very eyes; you know it can't really be done because I've given you the explanation in advance so all suspense is impossible but I am still going to mesmerise you and fill you with suspense and you won't be able to help yourselves.' And so it is: the reader still wants to know exactly what happened, how and why, and reads on. And yet, at the end of the book, we still do not know whether Santiago Nasar was 'guilty' and 'deserved' to die (according to the local morality), and the fundamental questions of causality and what we call 'fate' or 'destiny' are as mysterious and as troubling as ever. Though of course by then we have thought about them much more than before we began the book.

Thus it is that many layers of irony and ambivalence are packed into a brief novel whose extraordinary complexities are skilfully orchestrated so that even readers who normally reject fancy narrative techniques and temporal manipulations are lured on from line to line and from paragraph to paragraph. To help them along, the novelist has packed the book with oft-repeated phrases that act like poetic or dramatic refrains ('The day he was going to be killed', 'It was the last time she saw him', 'I would have said the same', 'The hooting of the archbishop's boat', etc.).

There are interesting and illuminating contrasts with the three short novels written more than a quarter of a century earlier and discussed in Chapters 2 and 3. In those chapters we said that *Leaf Storm* was 'modernist' and that *In Evil Hour* and *No One Writes to the Colonel* were 'neorealist' works. *Chronicle of a Death Foretold*, by comparison, is usually considered a 'postmodernist' work because although full of literary knowhow it seems – the verb is important – simpler than a book like *Leaf Storm*, even though it is written from a world view that is actually much more complex.

Leaf Storm and *Chronicle of a Death Foretold* – the one modernist, the other postmodernist – are both autobiographical in a significant sense, although the metafictional aspect is handled differently in each case. *In Evil Hour* and *No One Writes to the Colonel* are much less directly autobiographical, relying much more on social observation and much less on personal memory, and are fairly traditional in technique, although still extremely skilful 'realist' and 'referential' works. (Even within this distinction, however, the matter of *In Evil Hour*'s chain-like – metonymic – structure as against *No One Writes to the Colonel*'s poetic – metaphorical – structure is a useful comparative concept.)

To pursue the point, in the modernist *Leaf Storm* it is the philosophical-epistemological questions about time, consciousness and memory itself which necessitate the technical complexities and which give rise to the complex narrative form. In other words, narrative manipulations are *functional* in the way that the 'New Criticism' of the 1940s and 1950s proposed: the novel is the 'form of its content'. These strategies show the problematical question of time itself, its relation to consciousness (subjectivity), to the relativity caused by multiple points of view (synchronicity, simultaneity), the inherent relation between memory and myth, and the disjuncture between myth and history themselves.

In that sense *Leaf Storm*, as mentioned before, is very like a novel of the 1960s 'Boom' (always remembering that the 'Boom' was in part a delayed version of 1920s European modernism and that *One Hundred Years of Solitude*, much more postmodern, is by no means a typical novel of the 'Boom'), though without as yet an exploration – which in García Márquez's case would arrive with 'Big Mama's Funeral' – of the Boom's twin themes of the Nation and Identity. Despite the attacks of both liberal and Marxist critics upon them, the 1920s modernists never saw their way of writing as a form of escapism or a negation of reality, even if it was a negation of conventionally understood 'time', 'history' and 'consciousness'; on the contrary, they believed that their perception of reality was more realistic than that of either nineteenth-century 'classical realism' or early twentieth-century 'socialist realism'; and this of course is why the nineteenth-century impressionists, on the one hand, and Gustave Flaubert on the other – literary 'artists' all – are the essential predecessors of Joyce, Woolf and Faulkner, not Flaubert's contemporaries and heirs like Balzac, Dickens, Zola or Tolstoy.[5] This is also why, although *Leaf Storm* is profoundly autobiographical, its author did not feel the need to indicate this inside the text, as he would in the later *Chronicle of a Death Foretold*; on the contrary, he would have felt this inappropriate, because he was still in the modernist phase of conceiving even such a socially committed novel (simultaneously advancing and undermining a 'patrician' vision, as William Faulkner had in the 1920s and 1930s) as an autonomous 'work of art' and thereby concealing his literary clockwork: the work should explain itself and reality should be 'rendered', not 'reported'.

Even in *In Evil Hour* and *No One Writes to the Colonel*, the very sophisticated versions of 'realist' technique (*In Evil Hour* extensive, *No One Writes to the Colonel* intensive) show an evident self-consciousness and an implicit self-critique which one finds in few other writers within this discursive practice – realism – and its associated rhetorical strategies. Moreover, the persistent emphasis on communication or its absence – almost no one in *Leaf Storm* could understand, still less sympathise with, anyone else's point of view, a social problem which would become almost the shaping theme by the time of *One Hundred Years of Solitude* – is very firmly emphasised in both works: in *No One Writes to the Colonel* the central motif is a letter which never comes, symbolising a more general absence of communication in the small, isolated town; and in *In Evil Hour* we have the *pasquines* (anonymous flysheets), illegitimate messages without an author which almost nobody reads and which in the first half of the novel function as both a sign and a catalyst of social violence, and the *hojas clandestinas* (political leaflets), which function in the second half as a sign of political violence. Power, repression and solitude, on the one hand; love, liberation and solidarity, on the other – these seem to be the parallel impulses of this author's work at this stage in his life.

If we return, however, to *Chronicle of a Death Foretold*, a tragi-comic work, the inability of the townsfolk to communicate is laughable at times but contributes dramatically to the horror of an atrocious murder. Behind the stupidity, illogicality or irresponsibility of many of the characters, there lie deeper problems which were scarcely present in those earlier works: What is truth? Can anything be known at all? Do stories change if the narrative method changes? And many others besides.

In *Leaf Storm* the characters talked directly to the reader; there was no narrator outside of the boy, his mother and his grandfather. Here the journalist-narrator stands between the reader and the content of the story: he is omnipresent, and nothing in the book is narrated outside of his consciousness and voice, that of a man who 'came back to this forgotten town trying to reconstruct with all these haphazard fragments the broken mirror of memory'.[6] As in *Leaf Storm*, the novel itself is temporally (and therefore narratively) extremely complex, but here there is no sense in which once we have solved the detective-story puzzle of the timeline we will have reached the centre of its meaning; on the contrary, we are left with more of a disjuncture than ever between the events themselves – above all the naked climax of Santiago Nasar's eventual murder – and the already profoundly problematised construction and meaning of those events. In *Leaf Storm* – to insist – resolving the temporal puzzle resolves most of the problems posed by the book, and further elucidation is prevented mainly by the limitations of the point of view of the characters themselves. In *Chronicle of a Death Foretold*, by contrast, the painstaking reconstruction of the point of view of many individuals finally solves almost nothing – we are left not so much with the epistemological problem of the nature of reality and truth, which *seemed* to have been the obsessive purpose of the novel, but the ontological problem involved in the nature of events themselves – any events – and of narrative itself. This leaves us with a *discursive* problem, more Hayden White (narrativity) one might say than Henri Bergson (temporality), more Linda Hutcheon (postmodern parody and perplexity) than New Criticism (modernism's aestheticising complexity), in the sense that none of the characters are taken entirely seriously – not now because they are Latin Americans living in the false consciousness of their repeatedly colonised and almost permanently subjugated continent, but because nothing is taken seriously; even that earlier point of view is itself parodied.

Indeed, none of García Márquez's novels after *One Hundred Years of Solitude* and *The Autumn of the Patriarch* offer clear political-historical explanations for the absurdity – in Camus's or Beckett's sense – of Latin American life. Life itself, no longer analysable, in the modernist way, as 'experience', no longer texturally interesting in the same way, is everywhere absurd and unjust – García Márquez would have found this idea mystificatory in the 1950s – and therefore narrative and indeed all discourse begin to question their own status in quite different ways. They are no longer separable from the world they represent; such a space – like the space between history and myth – no longer exists. García Márquez's 1982 Nobel speech, of which more in the following chapter, would be the last effort to impose his earlier world view on reality, whereas he could no longer write from that earlier view when engaged in the business of fictional creation. (This loss of a philosophical vision is in his case closely related to the theme of Cuba as an extra-literary means of holding on to the world view otherwise unsustainable after his 1957 visit to the USSR. García Márquez at first attempted to believe in Fidel Castro as a successful reincarnation of Bolívar 120 years later, but eventually came to see him as yet another magnificent Latin American chaser after chimeras.)

So much for more general comparisons with earlier novels. Let us now return to the details, beginning with character, structure and technique and moving on to theme and ideology. *Chronicle of a Death Foretold*, like, for example, *In Evil Hour*, has an astonishing number of characters for so short a book – well over sixty – and their personalities, appearances and statements are expertly introduced and beautifully orchestrated. The hapless Santiago Nasar – a mere object of fate, violence and other people's pity – appears as an actor only in the first twenty and the last twenty pages, though of course he is mentioned all the time by the narrator and by others in the pages in between – because, in reality, this is more a book that concentrates on the narrator's reconstruction of the events than it is a book about the events and motives themselves since those events and motives, like all stories, all reality, all history, we come to see, are ultimately irrecoverable.

The novel has five unnumbered chapters, each of which divides quite noticeably into two sections. In the very middle of chapter 3, on the day he is destined to die, Santiago Nasar arrives at his house, after a night of carousing, at 4.20 a.m. – one hour before the formal beginning of the novel, when he gets up again at 5.30 a.m. to see the archbishop's boat go by. In other words, up to here the narrative has effectively gone backwards. Since the end of the novel will involve him trying desperately to get home again before the Vicario twins can kill him, it can be easily agreed that this poignant narrative device – Santiago going home earlier in the day – is crucial to the structure of the novel, even though it was not crucial to the unfolding of the events themselves. Thus the first return home, halfway through chapter 3, divides the book in half with the same *enjambement* device that we have previously noted in *No One Writes to the Colonel* (signalled by the bitter argument between the colonel and his wife).

As we are beginning to see, this most accessible and apparently simple of novels is fearsomely complex. The very first sentence – 'On the day they were going to kill him, Santiago Nasar ...' – is reminiscent in its structure of the famous first sentence of *One Hundred Years of Solitude*. And just as in that earlier novel the first sentence does not clarify whether the colonel died in front of the firing squad (he did not), so here it is not entirely clear whether Santiago Nasar was killed (he was, as the title of the novel itself suggests): 'they were going to kill him', not 'they killed him' or 'they would kill him', both of which would be conclusive.

If we look now at the first five sentences, sentence 1 (preterite tense) begins the narrative of the original events themselves with Santiago Nasar rising from his bed at 5.30 a.m. to wait for the arrival of the archbishop's boat; at this point we are not yet aware that there is a first-person narrator framing this third-person narrative. Sentence 2 (pluperfect) is an immediate flashback to Santiago's dreams during his brief sleep. Sentence 3 (preterite/imperfect) is a flash-forward twenty-seven years to his mother remembering his dreaming habits all that time ago. Sentence 4 (pluperfect) is a flashback from 3 to a week before sentences 1 and 2 (his mother recalling another dream Santiago Nasar had around that time). Sentence 5 (imperfect), explaining her reputation for dream interpretation, could refer, when it begins, either to the time twenty-seven years before or the time twenty-seven years later – and turns out to be the former and thus a return to the time of sentence 1. This is not only extraordinarily complicated for a first page but also already begins the novel's entire structural alternation between the events leading to the murder and the narrator's reconstruction and narration of them 'many years later'. Ordinary readers have no need to attend to all of this: the author guides them through with expert ease and their unconscious does the rest. The narrator, by contrast, is hesitant and unsure, and we feel no particular need to accept his interpretation when he says of Santiago Nasar late in the novel, 'My personal impression is that he died without understanding his death.'

The technical prowess by now is unmistakable. This is not only one of the world's great storytellers in the oral – elemental, dramatic, hypnotic – sense of the concept; he is also one of the most brilliant *literary* craftsmen. But ironically enough, this ultra-modern sense of literary expertise is here applied to the most traditional, and in many senses the most conservative, subject matter that García Márquez had ever taken on: that nexus of themes we think of as essentially 'Hispanic'. (The next book, *Love in the Time of Cholera*, would be more 'French'.) These themes go all the way back to the Golden Age of the sixteenth and seventeenth centuries – and even to the medieval troubadours before – and then forward to the works of Valle-Inclán and Lorca in the early twentieth century. They involve not only the well-known honour and shame syndrome but also an equally familiar cluster of motifs relating to destiny and fate.

In this traditional Hispanic world, typically, the relation between men and women is seen not as essentially individual and loving but as inherently social and prescriptive, and therefore violent and conflictive. Of the Vicario family, the narrator says: 'The brothers were brought up to be men. The girls had been educated for marriage.' The narrator's own mother comments, 'Any man would have been happy with them, because they had been brought up to suffer.' Such attitudes remind the reader of Lorca's Andalusian tragedies, like *The House of Bernarda Alba*, *Blood Wedding* and *Yerma*. And as we look further back, we think inevitably of works like Lope de Vega's *The Knight of Olmedo* (*El caballero de Olmedo*) on honour, fate and a death foretold, and *Fuenteovejuna* (in which a whole town proclaims itself guilty of the murder of an aristocratic rapist, out of solidarity), as well as Tirso de Molina's *The Trickster of Seville* (*El burlador de Sevilla*), which inaugurates the entire Don Juan syndrome, still relevant to the present day. In García Márquez's *Chronicle*, when the two murderers talk to the local priest they protest: '"We killed him in full awareness ... but we are innocent." "Perhaps before God," said Father Amador. "Before God and men both," said Pablo Vicario. "It was a question of honour."'[7]

In fact, the famous Mediterranean double standard can cut – so to speak – both ways. Don Juan, the *trickster*, is not blamed for trying, though the women he pursues are blamed for succumbing (even though women are also thought to be weak and susceptible); but even though the seducer is not blamed he must be killed, to wash the affront away. (In the Golden Age, and in many rural – especially Islamic – societies today the woman was and is also frequently killed.) Usually, of course, if the man is from a higher class, as in this case (remembering the epigraph, 'The hunt for love is high-flown falconry'), an embittered shrug of the shoulders is the more usual reaction. But García Márquez's implicit message appears to be that men should not be 'haughty' and that even if he didn't seduce Angela Vicario, Santiago Nasar had seduced others (we see him routinely harassing his servant Divina Flor), and he and all his class always 'ask' for what they only occasionally get. The novel draws attention to the ambiguity in the most usual symbol of love: 'a heart pierced by an arrow'. When Santiago Nasar is named by Angela Vicario as her seducer ('my author'), he too is impaled: 'She looked for him in the darkness, she found him at once among all the many names confused together in this world and the other, and she left him fixed to the wall with an unerring dart, like a helpless moth whose sentence had been laid down since the beginning. "Santiago Nasar," she said.'[8]

Themes relating to fate – destiny, chance, coincidence, premonitions, dreams – are closely related to the honour and shame thematic, because the question is to what extent social pressures, for the individual, are as much a part of destiny and the nature of things as any other agency. To what extent are we responsible for our actions, in control of our fate? Irony thus functions at every level: the ultimate absurdity here is that Santiago Nasar may not have done the deed and the brothers don't want to kill him! And to compound these ironies, many years later Angela and Bayardo get back together! It is the combination of fate and human fallibility, and above all the confusion of the two, which brings about the death. The agents themselves do not feel responsible: "'This cannot be helped,' he said to him. "It's as if it had already happened.'"

Many of García Márquez's titles have been extremely influential and are often quoted or paraphrased in newspapers and magazines. *Chronicle of a Death Foretold* is perhaps the most quoted title of all. The reason, of course, is that it implies that whatever is announced can be prevented and that human agency can predetermine the course of the world. All novels – all histories – have to address this problem, implicitly or explicitly. (Consider Tolstoy's 'second epilogue', on the nature of causality, in *War and Peace*.) On the whole, García Márquez's earlier work tended to imply that more things were subject to human agency than Latin American popular consciousness tended to believe; on the whole, the later work tends to question more sceptically what is and is not subject to human agency and tends to show that most things are not: 'Never was there a death more foretold' – but nobody could stop it.[9]

The particular genius of this novel is that the theme unites form and content, the story told and the way it is told, in a uniquely effective way. The forthcoming death of Santiago Nasar was announced by the would-be murderers and still nobody did anything about it; fate seemed to have given them the role of killers and nothing, it seems, could be done. Yet the 'fate' involved was a fate dependent on human ideology and agency – the honour code – which, being human, could be changed and is nevertheless construed as leaving nobody any choice. This leaves a circularity of fate and agency, responsibility and irresponsibility, which makes the reader almost dizzy. Even then, despite all the unfortunate coincidences and all the personal idiocies, the victim could still have escaped at the last but his own mother unwittingly caused his death by locking the front door.[10]

Are violent deaths fated? Is the day of our death determined on the day we are born? Do we have lifelines on the palms of our hand? Can our destiny be read in the stars? The name 'Nasar' in Latin American Spanish includes the word 'Azar' (pronounced 'asar'), 'fate', a word of Arab origin, which every native reader must unconsciously register. Santiago Nasar is a hunter; the two brothers fated to kill him are butchers. The first few pages are full of images of violence (Nasar's servant Plácida Linero cutting up rabbits, for example), in order to establish the theme and atmosphere, though the rest of the novel is not, until the very end, especially violent.

The end itself, however, is deeply shocking. And not the least shocking part about it is that it is also comic. The brothers who commit the act have been cast as comic characters until now; and many others have shown a tendency to say illogical things and to appease their consciences however they can by using every contradictory excuse under the sun. Now those same people turn up, as in a Western or, more appropriately, as in a Spanish bullring, and begin to 'take their places in the square to witness the crime'. Even more sinister, perhaps, is the fact that the author himself 'plays' with Santiago Nasar's death, as a bullfighter plays with a bull; and, as in a bullfight, the inevitability of that death is the precondition of the ritual or, in this case, the way in which this novel is to be narrated. (After all, since the death which has inspired his novel is the death of a close friend, many years before, the presupposition of the narrative is that the death was not inevitable then – or was it? – but is unavoidable now.) Thus in a novel which critiques 'machismo', García Márquez himself goes in for the literary version by declaring in advance that he is giving the end of the story first and challenging his audience to stop watching (i.e. reading). He, the insouciant author (a supremely confident contrast to his uncertain narrator, who is nevertheless based on him and has a similar but not identical biography), has conceived his novel quite consciously as a tour de force, like a bullfighter who is going to kill his bull in an unforgettable fashion, with a flourish at once dramatic and aesthetic. The result, on one level, is as populist, compulsive and irresistible as that well-known Hispanic pastiche, Ravel's *Bolero*; but it is also, because of the subtle counterpointing, profoundly unsettling and disturbing.

The typical postmodern work is light, parodic and quite often heartless. And this is what we feel we are getting, at the hands of a literary master, for most of this book. ('Don't bother, Luisa Santiaga. They've already killed him.') But García Márquez gives us both the comedy and the tragedy. Santiago Nasar staggers towards his house with his intestines in his hands, sees Wenefrida Márquez cutting up a fish and announces the blindingly obvious (even though it is not – yet – true), 'They've killed me, Missy Wenefrida.' But here we are at 'The End', Death itself, and finally, as this victim of fate falls dead to the floor, there is no further comment. We have been given a brilliant, horrifying, hallucinatory ending, with nothing more to say. All the clues, all the arguments, all the complexities, are behind us. (Or so we feel.) This is the fact, the only certainty, the moment of truth and yet the ultimate mystery, beyond all explanation, in the realm of myth itself.

Chapter 7

Love in the Time of Cholera (1985): the power of love

Six years had passed between the publication of *The Autumn of the Patriarch* and *Chronicle of a Death Foretold*. The new book, brief as it was, sold in its millions around the world and convinced the critics that García Márquez was back with a vengeance and capable, literarily speaking, of almost anything. In December 1982 the award of the Nobel Prize in Literature to the Colombian was probably the most popular decision made by the Swedish Academy in the second half of the twentieth century. In his acceptance speech in Stockholm, he pleaded for greater sympathy for the Latin American continent from which he came and which, by now, he felt entitled to represent. He spoke of a region still unknown and neglected, a region which was indeed magical but not in an irrational way, a region consistently subjected to the travesty of being judged by the standards of Europe in terms of culture and politics when Europe, which had many unhappy ghosts walking its corridors and skeletons rattling its closets, had taken a thousand years to achieve what it expected Latin America to have achieved in two hundred. 'Allow us to live out our own Middle Ages,' he declared, 'so that our peoples, despite all their misfortunes, may have a second chance upon the earth.'

The tacit reference to the ending of *One Hundred Years of Solitude*, with its implicit faith in social and political progress (giving credence, incidentally, to my positive interpretation of that ending outlined in Chapter 4), was already anachronistic. The García Márquez who spoke those inspiring words would continue to work for the Cuban Revolution, and for international solidarity and political progress, yet, despite those words, he was no longer as optimistic as he had been. *Chronicle of a Death Foretold* had demonstrated this – for those who wished to read between the lines. Yet again García Márquez was moving in two different directions at the same time. And like the Soviet Union he was no longer talking of victory but implicitly suing for peace. Up to now his books had been less about the grand theme of love than about the incapacity for love, which seemed to apply not only to individuals but to countries and even continents: solitude and power had dominated his literary world. Now, since his political world view seemed increasingly unlikely to prevail – and as a reader of political reality he was second to none – he decided to bestow cheer on the world. This socialist, this friend of Fidel, would adopt a new mask: the Bringer of Love.

He had begun a new novel before the prize was awarded and this, plus his extraordinary work ethic and unrivalled sense of vocation, commitment and concentration, allowed him to continue with his writing despite the notorious negative effect of the great Prize which, ironically, tended to blunt the creativity of those whose creativity had just been celebrated.

The new novel would have the curious name of *Love in the Time of Cholera*. Once again there was an image which acted as catalyst, that of two old people fleeing in a boat, because he had read about two aged lovers who had been murdered by a boatman. The murder would not be included; instead, the image of two old people fleeing the world in a boat would climax a novel which would also be inspired by the courtship of his parents. This time he, who had tended to exclude his father – indeed, fathers in general – from his novels, would give a character based partly upon his father, the protagonist Florentino Ariza, a starring role. And, adding to the list of personal reconciliations which the novel was to embody, it would be set in the spectacular colonial port of Cartagena, until this point, owing to the conservatism of its traditions, his least favourite city on the Caribbean coast.

All of this on the Colombian side, so to speak. But it would also be a novel with a significant French input and appearance – García Márquez had recently bought apartments both in Cartagena and in Paris – in contrast with, as we have seen, the profoundly 'Hispanic' nature of *Chronicle of a Death Foretold*. He read or reread such French classics as Flaubert's *Sentimental Education*, Proust's *In Search of Lost Time*, and Larbaud's *Fermina Márquez*. (Other European classics from the book's timescale – 1880s to early 1930s – would also be useful for those wishing to research this novel's literary background: for example, Thomas Mann's *The Magic Mountain* or Axel Munthe's *The Story of San Michele*.)

The action of the novel takes place between the 1870s and the early 1930s. Western literature has rarely managed successful novels about love, especially novels with a happy ending, and it may be that even García Márquez would have found it difficult to carry off the trick had his novel been set in the 1970s or indeed the 1980s, when it was written. As ever, the chronology is intricate although, once again, the new post-*Autumn* García Márquez has gone to considerable lengths to make it reader-friendly in every way: in this book the reader will note the complex architecture but also congratulate herself that she can see it and that she can, so to speak, 'use' it.[1] The characters have huge expanses of time at their disposal and so does the author: this long novel – the opposite of dense – has no more characters than brief narratives such as *In Evil Hour* and *Chronicle of a Death Foretold*.

In essence, the plot of the novel is a time-honoured love triangle. In the 1870s a young man from the lower middle classes of Cartagena, seventeen years of age, illegitimate and of mixed race, called Florentino Ariza, who works in the post office as a telegraphist, falls in love with Fermina Daza, the thirteen-year-old daughter of a coarse but wealthy Spanish trader. Their lives are in a way symmetrical because he is a boy without a father and she is a girl without a mother. After much teenage gazing and moping they become secretly engaged, but when her father discovers the relationship he sends her away to relatives in the distant Guajira and they are separated for three years. When she finally returns she has lost all interest in Florentino, having, effectively, 'matured'; but he is devastated and decides to wait for her to change her mind – for ever, if necessary.

Fermina, however, is courted at the age of eighteen by a handsome upper-class doctor, Juvenal Urbino, nine years older than her, educated in France, and one of the most eligible bachelors in the city. He will become celebrated throughout the region for his contribution to saving Cartagena from the repeated scourge of cholera and it is because she has suspected cholera that he meets her in the first place.[2] Although he is well above her in social rank, they marry and travel to Paris for an extended honeymoon. When they return they live first in the old walled city and then move out to the elegant island of Manga (where García Márquez's parents lived the last decades of their lives). Ariza realises that waiting may be even more problematical than he thought but, as a classically romantic 'fool for love', he determines to persist, and in order not to be tempted to marry another he embarks on hundreds of brief sexual relationships with women of every type and class, above all merry widows. One of them says to him, 'I adore you because you made me a whore'. (Florentino's 622 sexual relationships do not deter him from assuring Fermina, near the end of the novel, that he has 'remained a virgin' for her.) At the same time he works in the riverboat company managed by the brother of his dead father, resolved to make money and establish himself in society so that when the time comes his suit may seem more persuasive to Fermina.

Finally he gets his wish, or rather the essential preliminary to his wish: Juvenal Urbino dies at the age of eighty-one as he falls from a ladder while trying to rescue the family parrot. Ariza, almost immediately, attempts to woo Fermina Daza once more and is violently rebuffed: how could he do this, she rages, at an age when she and Ariza can expect nothing more of life? But as he finds ways to be useful and also proves himself a wise and experienced companion, she begins to rethink and eventually, despite the outraged opposition of her children (Ofelia, Fermina's daughter, snaps that 'Love is ridiculous at our age but at their age it is disgusting!'),³ they set off on a cruise together up the Magdalena River at the ages, respectively, of seventy-six and seventy-two. There, romance begins anew ('the hands made of old bones were not the hands they had imagined before touching. In the next moment, however, they were') and there the novel ends, with Florentino Ariza replying to the captain's question – how long will they go on sailing up and down the mighty river? – just as the colonel had responded, in an earlier novel, when his wife demanded to know what they were going to eat now that their money had finally run out. In that novel, of course, the colonel, quite out of character, had replied, after seventy-five years, 'minute by minute', 'Shit!' In this later novel, totally *in* character, Florentino Ariza, after fifty-three years, seven months and eleven days and nights, replies, 'For the rest of our lives' (rendered as 'Forever' in the English translation).

This novel is in six unnumbered chapters. Since the plot is based upon the triangle involving Fermina and the two principal men in her life, we can easily see, given García Márquez's predilections for structure and symmetry, that the book will be a game of twos and threes. Any structure involving 6 and divided into two controlling halves can be 1–1–1–|–1–1–1; or 2–2–2; or 3–|–3; or, perhaps 1–4–1. In fact this novel is both 3–3, following García Márquez's favourite two-equal-halves obsession and 1–2–|–2–1. However, here there is also a variation: as if to confirm the importance of the number three in this book, the six parts or chapters divide internally not into two sections each but three, making a total of eighteen. Since the number of parts – six – is equal, there is no need for an *enjambement*. There is, however, always a sense that three will collapse into two because of course Juvenal Urbino has to die for the two original lovers to get back together: two turned into three early in the book and now three has to turn back into two again.

Let us look at the 1–2–|–2–1 design. Chapter 1 deals with the theme of the *Old Age* of all three characters, in the early 1930s, focusing above all on Juvenal Urbino, who dies – totally unexpectedly – near its end; Florentino Ariza is introduced only in the last pages of the chapter. Chapter 2, a flashback, narrates the love affair between Florentino and Fermina in the 1870s and is therefore focused on *Youth*; Florentino is brutally rejected by Fermina at the end of the chapter. In chapter 3, continuing the narration of their *Youth*, the young Urbino returns from Paris in triumph in the late 1870s and marries Fermina, to Florentino's complete dismay; the newly-weds travel to France and Florentino builds a new life for himself in the 1880s.

This is halfway through the novel; one might say that to this point the novel has shown a decisive defeat by Europe and Modernity of the backward, Mestizo world of illegitimate, lower-class Colombia and Latin America.

In chapter 4, set between the 1880s and the early 1900s, we alternate between the placid but somewhat boring bourgeois life of the distinguished couple and Florentino Ariza's secret but scandalous love life, as all three protagonists move into *Middle Age*. Chapter 5, continuing the theme of *Middle Age* forwards towards old age, and towards the 1930s, shows the marital ups and downs of the Urbino–Daza couple and Ariza's last important relationship, a shocking sexual affair with his fourteen-year-old niece and ward América Vicuña, which ends with her suicide when Ariza hears that Urbino has died and sets off in pursuit of the widow. Finally, in chapter 6, we return to *Old Age* by picking up where chapter 1 finished in the early 1930s and following the difficult road to romance and the emotional and indeed sexual fulfilment of two lovers well into their seventies.

The conclusion of the novel, a reversal, seems to show a rejection of European Modernity – or, at the least, a demonstration of its limitations – and some kind of triumph by a less vain, less repressed and less commercially motivated Latin America.

This novel, then, is as carefully designed overall as *The Autumn of the Patriarch* or the formidably delivered *Chronicle of a Death Foretold* but it is much less structured in terms of the intricate details of content and technique. Where the previous three novels – *One Hundred Years of Solitude* as well – drive onwards with an irresistible impetus and a silk-smooth mechanism like beautifully engineered limousines – or perhaps *Chronicle* would be a turbo-charged sports car – *Love in the Time of Cholera* is more leisurely, less urgent, more stately, more meditative, more contemplative, as is appropriate for a novel which is not only *about* the era of the carriage and the steamboat but in many ways reflects their momentum and indeed the momentum of the great realist novels written in those times ('I'd like to get you on a slow boat to …'), not only in France but in Russia and Germany.

That said, this novel, as we shall see, is as much a postmodern parody of those nineteenth- and early twentieth-century books as it is a tribute to them; and many of the characteristic García Márquez features are to be found here.[4] Again the novel begins with a death, to be followed by a burial. Again the novel is inspired by things which have happened in the life of García Márquez himself and members of his own family. Again the novel is about old people, like *No One Writes to the Colonel* and *The Autumn of the Patriarch* – indeed, this is one of the world's great novels about old age. (He once commented that he used to write about old people because his grandparents were the people he knew best in the world; now he had started again because he was becoming an old person too.)

But the novel also has evident postmodern features. When the first lines begin – one feels like saying 'when the first chords begin' – 'It was inevitable: the scent of bitter almonds always reminded him of the fate of unrequited love' – the reader gets up to dance to this García Márquez melody inviting her to romance but she is also immediately aware that the tone has changed slightly and she is meant to be both enjoying the song and ironising the idea of such melodramatic invitations. García Márquez was aware that he was risking his reputation with this book, which, at one and the same time, both parodies those profoundly serious nineteenth-century novels about love and takes seriously those twentieth-century sub-literary genres known as soap operas (and their literary predecessors, the *romans roses*) which thrill mass audiences with their absurd and 'impossible' dramas. It is a tremendously fine – and slack – tightrope he treads and his journey across it is not without its stumbles and hesitations, though the reactions of both the experts and the general spectators watching from below confirm that ultimately he triumphed over this mortal challenge and reached the other side.

He had also taken to quoting himself. It was one thing to build his characters and their experiences, silently, from characters chosen among his family and friends and events that may have happened to them, either literally or in composite form. Most novelists do this and have always done it; García Márquez began the process in his first novel, *Leaf Storm*. However, it was quite another thing to name himself and family members, or friends, in his works, metafictionally, as he did in *One Hundred Years of Solitude* – one of the aspects that made that book an obvious early example of a postmodernist text – or *Chronicle of a Death Foretold*. This practice, too, has a venerable history, most memorably exemplified in *Don Quixote*, but it was implicitly prohibited by the great deities of modernism, indifferently paring their nails, and only reappeared again in the much less dignified and indeed celebrity-conscious postmodern period – though of course writers justified their appearances in their own works not by claiming that it was more 'sincere', since sceptical postmodernists did not give much credence to sincerity, but because it was more 'straight-up', more honest as far as such a virtue could still be thought to exist in the world .

In this novel, written overwhelmingly in the third person, there is nevertheless, again, as in *Chronicle of a Death Foretold*, a first-person frame, though the narrator says nothing at all about himself: just as in the earlier novel the narrator was born and bred in 'the Town', despite having moved away for many years, so here too the narrator is born in 'the City' – evidently Cartagena despite some teasing from the author – and seems never to have moved away, though his first-person interventions are few and far between. Postmodern though it appears, this was a device used by Flaubert in *Madame Bovary*.

The beginning of the novel, set on a Pentecost Sunday, is a re-enactment of the beginning of García Márquez's first novel, *Leaf Storm*, and suggests that the day his grandfather took him to see the corpse of his friend Don Emilio, the Belgian doctor who committed suicide in Aracataca when García Márquez was a small boy, was a crucial point of reference in his life, one which probably shocked him to the core. Moreover, this novel begins – and the suicide therefore takes place – just a few years after the suicide in *Leaf Storm*, set in 1928 – and very possibly in the very same year in the early 1930s when the original doctor died.

Once again some aspects of Colonel Nicolás Márquez are transmuted into some aspects of another authority figure: in *Leaf Storm* it was a colonel, like himself; in this case he becomes the most important medical expert in Cartagena, Doctor Juvenal Urbino. The suicide, here called Jerónimo Saint-Amour, is again a foreigner – where the original suicide was himself a doctor, Saint-Amour is a photographer – and again a morally problematical figure whose last note reveals truths which shock and disillusion his rather strait-laced friend. This time, however, García Márquez goes further in his implicit critique of Urbino's conventional morality – though he remains a positive character overall – than he did in the case of the colonel in *Leaf Storm*. And now the wholly unconventional Florentino Ariza, based to some degree on the author's not entirely respected father, is not only much more sympathetically portrayed than Urbino but also much more so than the character Martín in *Leaf Storm*, unmistakably a first highly negative literary portrayal of the very same personage, García Márquez's own progenitor.

And what of love (and sex)? And in general the relations between men and women? And what of class (and money)? And race (and culture)? And nation (and continent)? All these themes, all these ways of looking at the world, are woven into this extraordinary novel: sometimes a symphony, sometimes a waltz, sometimes a *liede*, sometimes a *vallenato*. The epigraph to the novel comes indeed from a *vallenato* composed by the blind Colombian troubadour Leandro Díaz: 'The words I am about to express / now have their own crowned goddess.' The crowned goddess is Fermina Daza, a composite undoubtedly of several women in García Márquez's life (most notably his wife, his mother and his former lover Tachia Quintana), whose hand – and not only her hand – are desired by the two leading men in the book, Urbino and Ariza. We call them Urbino and Ariza here but one of the most characteristic García Márquez narrative traits is to call characters almost invariably by their full name, both the given name and the surnames at one and the same time. This means that the effect is neither fully intimate nor fully formal, neither the narrative equivalent of the Spanish 'tú' nor of the 'usted'.

And this wilfully ambivalent technique goes with an equally or even more significant and impactful practice in García Márquez, namely his habit of using the word '*amor*', 'love', whether he is talking of romantic – spiritual – love or of sexual – erotic and physical – love. This creates a very distinctive atmosphere in the Colombian writer's later novels which, in a strange tele-graphic way, points up a major question in his books: what is 'love' for García Márquez, a writer not given inside or outside of his books to disquisitions and certainly not partial to 'novels of ideas'? The topic is raised in a novel – a novel of ideas, if ever there was one – which undoubtedly had a powerful impact on the young García Márquez, Thomas Mann's *The Magic Mountain*, which examines the whole question of the relation between love's 'sacred' and 'pas-sionate and fleshly' aspects and goes on to note, near its end, that 'it is well done that our language has but one word for all kinds of love, from the holiest to the most lustfully fleshly.'

Love, then, for García Márquez takes up myriad forms and it is not an easy thing to describe it or indeed to critique it. In his culture – Catholic, Hispanic, African, Indian – sexual practices were diverse, chaotic and largely unregulated; maturity came early and girls, in societies sometimes shockingly unfair and unequal, would often be married young and have children as teenagers; those from rural or working-class communities would often be forced into prosti-tution as soon as they were sexually mature no matter what the Church, the Law or polite society might say about it; and the double standard and the hon-our and shame syndrome would operate busily and busybodily, and Don Juan and Don Quixote would do their worst and their best, but most men would betray the women in their lives and children would get born in and out of wed-lock and the whole unjust carnival of love and sex, of sacred and fleshly unions would continue, from long before García Márquez was a child until the present day. And on the whole García Márquez, who nevertheless has strong views on social justice, prefers, as narrator, to stand back and, in the general area of love and sex, to leave matters to explain themselves and readers to make their own judgements from their own perspectives – though it is a rare reader who, after consuming several of these books, does not find him or herself a little less sure of what love and, more specifically, sexual morality, may or may not be.

As a teenager, like most young women in the West since the time of the troubadours at the end of the middle ages, the privileged Fermina Daza first experiences love as an idea, an emotion, a desire that is above all sen-timental – an idea apparently free of those social moorings called class, race and religion. (This may not be the case with the apparently more idealistic Florentino: Fermina's class may well be part of her attraction for him, even if unconsciously.) Quite quickly, though, as soon as she has some experience of the world, and as soon as her female cousins teach her something rudimentary about the inseparability of love and sex, she comes to realise that love cannot exist alone, outside of the social world.[5] And here we see the possible influence of a novel perhaps fated to influence García Márquez, a little-read novel by the French polymath Valery Larbaud – instrumental in introducing Hispanic culture into French society between the 1910s and 1930s – entitled *Fermina Márquez* (1911). The eponymous heroine – a Colombian teenager, the daughter of a banker – enchants a generation of Latin American boys at a French boarding school in the late nineteenth century. Her surname is of course the writer's own matrilineal surname and the not entirely glamorous given name would be adopted by him as the name of his female protagonist.

At the beginning of Larbaud's novel the beautiful Fermina is ashamed of being rich, empathises with poor people and has a platonic, Christian conception of love. At this stage she is an impassioned reader of Latin America's chaste classic *María* (1867) by the Colombian Jorge Isaacs. But later she falls for the most imposing and wealthy upper-class boy in the group – precursor of Juvenal Urbino – and comes to appreciate her own background: 'such luxury was worthy of the king of her heart'. And the boy from a lower class who used to fantasise about her – the novel's Florentino Ariza – feels humiliated when he sees her again: 'She was more beautiful than ever and seemed to have grown taller. In her presence, he [Lenoit] felt that he was just a child. He was not made to be loved by her; he should never have loved her'. His sentimental education is a brutal one; hers is equally brutal but she is set to marry a man who is handsome, rich and blessed with a great social future: the way of the world.

For García Márquez, of course, the ending of *Fermina Márquez* is just the start of his story. Will Fermina Daza be happy (the narrator of *Fermina Márquez* wonders precisely this about its heroine)? Yes, but not entirely. Do money and social position bring true fulfilment? No, not really but they certainly help. (Urbino is pleased with his wife, but García Márquez notes of their early times together, 'He was aware that he did not love her.') We have seen that the epigraph is from a popular song. García Márquez, now a successful man himself, with all kinds of honours, satisfactions and pleasures available to him, is perhaps more circumspect than he would have been when he wrote his early novels. Indeed, he would not – for ideological reasons – and could not – he didn't have the experience – have written this novel before the 1980s. But there can be little doubt that, even though Florentino has had hundreds of opportunistic, sometimes shameful, sometimes scandalous sexual relationships, the author takes seriously his lifelong love for Fermina: from his adolescence Florentino is perfectly capable of spending long periods of each day in a brothel while writing the most idealistic romantic poetry. Is his love 'real', is it an obsession, is it a quixotic ideal? We can never know, but we take it seriously – just as we are also to take seriously the sense that the Latin American people, for all their difficulties, for all the poverty and oppression amid which they live, have well-springs of authentic emotion, of true love – whatever it may be – suffused by a carnival spirit, which largely elude the repressed, self-disciplined and guilt-ridden Europeans in whose footsteps Juvenal Urbino and, to some extent, his wife Fermina have followed. (At one point Fermina's cousin Hildebranda goes to the post office to take a look at Florentino and comments, 'He is ugly and sad but he is all love'; whereas Fermina is 'really just a de luxe servant'.) They have a good life, but not a great and authentic one; a good marriage, but not a great and sincere one.

Like this marriage between Fermina and Juvenal, the novel is a curious mixture of the bland and the banal, the ruthlessly realistic and the occasionally profound. It dares to explore the most familiar cliches involved in letters to agony columns and the desperate truisms inevitably offered in reply: You never really know anyone. You can't really judge people. People can change their behaviour and, to that extent, their personalities; other people can remain the same for ever despite the passage of time. You never ever know what is going to happen in life. You only understand life when it's too late – and even then you would probably change your view if you lived even longer. It is very difficult to moralise about love and sex. It is very difficult to separate love from sex. It is very difficult to separate love from habit, gratitude, or self-interest. You can love more than one person at the same time. There are many kinds of love and we can love people in many different ways.[6] It is impossible to know which is better, single life or marriage, bohemia or convention; it is impossible to know whether security is better than adventure or vice versa; but everything has to be paid for. There is only one life and no second chance; yet you are never too old. One life is no better than another … And yet …

The theme of agony columns, like that of radio and television soap operas, and popular poetry and songs, is a pertinent one. García Márquez is not Thomas Mann or Marcel Proust, though he has read and assimilated their works. He remains committed to the lives of ordinary people, the forces that shape and constrain them, and the cultural artefacts that give them meaning. In this novel Florentino Ariza reads every kind of poetry but above all cheap and vulgar popular poetry. When he gets a new job at his uncle's steamship company he is put to writing business letters, which he couches in the style of love letters, suggesting that Latin American culture is not adaptable to the requirements of trade, business and technology. But he also, in his spare time, writes love letters in the Arcade of Scribes for illiterates to send to their dear ones.

Letters, indeed, are important in most of García Márquez's works. As a child he had no contact with his parents; once reunited with them, he won scholarships to boarding schools and wrote to his mother between the ages of eleven and nineteen and then beyond, continuing to write from university and from Europe. While in Europe and Venezuela he wrote regularly to his fiancée Mercedes for almost three years and was always in regular correspondence with his numerous friends, who were always enormously important to him. (What an irony that he had to give up writing letters when he became famous because some of his friends started to sell them!) Late in the novel, when Florentino discovers that Fermina Daza, newly widowed, is in no mood for love letters from an old – very old – flame, he embarks on a new mode of seduction, through letters that are ostensibly about life in general but which will actually capture her heart. One might say that where the narrator of *Chronicle of a Death Foretold* was journalist, detective and judge, the protagonist of *Love in the Time of Cholera* is a psychiatrist, counsellor, agony columnist, literary critic, a reader of texts and of people. And one might say that, despite his wilful romanticism and apparent illusions, his experience of life has made him a much wiser person than Fermina or Juvenal, despite all their advantages of culture and education, which have only blinded them with conventions and appearances. Florentino sends Fermina a six-page letter, an extensive 'meditation on life, love, old age, and death',[7] based on his ideas about and experience of the relations between men and women. One might say that, just as Melquíades has effectively written the book in which he appears, *One Hundred Years of Solitude*, Florentino Ariza has in a way written the story of *Love in the Time of Cholera*, in order to explain their own lives, and therefore Life itself, to Fermina. A reader of the novel might object that we can accept that Melquíades wrote the former because it is difficult to imagine that his book can have been more 'magical' than *One Hundred Years of Solitude* itself; whereas in *Love in the Time of Cholera* we do not get to read the wisdom in the letters. But of course, the wisdom in the letters is, we can be sure, merely a distillation of the wisdom in the book.

By the time the two ancient lovers make their river journey, the world itself is showing signs of being old and tired. The forests along the River Magdalena have been cleared both for agriculture and, ironically, to provide fuel – wood – to drive the very steamboat voyages which Florentino and Fermina are so enjoying. García Márquez had always seen love as a kind of sickness – another idea explored in Mann's *The Magic Mountain* – and this novel allows him to develop this conceit at length. The tropics, with their accelerated cycle of growth, corruption and decay, only underline the idea that death is always at the very heart of life; and all the love affairs in this novel are played out against the background and in the full knowledge of this gloomy truth.

The book is undoubtedly, for García Márquez himself, a reconciliation with people and cities he has been estranged from. But, as mentioned before, it is a reconciliation above all with love and, therefore, with life. The first half of his literary trajectory, then, deals more with solitude, power and death; the second, more with love, acceptance and the affirmation of life. In fact, the ingredients are the same; it is the distribution and the emphasis which has changed. Here, in a novel which ought, given its elements, to be sombre and discouraging, we find García Márquez affirming life as never before. He has used the conventions of soap opera and romantic fiction, with serious intent, to bring diversion, pleasure and optimism to a grey and disenchanted world.

Chapter 8

More about power: *The General in His Labyrinth* (1989) and *News of a Kidnapping* (1996)

The General in His Labyrinth (1989)   102
News of a Kidnapping (1996)   107
Epilogue: the later journalism   114

Love in the Time of Cholera was one of García Márquez's most successful novels with both literary critics and general readers, thereby not only repeating the achievement of *One Hundred Years of Solitude* but also demonstrating beyond all doubt that he had survived the stresses and the temptations which inevitably follow the award of the Nobel Prize. He was by now a Latin American institution – almost as famous as Castro, Guevara, Evita, Pele and Maradona – and felt able to turn his attention to the greatest institution in Latin America's entire history, the great Liberator, Simón Bolívar.

The General in His Labyrinth (1989)

By this time, indeed, García Márquez was a close friend of Cuban leader Fidel Castro and other politicians such as socialists Felipe González of Spain and François Mitterrand of France. He had always had a feel for power in his literary imagination but by now he had seen it from the inside over a considerable period of time. He set out to meet the ultimate challenge by writing a novel about the last months of Latin America's most famous figure, Bolívar. Inevitably, the book caused great controversy in Latin America, especially in Colombia and Venezuela, where those who idolise the Liberator do not approve of people, even great writers, tampering with his image.

Although García Márquez's audacity as a writer was second to none, he took the responsibility of writing about Bolívar extremely seriously. Most of his novels implied some understanding, direct or indirect, of Colombian and Latin American history but he had never had to consider the methods involved in investigating and writing history as such. Now he felt that every event in the novel had to be verified historically and every thought, declaration or eccentricity of Bolívar appropriately and persuasively researched and contextualised. In short, if an event was known to be true, it had to be accurately narrated; and even where there were gaps in the historical record, the writer's inventions had to be historically authentic and convincing. He read dozens of books about Bolívar and thousands of his letters, as well as consulting a range of historians and other experts ostentatiously thanked in the writer's first ever list of acknowledgments. Nevertheless the undertaking remained extremely risky. Georg Lukács had famously said, in his classic *The Historical Novel*, that such novels should take as their principal personage some invented secondary character, not the most important figures of the day; whereas García Márquez portrays one of the most iconic and most heroic characters in all of Latin American history and plants him centre stage, where he will remain throughout the book, without hesitation or embarrassment.

In fact the period chosen by García Márquez as the vertebral spine of his novel was the last eight months of Bolívar's life and in particular the journey, most of it down the Magdalena River, from Bogotá to Cartagena between 8 and 23 May 1830, after he, formerly the president of Colombia, had been rejected by the people of the capital:

> He had wrested from Spanish dominion an empire five times bigger than all of Europe, he had waged war for twenty years to keep it free and united, and he had governed it with a firm hand until the week before, but when it was time to leave he did not even carry with him the consolation that anyone believed that he was going.[1]

This gloomy voyage was perhaps the least documented journey of Bolívar's entire life and it has always intrigued historians and novelists. Indeed, García Márquez's close friend Alvaro Mutis had long expressed a wish to write a novel about it but had never put his wish into practice; García Márquez finally asked his permission to take the project over, and the book is dedicated to Mutis. This unknown journey would become the first half of his book and the second half would be Bolívar's agonising last months as his health failed and his dreams of Latin American unity collapsed.

A member of the Creole aristocracy, Bolívar was born in Caracas, Venezuela, in 1783. When he was born, the whole of the South American continent was in the possession of Spain and Portugal while the islands of the Caribbean were shared by Spain, France, England and Holland. Slavery existed in every country in the region, as also in the recently independent United States of America. By the time Bolívar died, only forty-seven years later, almost the whole of what would later be called Latin America was free of external rule, and slavery had been condemned and in some cases abolished. These achievements owed more to Simón Bolívar than to any other man.

This novel is divided into two parts but in two different ways. First, in typical García Márquez style, it is in eight chapters (unnumbered, as usual) divided into two equal halves. As mentioned, the first half, chapters 1 to 4, is occupied with the departure from Bogotá in May 1830 and the sixteen-day journey down the Magdalena River that García Márquez himself had so often sailed in his childhood and youth. The second half, chapters 5 to 8, addresses the last six months of Bolívar's life until the moment when he died on 17 December 1830 at the sugar plantation of San Pedro Alejandrino, outside Santa Marta. On the way to his last resting place – while hoping all the time that not only will he himself survive but the cause to which he has devoted his entire adult life will be reignited – he passes through many scenarios but especially Cartagena, Barranquilla and Santa Marta, those Caribbean cities which would be – which had been – so important in the life of García Márquez himself.

That explains how the novel is divided into two chronological halves (two intense and dramatic weeks and the following six months) and two thematic halves (the river journey and the coastal cities) in García Márquez's standard fashion. But he also returns to the pattern of his first novel, *Leaf Storm*, in which the 'present' plane of the narrative (half an hour in the afternoon of 12 September 1928) was constantly bisected, or invaded, by historical references going back almost seventy years and by similar flashbacks – or memories – in the lives of each of the three main characters, a structure achieved in the same way as cinema 'montage'. *The General in His Labyrinth*, similarly, has a brief central core – seven months: not as brief as in *Leaf Storm*, obviously – similarly underpinned by historical references and flashbacks going back through the previous forty-seven years of Bolívar's own life and of Latin America's dramatic history. As in his previous novels, García Márquez does everything possible to make this complex structure helpful rather than obscure, entirely negotiable to the reader who is flattered to feel that she is able, in a sense, to accompany the author by piloting her own way down the river of time and history.

Why, then, is the novel given the title *The General in His Labyrinth*, which suggests that the great Bolívar may be less able to find his way than we, the novel's readers? (It might also have been entitled 'The Autumn of the General' or 'Seven Months of Solitude'.) The reference is to a comment Bolívar himself made about his predicament only days before his death: 'How can I get out of this labyrinth?' It is not entirely clear whether the labyrinth in question was his life – or destiny – which appeared not to be heading for the expected outcome; or death itself, which none of us, ultimately, can escape. Such a weighty and essentially desperate cry is reminiscent of the unforgettable image bequeathed us by one of Spain's most famous poets, Jorge Manrique, who at the close of the medieval period wrote one of the country's best-loved and most characteristic poems, his *Verses on the Death of My Father*. Its best-known line, which could once upon a time, proverbially, be quoted by any Spanish schoolboy, runs: 'Our lives are the rivers that flow down into the sea which is death'. And its next best-known line states that death is the 'trap' or 'ambush' into which we inevitably fall. (Bolívar's most famous declaration was the disillusioned, 'He who makes a revolution ploughs the sea'; García Márquez includes it here but only as one of a list of celebrated quotations and not in any way emphasised.)

This novel, which takes Bolívar down the great river to the sea, where he will die, follows exactly the logic of Manrique's poem: as he leaves Bogotá, an English diplomat notes, 'The time he has left will hardly be enough for him to reach his grave'. It is hardly surprising, therefore, that this novel – this historical novel – bears such a powerful poetic charge, first returning its protagonist to the everyday physicality of ordinary life and then, having modernised and demystified him, successfully remystifying him and carrying him back again, fully restored, into the realm of myth. This is, it must be said, a minor miracle of literary achievement.

Bolívar is an unusually attractive figure because he not only embodied the ideals of the Enlightenment, which had already inspired the independence of both the United States and France – he had been present at Napoleon's coronation, though he disapproved of it – but was also a stirringly romantic thinker and leader.[2] His essential purposes were two: to liberate the whole of Spanish America; and to unite it as one country, 'the fantastic dream of creating the largest country in the world: one nation, free and unified, from Mexico to Cape Horn'. In New Granada – later Colombia – his great opponent in this endeavour was Francisco de Paula Santander, formerly a close associate but eventually an enemy. García Márquez portrays Santander as the stereotypical *cachaco*, indirect, hypocritical and self-serving, compared with Bolívar's more spontaneous Caribbean personality and behaviour. (Of Bogotá, Bolívar says, 'This isn't my theatre.') Santander, who stamped his 'formalist, conservative spirit' on Colombia for ever, is contrasted in the novel with Bolívar's greatest friend and ally, the self-effacing Ecuadorean general Antonio José de Sucre, whose assassination in June 1830 was a devastating blow for Bolívar both personally and politically. (This novel, including the many characters who actually appear in it, refers to an astonishing 130 historical personages, yet at no time does the reader feel overwhelmed.)

Bolívar was an inveterate womaniser, and although this book marks a return to the theme of power there are also many reflections on love, the thematic which García Márquez had been exploring throughout the 1980s. Bolívar's wife died after only eight months of marriage when he was nineteen, and García Márquez suggests that this loss triggered his 'birth into history' because, already an orphan, he became, 'without transition, the man he would be for the rest of his life'. After that his most important lover, and by far his most effective and loyal supporter, was the Ecuadorean Manuelita Sáenz; theirs was a scandalous affair – she was the wife of an English businessman – but legendary in Latin American historical romance. But many other women appear in the pages of the novel. Unfortunately, like his other talents, Bolívar's legendary lovemaking powers are on the wane and Manuelita discovers, early in the novel – and note here again the curious relationship between spirit and matter in García Márquez's conception of love – that 'he no longer had enough bodily substance to gratify her soul'.

Perhaps the most striking aspect of the novel, given that it retells the story of Latin America's most famous historical personage, is that Bolívar's life appears to bring together all the themes by now so familiar in García Márquez's previous books – as if all of them had really been inspired by the life of this archetypal Latin American. (García Márquez himself has often said that 'at bottom I have written only one book, the same one which just goes round and round and keeps on going'.)[3] The title suggests that even the greatest power is always limited, always temporary: even the powerful – even generals, colonels, patriarchs – cannot control fate and destiny. One proof of the limits of power is how long one has to wait for things: even the great Bolívar, like the unfortunate colonel waiting for his pension, has to wait for letters, for a passport and for permission to leave the country. On the other hand, some people wait because other people have the power to delay things; but, again, even the most powerful of men do not have the power to delay death ('the glory had left his body').

The theme of fame and glory takes us back to a complex of themes which had preoccupied García Márquez long before he himself had become celebrated, in particular the matter of identity and the solitude of power, including the distance between one's image and one's reality. The overwhelming majority of the references in the book, beginning with the title, are to Bolívar's official rank, which is in constant counterpoint with his intimate reality. The word Bolívar rarely appears and the word Simón hardly at all. Early in the novel Bolívar, rejected by the Colombian people, complains: 'I am no longer myself.' By the time we are halfway through the novel, the narrator observes, 'He could not master his soul.' And still later, the general himself remarks, 'I'll never fall in love again. It's like having two souls at the same time.'

Finally the moment comes for the great Liberator, imprisoned in his ailing body, in time, in fate, in historical circumstance, to die, as other men do. This unbearably moving scene – the imminent death of Latin America's greatest and most idealistic hero, going too soon, considering himself a failure who may even be forgotten – has been staged in dozens of plays and movies and might have been thought too much even for a writer as ambitious, and occasionally reckless, as García Márquez. But he himself had been destined to write this passage from the moment he was born. His protagonist is suddenly 'shaken by the overwhelming revelation that the headlong race between his misfortunes and his dreams was at that moment reaching the finish line' and exclaims: 'Damn it. How can I get out of this labyrinth!' Of course he won't, he can't, and so he observes 'the heartless speed of the octagonal clock racing toward the ineluctable appointment at seven minutes past one on his final afternoon', hears the slaves singing out in the plantation (the slaves, we know, who will be freed one day, thanks to him), and sees 'the final brilliance of life that would never, through all eternity, be repeated again' ...[4]

... because we all of us have only one life, even Bolívar, whose life has been narrated so many times but never – we are convinced as we read the final paragraphs – more expertly, more passionately or more unforgettably than this.

News of a Kidnapping (1996)

After *The General in His Labyrinth*, and the huge debate caused in Latin America, especially Colombia and Venezuela, by its maverick portrayal of a Caribbean Bolívar who occasionally farts and frequently curses, García Márquez turned to another novel of love, *Of Love and Other Demons* (1994), which will be studied in the next chapter. But before that novel was published he was already working on another political work, with a fully contemporary set of topics: drug-trafficking, terrorism and kidnapping.

Critics had been surprised by his audacity in studying the most famous and admired figure in Latin American history but accepted that it was not the first time he had written a historical novel. And it had been widely noted that García Márquez invariably – like most writers – took historical distance from his topics and tended to set his works twenty, fifty or even a hundred years in the past. Such was the condition of Colombia in the 1980s and 1990s, however, that García Márquez, by then a friend also of Colombian presidents López Michelsen, Betancur and Gaviria, began to spend more time in the country, especially from the early 1990s. He bought into a new TV news station and even looked for opportunities in print journalism.

His close involvement in the Cuban Revolution and international politics throughout the 1980s had left him little time to intervene in matters

Colombian; and in 1986 he had written a documentary work, *Miguel Littín Clandestine in Chile*, tracing the adventure of the well-known exiled Chilean cinematographer as he travelled his native land in secret filming its new reality under the dictatorship of General Pinochet. But after 1989, when the Berlin Wall fell soon after the two hundredth anniversary of the French Revolution and his aspirations for the spread of socialism appeared definitively frustrated, he took more and more notice of his own country, whose political situation was becoming ever more disastrous. Finally he set out to write a documentary work on what had happened to Colombia during the time when drug-traffickers controlled the destiny of the country at home and abroad: the book, a sort of documentary thriller in the tradition of Capote, in literature, or Costa-Gavras and Pontecorvo, in cinema, was called *Noticia de un secuestro* (*News of a Kidnapping*). This was a dramatic shift by any standards: the drug *capo* Pablo Escobar was a long way from Simón Bolívar.

In 1990 Colombia seemed on the verge of disintegration. A new Liberal government had come to power in early August led by an inexperienced young lawyer, César Gaviria. He had been running the election campaign of Colombia's most charismatic politician in many years, Luis Carlos Galán, who had vowed to put an end to the scourge of drug-trafficking and had been assassinated by *sicarios* (hitmen) paid by the great drug mafia godfather, Escobar, a man apparently richer and more powerful than the Colombian state. (The principal female protagonist of the novel, Maruja Pachón, was Galán's sister-in-law.) Yet although the drug cartels, which had unleashed a wave of bombings and assassinations over recent years, were the biggest problem, they were not the only one. Several powerful guerrilla groups defied the police and army in the mountains, jungles and villages of the country; and the police and army themselves were among the most ruthless in the continent and rarely confined themselves to operating within the law.

Colombia's situation was complicated by the position of the United States with regard to drugs. On the one hand it was the US which provided most of the demand for Colombian cocaine and yet was not entirely effective in preventing supplies from entering its territory. In concentrating blame upon the suppliers, the US made things extremely uncomfortable for nations like Colombia, whose traffickers, with huge paramilitary armies defending them in the countryside and in cities like Medellín, had become immensely rich and powerful. They had effectively declared war on the Colombian state when it threatened to extradite those it captured to the US, where they would be certain to spend the rest of their lives in jail. Luis Carlos Galán had been one of the principal advocates of sending the so-called 'Extraditables' to the US, and he had paid for it with his life.

This explosive situation was reaching its climax when Gaviria came to power in August 1990. At the end of that very month, as if to provide a first challenge to the new government, Escobar's paramilitaries began a new wave of kidnappings of prominent civilians by capturing Diana Turbay, the journalist daughter of a Colombian ex-president. It is here that the plot of *News of a Kidnapping* effectively begins, with other kidnappings in September, including that of Francisco Santos, the son of one of the country's leading newspaper proprietors, Hernando Santos Castillo, though García Márquez chooses to initiate the action with the kidnapping of government administrator Maruja Pachón and her sister-in-law Beatriz Villamizar on 7 November, only two days after the embattled government declared a state of siege.[5] Over the course of the next six months the government, acting on behalf of the families of the hostages, will negotiate with the drug mafias under the most difficult of circumstances; eventually some hostages are killed, but Francisco Santos, Maruja Pachón and Beatriz Villamizar are released after just over six months and Pablo Escobar agrees to go to prison as long as he will not be extradited. This is where the main action of the novel ends. There follows a kind of brief epilogue which accounts for the next six months, including reference to the fact that Escobar himself eventually escaped from prison and was finally tracked down and killed by the Colombian police in December 1993, when García Márquez was just beginning to do his research. Whether he would have published the book with Escobar still alive is open to speculation.

The book is a work of journalism (hence the word *News* in the title) but written like a novel – and in that sense the opposite of *Chronicle of a Death Foretold*, which is a novel masquerading as the result of a journalistic investigation. One is tempted to call it a 'documentary novel' but the truth is that almost none of it is fictional. This dual and indeed hybrid and problematical status explains both its undeniable virtues and some of the difficult issues it raises. Although its author was nearly seventy by the time it was published, it was notable for its extraordinary narrative momentum and the way in which the complexity of a painful and convulsive national situation had been condensed, narrativised and turned into a remarkably compelling political thriller. Probably no one else could have done it because not only was García Márquez still one of the world's greatest storytellers but only he, with his huge prestige in Colombia, could have gained access to so many top politicians and other leaders of Colombian society.

The book begins with a brief set of acknowledgments, which doubles as a prologue. It names Maruja Pachón and her husband Alberto Villamizar – one of the principal intermediaries between the government and the kidnappers – as his primary informants; it was they who proposed that he undertake this investigation. He declares that the 'autumnal task' of writing this book has been 'the saddest and most difficult of my life'. He admits that, horrific though it was, it was 'only one episode in the biblical holocaust that has been consuming Colombia for over twenty years' and then ends, somewhat bizarrely – and perhaps egocentrically – by hoping that 'this book will never happen to us again'. Was this a sign that the writer was now bigger than the stories he was telling, even when the story was the contemporary drama of an entire country?

Certainly there are reasons to fear that this brilliant journalist and storyteller may himself have become a prisoner: first, of his sources and in particular the larger-than-life couple who suggested the book and who, though important protagonists, may not have been quite as central as they and the book appear to claim; and second, of the genre that García Márquez employs in order to tell his story, that of the Hollywood thriller with its hackneyed conventions and rather rudimentary audience expectations.[6] It cannot be denied that the audience for the book would have been much smaller if the story had been narrated in a less exciting way; but it is also true that it might have been fairer to all the protagonists, major and minor, and that certain other distortions might have been avoided. In other words, García Márquez was by no means too old to research a story and to hammer out a compelling plot with a memorable point of departure and one of his familiar dramatic denouements. But a close reading of the story, held up against the political realities of the historical record, on the one hand, and the writer's own previous works and previous statements about Colombia's politics and the Colombian ruling class, on the other, suggests that the excitement of the chase, the expectations of his informants and the narrative requirements of the thriller may have led him astray in important and possibly decisive ways. Moreover, for a man who clearly does not know everything that has happened, and who has clearly not interviewed enough people, García Márquez suffers more than usually here from a personal weakness that he has famously turned into a literary-rhetorical asset, not least in *One Hundred Years of Solitude*: that of being a narrator with the tone of knowing everything. Here it is counter-productive.

For once he chose to number his chapters: there are eleven of them, telling the story of the abductions from the moment Maruja was kidnapped on 7 November 1990 to the moment she was released on 20 May 1991, followed by an epilogue which summarises the events leading to the surrender of Escobar a few weeks later and ends on a positive note as Maruja's ring, stolen by the kidnappers, is mysteriously returned to her in the last lines of the book. As in so many Hollywood thrillers, the heroine has been saved by the man who loves her and a sentimental ending guarantees that they at least will live happily ever after. Whether such a happy ending should have been imposed upon a book in which several of the other kidnap victims were in fact murdered is just the most obvious question to emerge from a reading of this nonetheless brilliant thriller.

There were four sectors involved in the drama of the 1990–91 abductions: the ten victims themselves, organised in four different groups; their families, desperately urging the government to have them released unharmed, at any cost; the kidnappers, from the ordinary criminals who actually carried out the abductions, to the top *capos*, most notably Escobar himself; and the Colombian government, led by the steely Gaviria, his ministers and the forces of law and order. García Márquez's method is a return to something like the time-bound organisation of his very first novel, *Leaf Storm*. The narrative alternates between the experience of the kidnap victims in the odd-numbered chapters and the behind-the-scenes efforts to release them, involving the distraught families, the ever more desperate government ministers and the ruthless kidnappers, in the even-numbered chapters. García Márquez largely suspends his usual critical perspective and leaves the story to tell itself (rather as he purported to do in that journalistic novel, *Chronicle of a Death Foretold*). At a deeper level, of course, the real struggle is between the Extraditables and the Government, with the hostages and their families merely as pawns, but García Márquez does everything possible to turn it into a 'human interest' drama, conceived as a traditional love story involving a crisis, a heroic struggle (knight rescues damsel in distress) and a successful return home at the conclusion.

It must be said that there are two largely unspoken realities hidden just below the surface of the text. First, the *narcos*, especially their leader Pablo Escobar, are human monsters (though Escobar was idolised in and around Medellin and it is important to understand why, though this is outside the scope of the book). Second, Colombia is a deeply unjust country with a history of violence that predates the recent drug-related atrocities by well over a hundred years and a governing oligarchy that also has two centuries of blood on its well-manicured hands (which might explain why many ordinary people admired Pablo Escobar, one of their own, when he managed to make a fortune even bigger than those of the ruling classes); some of the principal characters in the novel, here appearing for once as victims, are part of that ruling elite, and twenty years earlier would have been criticised – and indeed were criticised – by a different García Márquez in a different time. Yet despite some token statements about the Colombian 'political class', the narrator is careful not to blame anything that might be called the 'ruling class' for the emergence of the drug-traffickers during the twenty years which form the historical horizon of this book. One can only conclude either that the writer had changed his political ideology and hence his political analysis or else that he was unwilling to tell the whole truth for short- or medium-term reasons relating to the national interest or his personal relationships and that his book, therefore, lacking a full contextualisation, is unwilling to tell the whole story. When someone is as great a writer as García Márquez, this is an occasion for major regret.

In the standard English-language edition, chapter 1 and the Epilogue are twelve and eighteen pages long, respectively, while chapters 2–10 inclusive are all of roughly equal length (between twenty and twenty-eight pages). Having to deal with historical reality has evidently stretched García Márquez's ability to impose absolute order on a topic, but even here the chapters are of approximately equal lengths. Within each chapter there are several brief dramatic sections, some of them like scenes from a movie, others like radio news reports: some seventy in all, distributed throughout the book. Presumably this fragmentation explains why he decided to number the chapters and thereby deprive the reader of her usual – deceptive – sense of freedom.

Despite the odd–even alternation, reminiscent of *Leaf Storm*, he still more or less retains the practice he initiated after that first novel of having a midpoint dividing line between the two halves of each book. In this case, however, instead of there being a line, a moment, there is an entire chapter, a kind of pool, in the form of the whole of chapter 6, set in late January 1991. This allows him, first, to record the death of the only one of the ten hostages that the *narcos* deliberately murdered, Marina Montoya. Clearly, this exemplary assassination is the central dramatic moment of the book: if this innocent grandmother could be murdered, all the hostages could be murdered. The second function of this hinge-like chapter 6 is to allow García Márquez a meditation on what these abductions represented within Colombia's history over the previous twenty years, something he would not have done if this were really a novel and something which even here he only does after the dramatic outlines of his plot have been established. He begins this meditation by remarking that 'during that savage January [of 1991] Colombia had reached the worst circumstances imaginable' and was now in an apparently irremediable 'vicious cycle'. The position of the government was almost impossible:

> The government's credibility was not at the high level of its notable political successes but rather at the very low level of its security forces, condemned by the world's press and by international human rights organizations. In contrast, Pablo Escobar had achieved a credibility that the guerrillas never managed in the best of times. People came to believe more in the lies of the Extraditables than in the truths of the government.[7]

Again, although Gaviria was a good friend of García Márquez's by the time he wrote the book, there seems evidence that the narrator wants to talk up a real conflict of ideology and action between the families and the government rather than narrate the inevitable conflict of interest that actually existed – put simply, the government could not give in to any and all the demands made by the kidnappers whereas the families wished them to do precisely that – which the families themselves, inevitably, were too distraught to recognise. (García Márquez remarks at one point, 'Power – like love – is double-edged: it is exercised and it is endured.') As a writer he finds himself in the incoherent position of favouring the families' position simply to increase the dramatic tension in the book, when in reality one can be sure that as a citizen – and as a friend of the president – he would have approved the position of the government he supported.

Chapter 6 ends with the drama of the death of a second hostage, Diana Turbay, the daughter of ex-president Julio Cesar Turbay, apparently in an accident when the military launched a rescue attempt without the permission of the government. She and Marina Montoya would be the only hostages killed, and this dramatic development is, in effect, presented implicitly as the latest in the long series of violent events which have been plaguing the country since the 1980s. Again, however, it must be said that a previous García Márquez would not have started his interlude in the 1980s but would have gone back to at least the assassination of Gaitán – almost certainly by elements within the conservative oligarchy – in 1948, if not to the War of the Thousand Days at the beginning of the twentieth century or the betrayal of Bolívar by Santander in the 1820s.

Despite the deaths of Marina and Diana, the conventions of Hollywood prevail. One of the most elementary is that secondary characters have to die so that the danger facing heroes and heroines may be underlined. The entire momentum and framing of the book urge us to care desperately whether Maruja, the 'heroine', survives when a subsidiary character, her chauffeur, is killed on the fourth page of the narrative and never mentioned again. (The same occurs with Francisco Santos's chauffeur.) But these chauffeurs were real people, not characters, still less props, and some readers might care about them at least as much as the major characters.

Even more problematical – and frankly sinister – the unfortunate Marina Montoya is also turned into a similar secondary, sacrificeable character and, worse still, is treated quite deprecatingly on the basis of no other evidence than the testimony of the would-be heroine. (Montoya's characterisation, indeed, is more negative than that of the hostages who were rescued; one has to ask whether this is not because she would be unable to answer back when the book was published.) In short, it appears not to matter how many other, inferior people die as long as the stars survive. This is the cruel, even heartless art of the narrator of this book whose motives, plainly, were literary and rhetorical rather than historical and testimonial. And he then adds insult to injury by providing a happy ending for a not particularly distinguished middle-class couple – his key informants – when so many other characters did not have such an ending out in the real world and when the problems of Colombia itself and its millions of displaced and impoverished people continued much as before. (A cool historical analysis may eventually show that the – no doubt valiant – efforts of Villamizar to release his wife and sister have been much exaggerated in García Márquez's version, thereby distorting the entire story – indeed, there is internal structural evidence to support such a conclusion.) After getting her ring back Maruja, in the last line of the novel, muses: 'Someone should write a book about this.'

García Márquez never wrote tailor-made 'socialist novels', even in the 1950s, when there was much pressure upon him to do so – but even up to and including *The General in His Labyrinth* and *Of Love and Other Demons* (see following chapter) they were arguably novels written by a socialist. The narrator of *News of a Kidnapping* does not seem to be carrying this burden.

When the book appeared, however, most critics were 'blown away', as a Hollywood critic of the era might have put it. Even those unhappy with the political perspective conceded that the master narrator had done it again and produced the proverbial book one could not put down. Many said they were unable to sleep without completing it and some even paid it the highest compliment of all, mixing thriller with fairy tale: they said they felt that if they stopped reading even for a minute the magic screen would shatter and the hostages would never get away.

Epilogue: the later journalism

In the 1980s and early 1990s more journalists had been killed in Colombia than almost anywhere else in the world. There were also, unfortunately, many more spectacular and usually tragic stories to report in that country than almost anywhere else in the world. Nowhere had a higher murder rate. And almost nowhere else had Colombia's toxic and terrifying mixture of terrorism, drug-trafficking, guerrilla warfare and paramilitary activity, combined with police and military responses that at times were almost as violent as the ills they were seeking to eradicate. García Márquez responded to this situation in three ways, all closely connected to journalism. First, he took part in the founding of a new television station, QAP, with *El Tiempo* newspaperman Enrique Santos

Calderón and other journalists and investors. Second, as we have just seen, he researched a book, a documentary work, really an extended piece of journalism written up as if it were a novel, *News of a Kidnapping*. Third, with Unesco backing, he launched one of his most cherished projects, a journalism foundation, the FNPI, that would challenge the work of modern schools of communication which, in his perception, 'mean to do away with journalism'. It was inaugurated in 1994, with *barranquillero* Jaime Abello as director, and held its first 'workshop' in 1995.

In October 1996 García Márquez travelled to Pasadena, California, for the 52nd assembly of the Inter-American Press Society (SIP), where two hundred newspaper owners were present, as were Central American Nobel Peace Prize winners Rigoberta Menchú and Oscar Arias, as well as Henry Kissinger. Luis Gabriel Cano of *El Espectador* was elected president of the organisation and the next meeting would be held in Guadalajara. García Márquez, very concerned to front his new journalism foundation, gave a keynote speech declaring that 'journalists have become lost in the labyrinth of technology': teamwork had been set aside and competition for scoops was damaging serious professional work. He had three key recommendations: 'Priority should be given to talent and vocation; investigative journalism is not a specialist activity, so all journalism should be investigative; and since ethics is not an occasional matter, it should always accompany the journalist as the buzz accompanies the fly.' (This last phrase would become the motto of the FNPI.)

After García Márquez was deprived of his television station at the end of 1997 he purchased *Cambio*, a magazine originally connected to the Spanish magazine *Cambio 16*, so influential during the Spanish transition from dictatorship in the 1980s. By late January García Márquez was beginning to write long headline articles – mainly about big-name personalities like Hugo Chávez, the controversial president of Venezuela; Subcomandante Marcos, the leader of the Zapatistas in Chiapas; Bill Clinton; Javier Solana, the Spanish secretary general of Nato; US general Wesley Clark, the commander of the Nato attack on Yugoslavia; Cardinal Darío Castrillón, a Colombian cleric who might become the first Latin American pope; and the pop diva from Barranquilla, Shakira; as well as a major intervention in the Elián González tug of war between Cuba and Miami. He also, at a time when he was working seriously on his memoirs, wrote a number of reminiscences explaining the relationship between his own life experiences and his literary works under the byline 'Gabo Replies'. By now he was being broadcast on the internet.

He seemed to be revelling in this return to reporting but in mid 1997 his career in journalism finally came to an end when he was struck down by lymphatic cancer and for the rest of his working life he concentrated on getting his memoirs written and attending to the needs, both financial and inspirational, of his beloved journalism foundation. He would no longer get out and about in the way he had always loved to do and he would no longer write separate articles on his own account.

Chapter 9

More about love: *Of Love and Other Demons* (1994) and *Memories of My Melancholy Whores* (2004)

Memories of My Melancholy Whores   *120*

In 1994, between *Strange Pilgrims* (1992; see next chapter) and *News of a Kidnapping* (1996), García Márquez published the fifth of his brief novels – there would be six in all – this one entitled *Of Love and Other Demons*. His return to live in Cartagena had already produced *Love in the Time of Cholera* in 1985 and he turned to the city again to tell a compelling tale about an adolesecent girl tried by the Spanish Inquisition for sorcery. In the novel's prologue he asserts that he has been thinking about this story since October 1949, when he was a young reporter and his boss sent him to the convent of Santa Clara in Cartagena to see the old tombs being opened. (At the time that García Márquez was writing this story he was having a mansion built across the road from the convent, which was itself being rebuilt as a five-star hotel.) One of the tombs, that of an adolescent girl, contained a stream of bright red hair more than twenty-two metres long.

The girl's name – García Márquez asserts – was Sierva María. She was, he assures us, the daughter of the distinguished aristocrat the Marquis of Casalduero, who lived in one of the finest houses in the old walled city towards the end of the eighteenth century, during the last decades of the colonial period. Today this house is a must-see element of any tourist walk around the city; García Márquez has Juvenal Urbino's family live in it in *Love in the Time of Cholera* and Bolívar dines there during his stay in Cartagena in *The General in His Labyrinth*, in which a few words from García Márquez anticipate the novel he would publish five years later:

> That night Montilla brought together the cream of the city's society in the seigneurial house on the Street of La Factoría where the Marquis of Valdehoyos had lived out his miserable life and where his marquess had prospered by smuggling flour and trafficking in slaves.[1]

The marquis as characterised in *Of Love and Other Demons* is indeed a wretched character, and it happens that the point of departure of the later novel – an outbreak of rabies – was also mentioned in the episode from *The General in His Labyrinth* just quoted. It is another example of García Márquez's enduring interest in plagues – indeed, this novel might have been called 'Love in the Time of Rabies'.

Sierva María is bitten by a rabid dog on her twelfth birthday. She shows no sign of having been infected but her feeble and unloving father, himself the decadent son of a distinguished but overbearing progenitor, becomes increasingly anxious. Her mother, his debauched and addictive second wife, is indifferent to the girl's fate. Indeed, because of this parental neglect Sierva María has been brought up and educated in the slave compound rather than in the family mansion. This, inevitably, has made her very obviously 'different': she knows little about European culture, almost nothing about Christianity and speaks in African languages in preference to Spanish. Three months after she is bitten she has a fever and the marquis, fearing that rabies is developing, hires an Indian curer to resolve the problem. The girl is terrified, and so violent are her protests – in one of the African languages – that the rumour spreads that her problem is not that she has rabies but that she has been taken over by the devil.

The marquis, whose lost humanity has been reawakened by concern for this daughter he has previously ignored, decides, on the advice of the bishop, to send her to the local convent in order for her condition to be tested and for an exorcism to be carried out if she proves to be infected not by a dog but by Satan himself. The marquis regrets his decision immediately, and continues to do so for the rest of his life. His daughter will never leave the convent again. Just as she has been alienated and coarsened by her treatment at the hands of her own family, now she is repulsed and enraged by the brutal remedies of a still medieval religion. The Church's most talented young theologian and the bishop's favourite, Cayetano Delaura, sees the truth and tells it to the bishop: 'I think what seem devilish to us are the customs of the blacks, which the child has learned because of her neglect by her parents.'[2] This ingenious conception, at the heart of the novel's logic, is brilliantly developed by the novelist.

Equally ingenious is the development of the love interest, which demonstrates that the Church is not only barbaric but hypocritical. Delaura, a man of thirty-six, convinces himself that he has the young woman's spiritual salvation at heart when in fact he has fallen head over heels in love with her. Here as elsewhere the writer suggests that love itself is a sickness or even a plague – rabies being perhaps the best comparison – and that there is rarely anything that we can do about it. The novel's rationalist intellectual, the Portuguese Jewish doctor Abrenuncio, believes in abstinence: 'love was a sentiment contra natura, which condemned two strangers to a miserable and unhealthy state of dependence, as fleeting as it was intense'. Gradually, the two lovers evolve towards a physical relationship – given the girl's age, García Márquez is careful not to take it 'too far' – but Delaura is eventually discovered – after his secret way in to her cell is unfortunately blocked off – and the girl, who responds with violent dismay to his disappearance, which she never understands, is restrained and subjected to a terrifying exorcism. To this she reacts as if the devil himself were indeed tormenting her, and the self-fulfilling prophecy of Christian superstition is dramatically and tragically enacted. Soon she stops eating, loses her will to live and wastes away (she has realised, like Eréndira, that she needs not just love but also freedom), while Delaura, condemned by the Inquisition, spends his days atoning by caring for the poor or deranged.

By García Márquez's standards this is a minor work and suggests that *The General in His Labyrinth* was indeed his last genuine masterpiece. Yet critical opinion was overwhelmingly positive, most notably in the English-speaking world. Not the least enthusiastic were the academic specialists, delighted to note that this former 'Boom' writer was now giving full-frontal attention to their 'postmodern' concerns with sexuality, feminism, race, religion, identity and the legacy of the Enlightenment as it reflected upon each of these matters.

It must be conceded that with this book García Márquez had taken another huge risk in the sense that here he was reinventing a historical world that was completely outside of his purview and that involved imagining a series of characters into whom he can have had very little personal insight when he began to compose the book. It is the closest thing he has ever written to a traditional, conventional novel. It required a familiarity with Catholic doctrine and the practices of the Inquisition, as well as some knowledge of eighteenth-century medicine and African culture in the colonial period. The book has a sort of bleak, heavy immobility to it, that of a society full of illusions and superstitions. Although it recreates a world more than two centuries old – *the world before Bolívar*, one might note – it is conceived from the disenchanted perspective – disenchanted for García Márquez, that is – after 1989. It was the first novel he had written after the fall of the Berlin Wall and the triumph of almost everything he had opposed in his life. What he saw was a world going backwards for the first time since the French Revolution two hundred years before. In other words, he was here making the adjustment necessary if he was to write about a world without any conceivable revolutionary horizon.

Abrenuncio the physician is an Enlightenment man in a world of religious fanaticism, a free-thinker, an agnostic and, as far as we can tell, a materialist. One intuits that much of what he says conveys García Márquez's own beliefs. For example, he remarks to Delaura: 'You have a religion of death which gives you the courage and the happiness to confront it. I don't: I think the only essential thing is to be alive.' On the other hand, he has never had any interest in sex, considers love irrational and invariably dangerous, and supports suicide and euthanasia. It would be simplistic to consider him a 100 per cent reflection of his author, given that their ideas are two hundred years apart; but García Márquez too would consider himself free of prejudice and dogmatism, ideologically independent and broad of mind, difficult to shock and always ready to forgive.[3]

Cayetano Delaura, the young priest thought destined for a brilliant future at the Vatican, and purportedly a descendant of the great Renaissance poet Garcilaso de la Vega, is unable to escape the fanaticism of his religious era, hard as he tries. Intoxicated by love, he will eventually cry out that 'It is the devil … The most terrible of them all.' Unused to women, and indeed afraid of them, he finds himself dreaming about Sierva María even before he meets her. He sees her in the room he had as a student in Salamanca, looking out of the window onto a snowscape as from her lap she eats grapes that must never run out or she will die.

This image, in fact, marks the novel's halfway point, in the middle of the third of five chapters (that is, a halfway point marked by *enjambement*), as the confident young priest has this premonitory dream about a girl he doesn't even know. (Later, Sierva María herself has the same dream and is unwilling to tell Delaura how it ends.) At the conclusion of the novel, after refusing all food, her head shaven and dying for love of Delaura, who she believes has forsaken her, Sierva María has the dream again. As she gazes out at the snow she crams grapes into her mouth, two at a time, impatient to devour them down to the very last one. When her lifeless body is found the next morning, red tresses are gushing back in streams of bubbles – or grapes? – over her newly covered skull. As at the end of a film by Hitchcock, the reader's blood runs cold.

Memories of My Melancholy Whores

In 2004 García Márquez published his first novel in ten years, with the somewhat shocking title *Memoria de mis putas tristes* (*Memories of My Melancholy Whores*). In between *Of Love and Other Demons* in 1994 and this new work on love and the relations between men and women, his political thriller *News of a Kidnapping* had appeared in 1996, followed in 2002, after he had fallen seriously ill, by the first and long-awaited volume of his memoirs, *Living to Tell the Tale* (see next chapter).

Memories of My Melancholy Whores was not a new project. He had been thinking about its – highly problematical – topic for more than twenty years and had lately been planning to make it one of a trilogy of novellas on the general theme of love, possibly to be published all together or perhaps separately. In the event, *Memories* appeared first and no further novella has yet appeared. (The same thing would happen with his memoirs: in the late 1990s he announced that he would be publishing up to six volumes of memoirs but by 2011 only the first, *Living to Tell the Tale*, had appeared. Old age is no doubt part of the explanation; illness is another, related possibility; and whether to go on with difficult and maybe controversial topics is probably another.)

Perhaps surprisingly, the calamitous love affair between a thirty-six-year-old priest and a twelve-year-old girl suspected of demonic possession caused little controversy when *Of Love and Other Demons* appeared in 1994 – possibly because the story was set two centuries before or perhaps because the essential presupposition of the plot was that the desire and love depicted in the novel were overwhelming passions which the protagonists were helpless to resist. Cayetano Delaura knew that he was transgressing and – although the reader feels that Cayetano himself feels justified by his passion – he spends many years paying for his crime and atoning for his sin.[4] *Memories* is quite different: if the earlier novel was centred on the twelve-year-old girl, and her lover was shown not to be able to help himself, it is the male lead who is the protagonist of this novel and, far from being unable to help himself – in the beginning at least – he chooses, on the day of his ninetieth birthday, to 'give [himself] the gift of a night of crazy love with an adolescent virgin'. (Presumably he had decided against the idea of a ninety-year-old virgin …) The girl turns out to be fourteen and is delivered to him naked and unconscious, having been drugged by the brothel keeper who supplies her. Of these lurid materials García Márquez sets out – audaciously? outrageously? brazenly? – to build a fairy-tale romance.

As we know, love makes the world go round; but although popular literature and song are always at pains to suggest that happy endings are possible and tend, therefore, to end at the point of betrothal, serious literature is more likely to show us that betrothal is not always attained and marriage is not always happy and successful, though of course children have to be born and the society in which they are to grow up has to be appropriately managed. In García Márquez's works love is always a serious matter and nearly always a problem. Few serious twentieth-century writers have explored it in so many ways, in such depth and with such breadth.

In his early novels, as we have seen, love tended to be frustrated by the requirements and restrictions of power, and solitude seemed to be the almost inevitable outcome. In *In Evil Hour* there was little love to be seen but plenty of adultery, and the whole point of departure was an honour killing carried out by a vengeful husband who, as he rode away from his house in the early morning, had read, fixed to his front door, an anonymous letter denouncing his wife's alleged infidelity. In *One Hundred Years of Solitude* there are many affairs of love and sex – all filed, of course, under the single word 'love' – but very few of them end well, and the protagonist of *The Autumn of the Patriarch* is effectively defined by his incapacity for love for any man or woman apart from his mother. Up to this point politics – power, solitude – had predominated and love had not only come a poor second but its problematical – even impossible – aspects had been repeatedly emphasised.

The big change came in the 1980s, after García Márquez had not only taken politics as far as it could go in *The Autumn of the Patriarch* but had also, in his work with *Alternativa*, spent six long years devoting himself to political journalism at a time when everything in the political world was moving in what for him was a negative direction. And his political antennae told him that things were only going to get worse. Moreover, he had become increasingly aware that, although there was nothing dour about his books, it had become a cliché that socialists, communists and revolutionaries – the 'Left', in general – were too concerned with ideology and not with the topics that interested – and consoled – ordinary people, love chief among them. Perhaps the time had come for solitude – the lament about the political fate of Latin America and its people – to be superseded by that other socialist slogan, solidarity. Perhaps García Márquez should speak more directly to his audience: indeed, perhaps he should widen that audience by dealing less with ultimately demoralising political matters and more with the topic that had illuminated the individualism of the Western world for an entire millennium, the question of love. But not just in a vulgar, reductive way: love in all its forms.

So in 1980, when he started work on the first new novel he had begun for fifteen years, García Márquez had new perspectives. The subject matter of *Chronicle of a Death Foretold* was as horrifying as anything he had addressed before, but the writing itself had a new radiance and the narrative tone was agile and almost jaunty. And although the novel follows the protagonist Santiago Nasar to the – terrifyingly – bitter end, it also has a brutally ironic alternative ending in which Santiago ceases to be the protagonist when the original lovers, Angela Vicario and Bayardo San Román, come together again – in the middle of the novel, though in reality it is an epilogue – with every sign that all is forgiven, that love is to be given another chance, that a happy ending is on the cards; and so, the reader may conclude, you never know what may happen where love is concerned.

During that novel the narrator, someone very like Gabriel García Márquez, recalls that he proposed to his future wife Mercedes Barcha, 'when she had barely finished primary school', which is true of the real García Márquez, who fell in love with Mercedes when she was nine (Beatrice's age when Dante fell for her) and he was fourteen. This does not deter the narrator of *Chronicle*, in love with this not yet adolescent schoolgirl, from spending much of the novel in bed with the local prostitute, María Alejandrina Cervantes, and indeed the real García Márquez had his first sexual experience with a prostitute, arranged by his father, when he himself was only thirteen.

Love, and sex, then, in the works of García Márquez, are matters of extremes – not only in the content of the sexual episodes, though there are plenty of scabrous scenes, but also in the ages of the participants. This applies even to Bolívar, who in *The General in His Labyrinth* has several one-night stands with teenage girls. Few novelists have explored old age as regularly and with such originality as García Márquez has, beginning with *No One Writes to the Colonel*. Still fewer have written novels like *Love in the Time of Cholera*, in which a man waits more than fifty years to get his girl and first has sex with her when she is seventy-two and he is seventy-six; and in which, even more startling, he seduces his own fourteen-year-old niece, who is also his ward, and has a sexual relationship with her which ends in her suicide when he abandons her for his original love.

Sex between old people may be shocking to some (though perhaps less so after a few doses of García Márquez); sex between old men and very young girls – though not pre-pubescent children, one hastens to add – is shocking to many, and we are much less likely to get used to it or to get over it. The three most sexually controversial novels of the twentieth century in the English-speaking world were Joyce's *Ulysses*, Lawrence's *Lady Chatterley's Lover* and Nabokov's *Lolita*. The first two have by now been fully assimilated into the culture but *Lolita* retains most of its power to shock – and the fact that Nabokov's interest in the topic of older men lusting after under-age girls has been shown to extend well beyond that one novel has only added to the scandal. García Márquez is a professed admirer of the novels of Japanese author Yasunari Kawabata, especially his *House of the Sleeping Beauties* in which old Japanese men pay to lie alongside young drugged women, though they are not permitted to approach them in any sexual manner. In fact, García Márquez takes the epigraph to his own novel from Kawabata's book.[5]

García Márquez, for his part, juxtaposes the concepts of sex and little girls in *One Hundred Years of Solitude*, in which the second José Arcadio has sex (consensual) with 'a very young gypsy girl, almost a child', and runs away with her; in which Aureliano wishes, but is too shy, to do the same with 'an adolescent mulatto girl', a prostitute (the prototype of Eréndira), who has already had sex with sixty-three men that evening; and the same Aureliano, by then a grown man, falls in love with Remedios Moscote, 'only nine, a pretty little girl with lily-coloured skin and green eyes', and he marries her as soon as she reaches puberty, which she does 'before getting over the habits of childhood'. In *The Autumn of the Patriarch* the dictator not only regularly rapes every woman who comes into contact with him but also has an intense – indeed porno-graphic – relationship with a twelve-year-old schoolgirl when he is already demented and apparently more than two hundred years old. In short, given that we have already noted the stories of fourteen-year-old América Vicuña in *Love in the Time of Cholera* and twelve-year-old Sierva María in *Of Love and Other Demons*, it might be said that we should be ready for that of the 'barely fourteen'-year-old Delgadina, naked and unconscious, in *Memories of My Melancholy Whores*.

Clearly, the attraction of teenage girls for older men is an obsession with García Márquez; and clearly, as we have seen, that obsession, in his case, emerges from his own biography (his own first experience at thirteen; his love for Mercedes when she was nine and he was an 'older man' of fourteen) and indeed from a culture – the Hispanic–Islamic rural nexus – in which girls were expected to come to sexual maturity very early and were betrothed and married in many cases when they were still children. It is rumoured, after all, that the Virgin Mary was only thirteen when she was impregnated by the Holy Ghost. And Muhammad's wife Aisha was traditionally thought to be six years old when betrothed to the Prophet, and nine or ten when the marriage was consummated. Even in our own contemporary culture, the weakness of older men for 'schoolgirls' is well known; however adolescent schoolgirls, though capable of child-bearing, have to be protected in Western culture both from sex itself, as far as possible, and certainly from becoming pregnant. And yet there has recently been a curious and contradictory development: on the one hand, an increasing awareness of the rights of children not to be abused; on the other, an increasing sexualisation of almost everything through advertising, the media and the internet, not least the images of adolescents and little girls.

The question – one of the questions – is whether García Márquez manages to objectify his obsession and turn it into something more general, indeed 'universal'. Certainly, the 'Lolita' topic had never scandalised readers of his earlier novels – though most had not registered how frequently he returned to it – but the times were very much changing when *Memories of My Melancholy Whores* appeared in 2004; and with the plot of that novel, outlined above, involving a ninety-year-old man and a fourteen-year-old girl, it could be said that the seventy-seven-year-old novelist was certainly pushing the sexual envelope.

Because this time there are no mitigations provided. The girl is a prisoner, a reluctant and possibly involuntary prostitute, supplied by a procuress and paid for, drugged and denuded; her seducer – we do not wish to say abuser – is very old, but he is certainly not gaga, and he knows exactly what he is doing; we are not in the late eighteenth century, when morality may have been different, but in the second half of the twentieth century. But this, of course, is only the beginning of the story; our aging lothario soon falls in love with the girl – having never known this emotion before – and eventually decides, like many an old fool, to leave all his worldly goods to her; and he persuades himself that his emotion may be reciprocated, so that we the readers may be in the presence of a – somewhat improbable – fairy tale. (Up until now this unattractive fellow has never had sex without paying for it, including a monthly episode with his servant, and for a long time he kept a note of all the women he had enjoyed, just as Florentino Ariza does in *Love in the Time of Cholera*.)

In due course the protagonist, known only by his nickname of Mustio Collado, decides to call the girl 'Delgadina', inspired by a famous medieval Spanish ballad about 'the king's youngest daughter, wooed by her father'.[6] The word 'wooed', of course, is a euphemism, and it would be interesting to know if the euphemistic desire of the medieval protagonist is in fact shared by the author. At any rate, the man names the girl. He has no desire to know her real name: she is to be, as far as possible, his fantasy creation, his living doll. (He has already revealed that his birthday is 29 August, the day of the Martyrdom of St John the Baptist: in other words, the day of the symbolic castration – the beheading – of an older man through the wiles of a dangerous young virgin.)

As for the naming, 'Delgadina' would have been a much better title for the book. There are not many 'whores' in it, and almost none of them are 'melancholy'.[7] The title is best understood as an example of the phenomenon known in Spanish as hyperbaton, most associated with Luis de Góngora (1561– 1627), which for poetic effect separates words that normally go together. This title really means 'My sad memories of whores', or perhaps 'I, sad, remember whores'. There is another striking example of this procedure in the novel when the narrator refers to 'Delgadina's happy bed', which illustrates very neatly the old man's capacity for self-deception: I leave my readers to deconstrue it.

Surprisingly enough, this brief work is the only novel that García Márquez has ever set in what he has always insisted is his favourite Colombian city, Barranquilla, though it is never named in the book. It is also the only one narrated throughout by a single first-person narrator (which is, naturally, the format of his memoir *Living to Tell the Tale*). Mustio Collado is a second-rate though popular newspaper columnist who was born to privilege and has never had to work hard for a living. (In other words, he is *not* Gabriel García Márquez, though one is tempted to say, cattily, that García Márquez's writing has never been more mediocre.) The novel is in five numbered parts and the mid point is marked once more by a symbolic moment halfway through the middle chapter, in this case by an *enjambement* in chapter 3 as the infatuated narrator announces that, thanks to love, 'I became another man.'[8] This is underlined by the fact that four months now pass before the next events, when the first two and a half chapters have been taken up by just two days.

At the end of the novel, after a few ups and downs, the narrator has made it to ninety-one. He is convinced that his teenage sex object now loves him back, and he has therefore apparently demonstrated, like Florentino Ariza and Fermina Daza before him, or like Angela Vicario and Bayardo San Román before them, that 'life is never over until it's over', that 'you're as old as you feel' and love may appear in the most unlikely places at the most unlikely times – and indeed to the most unlikely people. If this conclusion is to be taken literally it is an interesting one, even though not every reader is likely to identify with Collado's joy. (In truth, the book raised few politically correct eyebrows when it came out, though gradually talk of child abuse has become more frequent and may be expected to grow louder over the years.)

But there are at least two other possibilities. The first is that the madam, Rosa Cabarcas, and the girl, Delgadina, have been stringing the old man along in order to get his money; there are some textual indications which seem to make this plausible though by no means certain. The fact is that absolutely everything the protagonist knows about the girl comes through the mediation of Cabarcas, who may have made her up like any Hollywood director or scriptwriter giving the audience what it desires. This interpretation would make the novel not dissimilar to Cervantes's classic comedy, *The Jealous Old Man* (*El viejo celoso*) – though even that man is not as old as this one nor his bride as young (she is fifteen – and Cervantes clearly disapproves). The other possibility is that the old man is to be seen not as a normal guy with normal instincts but as a damaged personality because we discover in the very last pages of the book that when he was only eleven, while waiting for his father to come out of his office, he was sexually initiated 'by force' by a prostitute before he was ready for the experience and, after an initial trauma, became a sexual addict for the rest of his life and a man incapable of love and indifferent to sex without payment.[9]

Now, almost eighty years later, love has made Collado a changed man. If in the first line of the novel he confesses to the desire for 'crazy' love, the last line claims that he now understands 'good' love: 'It was, at last, real life, with my heart safe and condemned to die of happy love in the joyful agony of any day after my hundredth birthday.' We are reminded here that the Gongoresque title and the ballad *Delgadina* are not the only echoes of classical Spanish literature. The malign madam, Rosa Cabarcas, inevitably recalls *The Spanish Bawd* (*La*

Celestina) by Fernando de Rojas; and the distinction between crazy and happy love is clearly a reference to the – famously ambiguous – late medieval classic, *The Book of Good Love* (*El libro de buen amor*). Only now, aged ninety-one, has Collado come to a true understanding of real love and therefore of real life and we thus, in a sense, also have an optimistic version of the ending of *Don Quixote*: like the knight of the sad countenance, Collado has been sick all these years. Don Quixote has to die but Collado lives on. He now has his 'heart safe', not because Delgadina is his but because he has a 'healthy' love for her.

Chapter 10

Memoirs: *Living to Tell the Tale* (2002)

Strange Pilgrims   *129*
Living to Tell the Tale   *133*

There was great expectation worldwide when Gabriel García Márquez announced in 2002, after surviving a serious illness, that the first (and by 2011 only) volume of his memoirs was finally ready for publication. He had decided that the memoirs would have a semi-fictional status, which has delighted most readers but has caused academic critics a series of unusually difficult but also illuminating dilemmas. These begin with the epigraph: 'Your life is is not the one you lived but the one you remember and how you remember it in order to tell it.' This statement raises almost every question that can be asked about experience, observation, memory, language, truth and sincerity before the reader has even begun the narrative.

The fact is that, more than most novelists, García Márquez had been writing autobiographically even when he least appeared to be doing so. Excavating his own past had been the principal motivating force of his early writing, and he had been talking about writing his memoirs since the late 1960s, when he first became famous. At that time, weary of the endless series of repetitive interviews to which he was subjected, he began to embellish some of his stories, partly to stave off boredom by amusing himself but also partly, no doubt, to protect his biographical secrets. He would eventually say that his interviews should be considered a part of his creative fiction.[1]

It is usually assumed – naively, it has to be said – that memoirs or autobiographies are written to set a record 'straight'. This is certainly a frequent claim, but in truth these works are more often used to 'get one's message across', sometimes known as 'telling it my way'. This usually involves setting the record 'straight' by concealing one's 'deviations' from the conventional 'norm' and thus eliding one's real motivations and behaviour. As is well known, writers write their novels, to an important extent and in important ways, from the heart (or from the id, to be Freudian for a moment) but their memoirs from their heads (or from the super-ego).

Strange Pilgrims

García Márquez's final collection of stories, *Strange Pilgrims*, was published in 1992 to coincide with the commemoration of the so-called 'discovery' of the Americas five hundred years before. García Márquez had written almost eighty stories set in the Western Europe he had known in the fifties, sixties and seventies and set about cutting the great majority until he had reached a round dozen. Paradoxically, they are by far his most autobiographical short stories even though they are the only stories of his not set in Latin America. Indeed, it could fairly be claimed that they give as useful an insight into his life and times as *Living to Tell the Tale*. Some of them had already been published in preliminary form among the chronicles he wrote for *El Espectador* and *El País* between 1980 and 1984 and those chronicles, as we have mentioned, were themselves notably autobiographical in comparison with any that he had written in earlier decades.* Ironically enough, when he was living in Europe in the times to which the stories refer, he was writing not about Europe but about Colombia; now he looked back on Europe itself with a distant, ironic but essentially benevolent gaze. All except two of them ('The Trail of Your Blood in the Snow' and

---

* The stories are *'Bon Voyage*, Mr. President' ('Buen viaje, señor presidente', June 1979), 'The Saint' ('La santa', begun August 1981; see intermediate version 'Margarito Duarte', in *El Espectador*, 20 September 1981), 'Sleeping Beauty and the Airplane' ('El avión de la bella durmiente', March 1980; see intermediate version in *El Espectador*, 19 September 1982), 'I Sell My Dreams' ('Me alquilo para soñar', March 1980; see intermediate version in *El Espectador*, 4 September 1983), '"I Only Came to Use the Phone"' ('"Sólo vine a hablar por teléfono"', April 1978; see intermediate version in *El Espectador*, 'María de mi corazón', 3 May 1981), 'The Ghosts of August' ('Espantos de agosto', October 1980; see intermediate version in *El Espectador*, 'Cuento de horror para la Nochevieja', 28 December 1980), 'Maria dos Prazeres' ('Maria dos Prazeres', May 1979), 'Seventeen Poisoned Englishmen' ('Diecisiete ingleses envenenados', April 1980; see intermediate version in *El Espectador*, 'Roma en verano', 6 June 1982), 'Tramontana' ('Tramontana', January 1982; see intermediate version in *El Espectador*, 'Tramontana mortal', 29 January 1984), 'Miss Forbes's Summer of Happiness' ('El verano feliz de la señora Forbes', 1976), 'Light is Like Water' ('La luz es como el agua', December 1978), and 'The Trail of Your Blood in the Snow' ('El rastro de tu sangre en la nieve', 1976). Those published first as newspaper pieces and/or films give us a rare opportunity to see García Márquez's process of creation. Five are based on his experiences in the 1950s; six on his experiences in the 1960s and 1970s (though 'I Sell My Dreams' and 'The Saint' have updates into the 1960s and 1970s; and 'I Sell My Dreams'

'Miss Forbes's Summer of Happiness'), García Márquez states, were completed in April 1992, though some of them had been started in the 1960s.[2]

Taken as a whole, they give implicit testimony to the conversion of García Márquez from the inexperienced and impoverished traveller he was in the 1950s to García Márquez the 'Man of the World' in the 1980s and 1990s. They attest to the achievement of an imperturbably ironic perspective on Europe. By this stage one could hardly speak of influences upon this globally renowned writer, but these stories seem to hark back to more traditional times and to the kind of stories that W. W. Jacobs or Somerset Maugham had written in times long past. In the 'Prologue' he notes that he had felt that he needed to go back to Europe to refresh his memory; but Europe was totally changed. Then he 'rewrote all the stories in eight feverish months', indifferent to questions of truth and authenticity. They seem to have been written more for himself than for his audience, full of coded messages about his personal life. Some readers saw them as a kind of nouveau riche vision of travel and cultural contact. It is, in retrospect, astonishing that he was working on some of these whimsical and in some cases rather slight – even trivial – creations at a time when he was interacting closely with Fidel and Raúl Castro and still writing politically committed diatribes against the policies of the United States and the Colombian ruling class.

The stories were organised in no discernible order, whether chronological or thematic. The first, '*Bon Voyage*, Mr President', narrated in the third person, is many readers' favourite (many others like the last, 'The Trail of Your Blood in the Snow', best), and is set in the 1950s in Geneva, the first place García Márquez visited in 1955, directly after landing in Paris. The protagonist, ex-president of the Caribbean republic Puerto Santo, has come from exile in Martinique to have medical tests in Switzerland. Like 'Maria dos Prazeres' and his last novel, *Memories of My Melancholy Whores*, it tells the story of someone who discovers that death can always be postponed and is best forgotten about – a story, then, that perhaps became more relevant to the author in the final stages of preparing the collection as he was recovering from cancer.

'The Saint', previously a newspaper chronicle masquerading as a true story, had by this time also been filmed (*Miracle in Rome*, 1988), and is narrated in

seems to continue into the 1980s); and one, 'Sleeping Beauty and the Airplane', is contemporary and will eventually be totally transformed into the novel *Memories of My Melancholy Whores*. One is set in Geneva, one in Vienna (though also in Barcelona and Havana), four in Italy (Rome, Naples, Arezzo, Pantelleria), four in Spain (two in Barcelona and Cadaqués, one in Zaragoza, one in Madrid; also, partially, 'I Sell My Dreams' and 'The Trail of Your Blood'), only one, surprisingly, in France ('The Trail of Your Blood'); and one takes place between Paris and New York, in a plane ('Sleeping Beauty and the Airplane').

the first person. It begins in Rome in 1955 and gives walk-on parts to Zavattini (a 'machine for inventing plots'), and three different popes. 'Sleeping Beauty and the Airplane' is a tale set in the late 1970s or early 1980s, and written at the same time, about a plane journey from Paris's Charles de Gaulle airport to New York, sitting next to the most beautiful woman the narrator – more like García Márquez than ever (though reportedly the experience actually happened to his son Gonzalo) – has ever seen. She spends the entire journey asleep and he is awake the entire time, watching her and thinking of Kawabata's famous novel and Gerardo Diego's erotic poem 'Insomniac' ('You and your naked dream. You don't know it, you dream it', etc.). *Memories of My Melancholy Whores* would, in effect, be an expanded version of this story, one which takes the ecstasy of sadomasochistic contemplation much further.

'I Sell My Dreams', which by this time had inspired a television series, begins at the time of García Márquez's visit to Vienna in 1955 and features a Colombian woman who hires herself out to families to explain their dreams to them. '"I Only Came to Use the Phone"' is one of the best of these stories, narrated in the third person, about a Mexican woman who drives from Zaragoza to Barcelona, but her car breaks down on the way and she becomes trapped in a lunatic asylum where all she wanted was to use the phone.

'The Ghosts of August' is the most directly autobiographical of all, since the first-person narrator has a wife called Mercedes and two boys of 'nine and seven'. It originated in the García Barcha family's 1969 journey from Pantelleria to Paris, when the family stopped over in the home of Miguel Otero Silva in Arezzo, Italy, on the way. It tells the legend of the castle's first owner, the great Ludovico, who murdered his wife after making love to her and was then torn to pieces by his own dogs. 'Maria dos Prazeres' is set in 1970s Barcelona. A Brazilian ex-prostitute who lives in the Gracia quarter of the city is feeling very old (she is seventy-six) and becomes obsessed with death, but once again we learn that life is never over till it's over and Maria even has one last sexual thrill – though of course the reader asks herself, as the old lady and a handsome young man mount the stairs to her apartment at the conclusion of the story, whether he may be a serial killer, a theme in which García Márquez's later stories began to take an unhealthy interest.

'Seventeen Poisoned Englishmen', another third-person narration, is set in Naples in 1955, when García Márquez first went to Italy; it is rather weak and makes little sense overall. The same may be said of 'Tramontana', set in the Catalan beach resort of Cadaqués, in the 1960s or early 1970s, this time with eleven Swedes. Like the seventeen Englishmen, and indeed like all the Europeans included in the collection, they are ferociously stereotyped – right down to all looking the same – though of course it is they, the Swedes, who are accused by the narrator of stereotyping – exoticising – the young Caribbean protagonist. They force him to return to Cadaqués against his wishes and he dies in an accident on the way.

'Miss Forbes's Summer of Happiness', by then a movie (1988), was narrated in the first person, as if by García Márquez's son Rodrigo (though naturally the story does not say this). It is set in Pantelleria in August when the narrator, elder of two brothers, was about nine, roughly Rodrigo's age when the family holidayed there in 1969. The boys' parents leave them with an obsessively repressed and sadomasochistic German governess, Miss Forbes (another stereotype). The boys want Miss Forbes dead and get their wish, though their own efforts are not successful and she is stabbed to death by some crazed lover. In 'Light is Like Water' there are again two boys, again nine and seven, but this time the events take place, curiously, in Madrid, where the boys insist on a boat as a Christmas present. They sail in the light which floods their house while their parents are away and the thirty-seven classmates they invite to the house all drown.

Finally 'The Trail of Your Blood in the Snow', which many readers consider García Márquez's greatest story, is a fantastic version – like a fairy story – of something that really happened to him,[3] though the two protagonists are both wealthy upper-class Colombians from Cartagena, the young woman 'almost a child', at eighteen, and the young man a year younger. They are married on arrival in Madrid – she secretly two months pregnant – but she pricks her finger on a rose and it bleeds all the way to Paris. They park their convertible 'outside the emergency entrance of a huge, gloomy hospital'. The boy, helpless in the vast unknown foreign city, gets lost and the girl dies two days after she is taken in, without ever seeing him again.

The critics were divided by these stories, and their division exemplified the debate that would follow: had García Márquez been spoiled by fame and turned into an ironic version of one of the many writers who had imitated his magical realist style? John Sturrock, writing in the *Times Literary Supplement*, evidently thought so: 'The time he has spent crowd-pleasing [writing movie and TV scripts] has done García Márquez no good as a serious writer: these are for the most part facile stories, too easy on the mind, soft-centred and poorly focused.' On the other hand John Bayley, in the *New York Review of Books*, argued that 'it might be said that Márquez popularised surrealism by making it such a pleasure to experience surrealist moments in his own lovingly exotic paragraphs. Here is an author who really enjoys what he writes about, and can be seen and felt enjoying it.' Much of his genius, Bayley went on, 'resides in a seeming unawareness of that plodding Anglo-Saxon distinction between a 'serious' writer … and a popular lightweight one … The fact remains that most of his works are undoubted masterpieces; and that may be true particularly of his novellas and stories, like most of the ones in the present collection'.* These two views between them sum up a large and ongoing debate about García Márquez's later work. Was he always a writer whose world view was unsophisticated and over-simplistic? Or one whose early work was sober, serious and illuminating but went downmarket after the Nobel Prize? Or is he simply one of those serious writers who are able almost effortlessly to modulate their writing in such a way that they can speak not only to the most sophisticated of critics but also to a much wider swathe of general readers than, for example, the modernists of the 1920s from whom García Márquez learned so much?

Living to Tell the Tale

As we noted in Chapter 6, the newspaper columns García Márquez wrote between 1980 and1984 are the richest source of biographical material available to students of this author; and we have just seen that *Strange Pilgrims* (1992), which draws on those columns to a significant degree, also contains many autobiographical ingredients. Earlier books of his have the words *relato* (account), *crónica* (chronicle), *diatriba* (diatribe) and *noticia* (report) in their titles. With *News of a Kidnapping* García Márquez produced a work of journalism written like a novel; now, with *Living to Tell the Tale*, he had produced a memoir also written like a novel. And it is surely 'telling' that although *Living to Tell the Tale* does not have 'memoir' or 'autobiography' as a subtitle, his next novel, *Memories of My Melancholy Whores*, does indeed have 'memoir' in its Spanish title, though unfortunately the English translation has

---

* García Márquez continued to write stories after 1992 and was evidently intending a further collection possibly connected to the *Difficult Loves* (*Amores difíciles*) series of film scripts he had written in the late 1980s. These stories include: 'Meeting in August', *New Yorker*, 6 December 1999 ('En agosto nos vemos', *El País*, 21 March 1999), in which the female lead has done a degree in literature (like Graciela, the protagonist of his play *Diatribe of Love Against a Seated Man*) – during a four-hour boat trip to her island of love she is reading *Dracula*. The story was reportedly one of five to appear in a new book (*Melancholy Whores* was supposed to be one of them for a time). Another was 'The Night of the Eclipse' ('La noche del eclipse', 2003), in which a woman has sex with an elegant young man who turns out to be a con artist, pimp and probable murderer. These stories are similar in theme to 'Maria dos Prazeres' and a film based on a sinister García Márquez script called 'I'm the One You're Looking For' (*Yo soy el que tu buscas*, 1989).

not carried this across, preferring 'memories', a linguistic 'false friend' if ever there was one.

As a matter of fact, shortly before publication the new book's title was announced as *Vivir para contarlo. (La novela de una vida. Memorias)*, or, literally: 'Living in Order to Tell It. (The Novel of a Life. Memoirs)'. The 'vivirlo' instead of 'vivirla' indicates that almost to the very end the writer was thinking of the abstract but more dynamic concept of 'living' instead of the concrete concept of 'life'. And the earlier and obviously contradictory subtitle 'The Novel of a Life. Memoirs' would only have highlighted the mischievous intent implicit in both versions of the epigraph. Together these differences not only underline García Márquez's ambivalence about 'telling the truth', or even 'telling it like it was' (as against going where the demands of a good story lead you) but also show that he was still having doubts about what he was doing, or at least how he wanted to present what he was doing, almost up to the last moment before the publication of the book.

This vacillation is evident in fact throughout his career: in few writers is the problematic status of truth and sincerity in storytelling exemplified as variously, as subtly or as profoundly as in the work of Gabriel García Márquez. Critics have often suggested that this is because he has a fundamental problem with honesty: in other words, a problem of character and ethics. But the problems are of course real – is life a dream? are we capable, post-Freud, of 'telling the truth'? – and it could as easily be argued that this writer is much more honest about the problems of honesty than many of his critics. Remember his warning in his very first article that his generation could not be relied upon to be 'men of good will'.

As mentioned, his next novel, which, had it been translated literally, would have appeared in English as *Memoir of My Sad Whores*, does indeed continue the autobiographical convention (it is a *fictional* autobiography, of course). Its narrator will confirm this intention at the beginning of chapter 2 when he notes, 'I am writing this memoir in what little remains of the library that belonged to my parents.' Unfortunately, the translator again renders 'memoria' as 'memories' (which would be 'recuerdos'); it has to be said that this is a curious decision when, after all, the writer was so insistently writing in autobiographical mode at this time in his life. Memories and memoir are quite different things.

Most writers have more interesting childhood biographies than their average reader can boast (or lament): indeed, these childhoods, sometimes traumatic but invariably at least involving some form of painful 'distancing', are often the reason why people become writers in the first place. And certainly García Márquez's childhood was more extraordinary than most. As we saw in

Chapter 1, he was born in his grandfather's house, the first child of a mother who would leave him there for six years from the age of one. (The cover of the memoir bears a picture of that one-year-old baby but the book, the least confessional of autobiographies, does not address this riddle: the photograph is a sort of question mark, entirely unexplained.) His first fully conscious memory of his mother was when she returned to her father's house when Gabriel, her eldest child, was seven: a story he has sometimes told in interviews but – surprisingly and significantly – not here in the memoir. After that her husband and the other children also returned to the town, but Gabriel continued to live in his grandfather's house until the old man fell ill when he was nine. Even after he was restored to his nuclear family – his parents and, eventually, ten brothers and sisters – he mainly attended boarding schools and then went straight on to university so that in fact he almost never lived with his family for more than a month or two at a time, even though the rest of them mainly stayed together.

It is not surprising, then, that in *Living to Tell the Tale*, which takes him from his birth to the age of twenty-eight, when he moved to Europe, García Márquez begins with the topic that has haunted him all his life – his relationship with his mother. (Neither García Márquez himself, nor any of the students of his work, has ever referred directly to this topic, which suggests that his diversionary tactics have been extremely effective.) His tone suggests that this relationship has been the most normal and natural thing in the world, yet how many mothers feel the need to say to their eldest child, 'I am your mother', as Luisa Santiaga Márquez Iguarán de García does on the very first page of this book; and how many writers would decide to begin such a book in such a way? (Later, the author notes almost matter of factly that he was putting the last finishing touches to it when his mother died, aged ninety-six, on 9 June 2002.)

And yet, in this climactic account of his life, putting what one might call the 'finishing touches' to a series of texts which he has been writing about his childhood ever since 'The House' when he was nineteen, he once again conceals the theme of the absence of his mother behind the somewhat less dramatic theme which he has been pursuing all his life as if it were infinitely the most important, namely 'the house' (the past, his childhood, Aracataca) – when the real, Hamletian question (to be or not to be his mother's son, not to mention his father's) is: Why was he in that house from 1928 to 1934 and his mother not? Few statements in the book raise more questions than the following one: 'for us there was only one [house] in the world'. *Why* did she leave him? *How* could she have left him? And then the Freudian question arises: Was it his father's fault? And of course the Freudian answer is that it is always the father's fault, and the son wishes to make him accountable for it, but that the mother is invariably guilty of collusion, and the son wishes – at first – to avoid this conclusion.

The memoir is in eight numbered chapters of even length,[4] each between sixty-six and seventy-five pages in the Spanish edition. It is striking to note that for the first time since *Leaf Storm*, and indeed the only time in his entire narrative trajectory (the next work, *Memories of My Melancholy Whores*, will return to the template), García Márquez fails to establish a functional symbolic dividing line halfway through his book, which means that he has failed – or declined – to create a book chronologically, narratologically and aesthetically structured in two halves. The obvious reason for this failure is that since he is constrained by truth and history, he is aware that such a division would be a falsification – whereas in fiction story and plot can always be manipulated according to all the immensely subtle requirements of the novelist's art. In point of fact the last chapter of each half, chapters 4 and 8, are the *least* compelling – and each is set in the highlands, in Zipaquirá or Bogotá.[5]

Of course, it could as easily be asserted that it is the need to manipulate not his literary story as such but the truth of his own life that has left him unable to impose his usual structural design, which – up to now and then afterwards as well – has been both an aesthetic and a psychological imperative. Symptomatic of this difficulty with establishing a chronological structure is the repeated appearance of phrases like 'so that' which connect paragraphs in his book but do not link events or establish causality in the real history to which he is referring. Here he cannot write the story he really wants or needs; he is constrained, at least partly, by what actually happened – despite the compositional freedom declared in the epigraph. Much of the humour of *One Hundred Years of Solitude* comes from the implicit scepticism about time and chronology, whose vagueness troubles the reader but means so little to the characters; or from the narrator's at times absurd omniscience and hyperbole, from his godlike, declaratory positioning, implicit in the magical realist perspective, which the content of the book itself hilariously undermines. Unfortunately all these techniques have become hardened – part of the García Márquez 'brand', perhaps – and in the memoir they work against the author's intentions.

So the halfway mark here comes between his time at high school in Zipaquirá and his time at university in Bogotá, which makes chronological sense but no kind of thematic sense – after all, it is the contrast between the coast and the highlands which gives structure to the memoir, as indeed to his life, and both Zipaquirá and Bogotá are in the highlands. Or one could say that it is the contrast between his education in school and university and his real education, as Mark Twain would have said, which structures this story, whereas both Zipaquirá and Bogotá relate to his formal education. Of course, another reason for this failure might be that García Márquez, after his illness, was no longer as in control of his material as he had previously been – but although *Memories of My Melancholy Whores* certainly confirms this suspicion, it does not confirm the larger thesis because, as mentioned above, it returns decisively to the two-part pattern.

We are left, then, with the blindingly obvious conclusion that one's own life is not as malleable as fiction. So the halfway signature principle is half abandoned. But that is because the story that García Márquez most wants to tell is the frankly mythological tale of how a boy who lost his mother soon after birth got her back, many years later, and how the two of them made a journey – a journey that neither Oedipus nor any of the other Greek heroes was privileged to make – back to the house where she gave birth to him, a journey which therefore returns to him not only his mother but his past, a journey at the end of which, like some male sleeping beauty – Narcissus, perhaps – he is brought back to life (brought *properly* to life, to real life, his real life, like Mustio Collado at the end of *Memories*) and can therefore start to live in the future as well as in the past. (A more ruthlessly Freudian reading might pass over both Oedipus and Narcissus and propose that what we have here is Ulysses travelling back to his lost Ithaca with … Penelope …)

Nevertheless, this memoir is, surely, a classic of the genre, beautifully written on the whole (one suspects that most of it had been prepared many years before it was published), but nevertheless an unbalanced narrative. This is because its best pages are the first pages, its best story is the first story, the story of how he and his mother Luisa went back in 1950 to try to sell the old family house of her father, Colonel Nicolás Márquez, the house where Gabriel García Márquez had been born almost twenty-three years before. This first chapter is an anthology piece: it starts in February, 'on the eve of Carnival', with his mother introducing herself to him in a bookstore in Barranquilla like a figure from Greek mythology – 'I am your mother' – as if he might not know her (after all, on the unmentioned previous occasion when she had introduced herself to him sixteen years before, in Aracataca, when he was seven, he really had not known her); the chapter continues with their arrival in Aracataca the next day, then goes back to the 1920s when his father and mother went through hell and high water to get married – in Santa Marta, not Aracataca – before leaving for Riohacha (this story had already been told, in a modified fashion, in *Love in the Time of Cholera*), and ends back in Aracataca in March, with his birth. It is impossible, of course, not to think of Proust's modernist classic *In Search of Lost Time*.[6]

As in most such memoirs the author miraculously remembers the smallest details of the events he is recalling, even things that people said when he was four or five years of age. Bizarrely he recreates Aracataca to some extent through his own fiction: there are numerous tacit references to *One Hundred Years of Solitude*. He gets a significant number of his facts wrong (despite sometimes leaning on information drawn from previous biographers).[7] And he misses out some of the most important ones: he never mentions that his father was not present at his birth; that his mother left him after little more than a year and did not return for a further six years (whereas in interviews he had occasionally stressed the fact that he 'did not know' his mother); that he was not baptised for three years; or that, as he had said so often in interviews, 'nothing important happened to [him] after [his] grandfather died' when he was a small boy.

As for his father, Gabriel Eligio García, to whom he had almost never referred in interviews (and never favourably), and who was evidently a problem for him throughout his childhood and youth – indeed, for much longer, to judge from his fiction – he is here, unexpectedly, presented as a good and honourable man with some perfectly normal and perhaps even natural faults (though the very facts submitted seem not to bear this out). Their confrontations in the memoir are not a matter of irreconcilable differences but a result of the father's quite understandable desire for the son to be a professional – a doctor, a lawyer or a priest – whereas the son wants nothing other than to be a writer. Indeed, the explicit and official central theme of the entire memoir is nothing to do with the subterranean – indeed, tragic – 'family romance' we have been discussing thus far but with the narrator becoming a writer through, on the one hand, a growing and irresistible vocation (the question of ambition is completely elided) and on the other an unusual and privileged experience of life (the deeply painful nature of this unusual experience is also largely attenuated). He was the victim, he recalls, of 'an overwhelming vocation: the only force capable of disputing its rights with love. And especially the vocation for art, the most mysterious of all, to which one devotes one's life without expecting anything in return.'[8] Readers of García Márquez's earlier fiction and journalism up to this point will be eager to read this story of the development of an artistic vocation but may be disappointed perhaps to note that it is not also the story of how he came to the political consciousness that would define his life and condition his activities for the next forty-something years: for the young man in this memoir, apparently, writing was all.

One of the touching ironies of the narrative as he tells it is that his mother has come to see him not only to ask him to accompany her but to pass on his father's fears about him wasting his life in trying to be a writer – whereas the journey that she takes him on confirms him for ever in the conviction that writing is the only thing he wants to do. Indeed, as soon as he leaves her after the visit to Aracataca (briefly touched on again in chapters 2 and 7), he heads straight for his typewriter and begins a novel which will become *Leaf Storm* with the same phrase – later suppressed – with which he has begun this memoir: 'My mother asked me to accompany her to sell the house.'

One of García Márquez's biographers, Dasso Saldívar, asserted in 1997 that García Márquez had always lied when he claimed that the journey with his mother was in 1950 – Saldívar says it was in 1952 – and lied again when he said it was crucial in the development of his vocation, not only because if the visit was in 1952 he could not have been inspired to start a novel he said he had started in 1950 but because he was also lying about the origin of that novel: *Leaf Storm*, in Saldívar's opinion, was started in Cartagena in 1948 or 1949.[9] This was a somewhat reckless allegation – I personally believe that in these instances García Márquez was telling the truth – because, after all, if a writer is insisting that his entire life was changed by a specific event a biographer really needs to have cast-iron evidence if he wishes to refute the story. Saldívar's evidence is far from cast-iron, and the more convincing evidence – including the evidence of the development and maturity of García Márquez's writing at different times – seems to be on the other side.

Indeed, in the very narrative which recreates the experience of mother and son walking together through the empty streets of Aracataca in February 1950, each sense impression striking a 'supernatural echo' inside the young man, the reader is stunned by the sudden impression of distancing and perspective which García Márquez himself evidently experienced and which is materialised for ever in the multiple points of view registered, condensed and unified in *Leaf Storm*.[10] Not the least interesting aspect of this is the way in which the multi-perspectivist techniques of modernist narrative, based after all on the apprehension of a much more complex and relativist modern reality after the First World War, allow García Márquez suddenly to see – really *see* – his own past and present in a quite new way and certainly a quite different way from the way most Colombian novelists of the time were seeing the world. This changes not only the form but the content of his novel: it becomes in part a novel *about* memory and point of view. He had finally become fully aware, he says, of 'the emotional burden I was carrying without realising it and that was waiting for me, intact, in my grandparents' house ... that earthly paradise of desolation and nostalgia'.[11]

Structurally, the book is very similar to *The General in His Labyrinth*. In addition to the rather unconvincingly conceived division in two halves – perfectly achieved in *The General* – the memoir uses the journey to Aracataca, like Bolívar's journey from Bogotá to the coast in the previous work, as its initial spine and then weaves a series of flashbacks into the narrative until the time when the flashbacks catch up with the journey; then the narrative proceeds on its way through the later Barranquilla period and the period in Bogotá at *El Espectador*, until the moment when its protagonist leaves for Europe. Then, just as on the first page his mother made him a proposition to return to the place of his birth, so on the last page he himself makes a proposal of marriage to Mercedes, the woman with whom he will eventually spend the rest of his life, on the day he sets off, like Ulysses, for foreign climes.

In the Bolívar book, when he and his entourage reach the coast, the narrator notes: 'For there was the sea, and on the other side of the sea was the world.' This – 'the world' – is exactly the same answer the marquis gives his daughter in *Of Love and Other Demons* when she asks him what is on the other side of the ocean. And in *Living to Tell the Tale* we find what is surely the origin of these answers when little Gabriel sees the sea for the first time and asks his grandfather what is on the other shore. His grandfather replies, 'On the other side there is no shore'. By this time in his life and career the writer was taking evident pleasure in repetition, self-quotation and variations on the same – old – themes.

The narrator, timid but insistent exhibitionist that he is, remains careful as to how and when he should expose himself. He dismisses both his early poems and his imperfect but remarkable first stories – admired by some of Colombia's leading critics at the time of their publication – as immature 'exercises' not worthy of consideration: 'inconsequent and abstract, in some cases quite ridiculous, and none of them based on true feelings'. This might seem to be an admirable degree of self-criticism and a perfectly understandable application of high standards by a mature writer but there is something in the insistence – protesting too much – that suggests that the embarrassment may be less aesthetic than personal: that this man, who has used his own autobiography in so many ways in so many works, is deeply troubled at the idea that he may be seen and analysed in works where, far from not expressing his real self, he had expressed his real self too transparently.

It is indeed striking – though not in the least unusual – to find a writer going far closer in his fiction to staging and confronting the real dramas and traumas in his life than he does in his memoir, which is relentlessly upbeat and very far from anything one might vaguely call 'confessional'. *The Autumn of the Patriarch* was painfully confessional but it turns out that, as far as the memoir is concerned, he had waited all those years to write it in order *not* to tell the truth about himself, in order *not* to tell life as he lived it, in order – in fact – to leave an 'official version' of his life, in order – incredibly – to neutralise or even negate the story, or the sub-story: the autobiography secretly, fragmentarily told by his novels. Rarely has the difference between 'memoir' and 'autobiography' been more starkly demonstrated. Here is a man whose life's biographical experiences can be found in hundreds of details in his works – he has said of himself, the world's most famous 'magical realist', that he invents nothing, he is a 'poor notary' who merely records what he sees in front of him – but whose memoir sets out to dilute and whitewash the dramatic and passionate emotions which had accompanied, inevitably, that extraordinary life.

Occasionally those emotions surface, and when they do the results are, for their very rarity, especially 'memorable':

> in those solitary weekends, when the others retreated to their homes, I was left lonelier than a left hand in a deserted city. I lived in absolute poverty and was as timid as a quail, which I tried to overcome by being insufferably arrogant and brutally frank. I felt that I was surplus to requirements everywhere I went and some of my acquaintances were pleased to make me feel it … I was convinced that my bad luck was congenital and irremediable, especially with women and money, but I didn't care because I believed I didn't need luck in order to write well. I was not concerned with glory, nor money, nor old age, because I was sure I was going to die young and in the street.[12]

These moments of true emotion are very much the exception, however. Usually, on the contrary, the writer is determined to set aside, or even suppress, the moments of pain and trauma. The García Márquez of the novels is notable above all for an almost unique achievement in *chiaroscuro*, through which a dark and often melancholy picture is finally overlaid by a dazzling radiance which not only offsets the darkness but gives it depth and relief. This memoir largely avoids darkness: the author has opted for a classical imperturbability; rather than recreate the dynamic and contradictory reality of life as it was actually lived, with all its pains and pleasures, he has written it from a great distance, from the summit where he, as an acclaimed and magisterial artist, has chosen to set his easel, on the sunniest of days.

It is quite natural that he should insist on *Leaf Storm* as the first fruit of his vocation: it was his first fully achieved work; but the reason why he insists on this so emphatically is because it completely refashioned his own true emotions while nonetheless recreating, in an equally satisfactory arrangement, the real world: art mastered emotion and wish-fulfilment secretly ruled. This was doubly, trebly therapeutic; and coincided with the liberated, emotionally healthy life he was leading, at last, for the first time, in Barranquilla as he wrote it. But we must note that what is also implicit in his idea of the fully achieved work is an equally implicit rejection of the concept of *écriture*, of writing as either linguistic exploration or self-searching. This is hardly surprising in the case of a writer who has always carefully avoided reading critical analyses of his work and has equally avoided participation in any kind of academic round-table situation. His declarative and constructivist approach to writing – which wishes to know nothing about the shadowy depths and the true wellsprings of his intuitions – makes it impossible for him to consider the question of writing as a form of self-exploration or self-knowledge. To put it at its crudest, he uses a world he knows in order to tell good stories. Everything else is the invention of the critics.[13] It doesn't matter how technically adept you are: writing should be to communicate something 'real' and not 'merely' the exploration of the autobiographical or cosmic unknown. He finds that idea not only morally otiose but also personally embarrassing.

Some of this is to do with an essentially anti-academic position. (Cervantes would probably have done and said the same.) And much of that anti-academicism has to do with a dislike of schemes, which he finds hyper-rational, essentially 'European' and above all French (he deplores 'Cartesianism'). Involved in this is a very Latin American dislike of planning as against spontaneity, of concepts as against life. But in his particular case it is obvious that the dislike of analysis strongly includes any form of *psycho*-analysis. Even though, paradoxically, he has returned again and again to the essential dramas and traumas of his childhood, he is most unwilling to look too closely at them and even more unwilling to encourage anyone else to do so. Narcissus wishes to look at himself but not too directly; he even wishes to expose himself to the gaze of others but he doesn't want to speak this desire out loud. Look again at the child on the cover of the memoir; his anguish is only explored in the most indirect fashion in the book. But it motivates everything inside it, if only by absence and avoidance, by displacement and condensation, and it structures the entire narrative design. Even so, the storytelling itself is as wondrous as ever.

Conclusion: the achievement of the universal Colombian

Gabriel García Márquez has had three major cultural passions in an extraordinarily busy and committed career: first, his narrative fiction, the novels and short stories which are his greatest claim to fame; second, his journalism, also a lifelong endeavour; third, the cinema – writing film scripts and adaptations and participating in production – which has been another permanent obsession but whose treatment would require another book. He was also a talented poet and graphic artist in his childhood and youth, as well as an accomplished singer and dancer. Later, he even wrote a work for the theatre, *Diatriba de amor contra un hombre sentado* (*Diatribe of Love Against a Seated Man*, 1988).

Looking back, the first half of García Márquez's career was spent in exorcising the traumas and recuperating the magic of his childhood. But the period in which he actually wrote his early works was dominated by the *Violencia* which followed the assassination of Liberal politician Jorge Eliécer Gaitán in 1948. This tension and interplay between the personal and the political would condition García Márquez's entire literary career; but few great writers have proved as adroit as he has in satisfying the aesthetic requirements of even the most demanding of 'bourgeois' critics whose normal position was that overt political commitment undermined the 'eternal' values of literary works.

In that first phase García Márquez was influenced above all by the novels of the great modernist writers of the 1920s: Franz Kafka (out of Dostoyevsky), William Faulkner and Virginia Woolf (out of Joyce), and Ernest Hemingway (out of Gertrude Stein), accompanied by the Italian neorealist movement in cinema (which García Márquez studied in Italy in 1955). He also began to read the works of Sophocles, most notably *Oedipus Rex*, which he would later consider the most perfectly plotted drama in the history of literature.

Up to then the historical events that had shaped his imagination were the War of the Thousand Days (1899–1902); the massacre of the banana workers in Ciénaga (1928); and the assassination in Bogotá of Jorge Eliécer Gaitán (1948), the very politician who had investigated that 1928 massacre – all Colombian events and all catastrophic from a progressive standpoint. The next major historical event, which would give his later novels a Latin American dimension, was the Cuban Revolution: García Márquez visited Havana only days after Castro's triumph and worked for the Cuban press agency Prensa Latina. After this he lived in Mexico for six years, during the early phase of the Latin American 'Boom'. *One Hundred Years of Solitude*, published in 1967, is still the novel which best encapsulates Latin America's historic identity and its dilemmas. At this point, surprisingly late in his trajectory, García Márquez's current influences were primarily Latin American: the Mexican Juan Rulfo, the Guatemalan Miguel Angel Asturias, the Cuban Alejo Carpentier and the Argentinian Jorge Luis Borges (though he had been reading Borges since the early 1950s).

From this moment on, however, García Márquez himself became one of the world's most influential writers and has remained so to this day. Although Asturias and Carpentier had invented the literary mode known as 'magical realism' between the late 1920s and the late 1940s, most notably with *Men of Maize* (1949) and *The Kingdom of This World* (1949), it is García Márquez who is most commonly associated with this way of writing and it is he who has influenced innumerable writers all over the world but especially in the post-colonial world.

García Márquez is one of the greatest figures in Latin American history in each of his three activities as a writer: that of novelist, short story writer and journalist. No other writer can claim as much, though Mario Vargas Llosa, another Nobel Prize winner, comes close (he is not a major short story writer), and he and Carlos Fuentes are also distinguished essayists, which García Márquez is not.

Most writers, particularly in Latin America, are unable to complete their 'natural' trajectory as authors but García Márquez, like other members of the 'Boom', has had the satisfaction of living a long life and writing throughout it in response both to events within his own experience and consciousness and events out in the wider world. His every work since 1967 has been greeted with the kind of anticipation given by fans to the next movie of their favourite film star – though such stars tend to be transient, while García Márquez has been in the public eye for four decades and yet has managed to maintain the admiration of most critics and serious readers from start to finish. The tenacity of his vocation, the clarity and brilliance of his conception, the mastery and control of his *métier*, have made his life a contrasting story of extraordinary patience until the writing of *One Hundred Years of Solitude* and of almost unparalleled critical and popular success ever since. His themes have remained much the same, his style is instantly recognisable, yet for the most part García Márquez has found, with uncanny resourcefulness, a way of refreshing his creative methods and intriguing his readers anew. Writers as different as the US's John

Barth, Latin America's own Isabel Allende, and the British Commonwealth's Salman Rushdie have all been marked by the author of *One Hundred Years of Solitude*.

Returning to the individual works, we can see that in *Leaf Storm* García Márquez was still exploring the legacy of his childhood, still obsessed with genealogy and illegitimacy, still wanting to be what he thought his grandfather was but beginning also to take his distance from that world and that world view. His material world is the Costa and Bogotá but beyond the horizon is the post-Second World War settlement and the Cold War.

When explaining and justifying *No One Writes to the Colonel* and particularly *In Evil Hour*, García Márquez talks about political pressures – especially from friends in the Communist Party – as if he might have written differently in other circumstances and as if, indeed, decisions on ideology and form were simply a matter of personal choice and conscience. He chose, then and later, to play down the extent to which the wider political context (rather than individual people or parties) affects a writer. His novels are the product of a long, complex relationship with, first, Colombia (including his own childhood memories), then the world, and then Latin America – in that unnatural order! – a relationship which involves him in a long assessment of politics and Latin America in the context of the world as a whole. By the time of *In Evil Hour* he has lived in Europe and been directly influenced by Italian neo-realism (whose basic ideology is also Communist Party-inspired). But he is never entirely satisfied with *In Evil Hour* – in part, perhaps, because there was not enough of him in it – and gives it up for *No One Writes to the Colonel* which, like *Leaf Storm*, is much more autobiographical though in a different, less visible way.

'Big Mama's Funeral' and *One Hundred Years of Solitude* are his two most 'Latin American' works – and also, not surprisingly, the two most 'magical realist' – together with *The Autumn of the Patriarch*, though the latter is more imbued, perhaps unfortunately, with a rather Spanish *goyismo* and *tremendismo*. The first two were written by a García Márquez who had already experienced the 'universal' but has only recently experienced the continental (Venezuela in the case of 'Big Mama's Funeral'; Venezuela, Cuba and Mexico in the case of *One Hundred Years of Solitude*). They are both globalised works which depict not merely Colombia but Latin America in the World.

The Autumn of the Patriarch in 1975 forced García Márquez, as he explored the political phenomenon most closely associated with Latin America – dictatorship – to also assimilate and explore his own celebrity and importance: the meaning of his motives for writing (glory, wealth, influence, power: to become on a large scale, perhaps, what he thought his grandfather was on a small scale);

and the meaning and implications of his success and the moral obligations it now placed upon him. Though carefully encoded, this dimension made this one of the most remarkable autobiographical novels ever written.

García Márquez was always notable for his subtlety and his ability to give balanced pictures of conservatives: the mayor in *In Evil Hour* is a classic example. By the time of *Chronicle of a Death Foretold* however there are not so many bad people in the world but there are infinitely fewer good ones: almost all of them are conditioned by the social ideologies that surround them – notably, in this novel, the deeply regressive honour code which brings about the murder – and almost no one does anything to prevent the crime. This may well communicate García Márquez's disappointment with not only the Colombian people but with the Latin American people as a whole who, eight years after the Chilean coup, had done rather little to fight dictatorship when he (through *Alternativa*, the Russell Tribunal, Habeas, etc.) had done so much. *The Autumn of the Patriarch* had shown something similar but this was a past-oriented novel and portrayed the people as confused by ignorance and 'false consciousness'. By 1981, when *Chronicle* appeared, it was no longer so easy to believe this explanation.

The award of the Nobel Prize in 1982 consoled García Márquez for his political disappointments as he began to move through middle age to old age. From *Love in the Time of Cholera* the pressure of nostalgia became irresistible, and he had clearly begun to grow weary of resisting the tide of history when there was no sign whatever of it turning any time soon. In that novel, which represented a new start, some degree of reconciliation with high culture – and the bourgeoisie that created it – is finally acknowledged, in a novel where elite and popular culture are both given their 'place', though there is still of course an instinctive and emotional preference for popular culture.

He was on safer ground politically with *The General in His Labyrinth*, both because it was a novel about the distant past – though a distant past which foretold a disenchanted future – and in any case Bolívar is from the start an aristocrat and a man of power. Nevertheless, the decision not to concentrate on Bolívar's extraordinary successes – the great military victories resulting in the independence of Latin America – is of course profoundly significant and, given that the book was published in 1989, the year which marked the anniversary of the French Revolution and the fall of the communist-constructed Berlin Wall, it shows García Márquez's prescience, good timing, relevance, contemporaneity and luck.

News of a Kidnapping was his first major work set mainly in Bogotá, though many of the protagonists, not least Pablo Escobar, are from the provinces. By now, 1996, García Márquez has been separated from the ideology that has conditioned his writing since the early 1950s: the influence of Marxist theory almost disappears with the collapse of the Berlin Wall in 1989 and Marxist political practice – above all as exemplified by the Cuban Revolution – almost disappears when the so-called 'Special Period' begins in 1990. At this point he begins to stress that he could never 'desert his friends' – Fidel and the Cuban people – but carefully avoids saying that he supports the Cuban Revolution as such.

When I first met García Márquez, in 1990, I asked him whether he was not depressed at all that was going on in the world, given his lifelong commitment to socialism. 'No,' he said, 'you can't afford to be depressed and anyway it makes no sense.' He looked at me and leaned forward: 'It's history, and history is what is. I think it will be a long time before we see things clearly but I feel now that we are at the beginning of a vast new era which will see the liberation of human thought, an escape from ideology into something different.' He may not entirely have believed this, but ultimately he is what Sebastiano Timpanaro would call a Leopardian pessimist. His philosophy, in this respect very close to that of the physician Abrenuncio in *Of Love and Other Demons*, follows Antonio Gramsci's slogan, borrowed from Romain Rolland and paraphrased: 'Pessimism of the intellect, optimism of the will'.

I had already been impressed by the way in which this writer, whose world view had been socialist since the early 1950s, had managed – indeed, had been determined, always – to write books which were not constrained by his extra-literary politics. The politics is always there, of course, it cannot be otherwise, but García Márquez had been utterly sincere when, to the exasperation of more explicitly committed leftists, he had so often insisted that 'a writer's revolutionary duty is to write well'. If you wrote with truth – your truth, what you felt, and the world's truth, what you saw – and applied your literary talent with every ounce of tenacity and commitment you could muster, the result would be the only justification you would need.

García Márquez has one of the most instantly recognisable literary styles and one of the most coherent rhetorical identities in the entire history of world literature. But he also has something even more important: a consistent body of themes, which he has explored since the very beginning of his literary trajectory, and which may be summarised in just two words: power and love. Without wishing to claim any kind of overall equivalence with Shakespeare for this great Latin American, it may be said that it is difficult to think of any other writer since the incomparable Elizabethan who has concentrated so tenaciously and obsessively on these two themes, which bring together the public and the private in a thousand different ways.

In the first half of his career – *Leaf Storm* (1955) to *The Autumn of the Patriarch* (1975) – a more political García Márquez concentrated on the themes of power, solitude and death. Each of these themes, naturally, was the nucleus of a cluster of related motifs; and equally, each of them also implied its opposite – power suggested vulnerability, victimhood or injustice; solitude suggested community, socialism or love; and death suggested life, creativity or art. In the second half of his career – *Chronicle of a Death Foretold* (1981) to *Memories of My Melancholy Whores* (2004) – a less political (or even post-political) García Márquez, aware that the 1982 Nobel Prize gave him both influence and increased responsibility, began to write works which, while continuing to explore the same themes, began to investigate the lighter, more optimistic side of them. As is well known, many writers devote themselves to the vision of a dark present in order to shock their readers and persuade them that a different future is possible; and similarly, if the present is dark and the future possibly darker, then some alternative vision might be in order.

The works produced during the first half of his career tended more to the diagnostic and the condemnatory, while those from the second half tend more to the exhortatory and the curative. Thus power, solitude and death continue to be central concerns but love, community and life are now more strongly stressed, and optimism and hope tend to dominate the later pages. As we have seen, when critics came across *Chronicle of a Death Foretold* in 1981 they were not at first aware that the novel was not only a love story – over the dead body of the hapless Santiago Nasar, one might say – but a love story with something like a happy ending. (That said, it is important to remind ourselves that García Márquez's treatment of love is multivalent, not in the least simplistic, and frequently disturbing.) The book was also written in a new, radiant style, still recognisably Garciamarquian but no longer either 'magical realist' like *One Hundred Years of Solitude* or 'modernist' in the way that *Leaf Storm* or *The Autumn of the Patriarch* had been. Clearly García Márquez was now postmodernist in style and positive in message.

At the end of *The Autumn of the Patriarch* the tyrant eventually dies, a man who, in the view of the people, as we have seen, 'never knew where the reverse side was and where the right of this life which we loved with an insatiable passion that you never dared even to imagine out of the fear of knowing what we knew only too well that it was arduous and ephemeral but there wasn't any other'. Later, a real politician lies dying, the great Liberator in *The General in His Labyrinth*; the world goes away from him, though he, quite unlike the Patriarch, has tried to do his best as an Enlightenment rationalist and has also, as a passionate romantic, drunk every last drop of life:

> Then he crossed his arms over his chest and began to listen to the radiant voices of the slaves singing the six o'clock *Salve* in the mills, and through the window he saw the diamond of Venus in the sky that was

dying forever, the eternal snows, the new vine whose yellow bellflowers he would not see bloom on the following Saturday in the house closed in mourning, the final brilliance of life that would never, through all eternity, be repeated.

There is only one life. This means that we are all entitled to justice from birth, and all of us should strive for this, both for ourselves and for others; but it also means that we must take every opportunity to live life to the full. The left-ist critics who condemned García Márquez earlier in his career for not making his works explicitly committed have always tended, similarly, to condemn the Bakhtinian view of carnival as a way in which the people can escape for a while from oppression (or power) and celebrate the intensity, the radiance and indeed the very transience of life (embodied above all in love).[1] No writer has ever communicated the elements involved more effectively than García Márquez, which is why we read him and why he will also, surely, be read by future generations long after ours has had its one and only chance on earth.

Notes

2 Early short stories, journalism and a first (modernist) novel, *Leaf Storm* (1947–1955)

1 *Vivir para contarla* (Bogotá, Norma, 2002), p. 324. All translations are mine unless otherwise noted.

2 There are in fact dozens of other short stories hidden away in the collected 'journalism' of Gabriel García Márquez (henceforth GGM): among all the different *crónicas* are stories made up one evening and published the next. It is perhaps surprising that they have not been pirated and collected separately, but very few of them could compare favourably with the thirty-eight stories that have been published in the four official collections.

3 Note that, this analysis notwithstanding, at all periods, rather like Cervantes with regard to Spain, GGM devotes very little time and space to describing or evoking Colombia (and to the extent that he does it, there is much more evocation than detailed description).

4 *Todos los cuentos* (Barcelona, Plaza y Janés, 3rd edn, 1976), p. 18.

5 *Todos los cuentos*, p. 25.

6 The story 'Tubal-Cain Forges a Star' ('Tubal-Caín forja una estrella'), published in *El Espectador* on 17 January 1948, was omitted from the collected stories, probably owing to an oversight: it bears an important thematic relation to others published at the time.

7 GGM's stories and newspaper articles have always been shamefully badly treated by anthologists and publishers – probably in part because GGM himself has simply not given the matter sufficient care and attention .

8 It is crucial to understand that in Spain and Latin America *modernismo* was the literary movement led towards the end of the nineteenth and early twentieth centuries by writers such as Rubén Darío of Nicaragua and José Martí of Cuba. It was inspired above all by recent developments in French poetry. *Modernism* in the Anglo-American sense coincides more closely with the Spanish and Latin American *vanguardismo* of the post-First World War period.

9 This first period coincides broadly with Jacques Gilard's classic collection of GGM's early journalism, which he divided into three volumes representing a natural subdivision of this first period into a further three, briefer periods: *Textos costeños*, 1948–1952; *Entre cachacos*, 1954–1955; and *De Europa y América*, 1955–1960.

10 They appeared in *El Universal,* Cartagena, May 1948–December 1949; *El Heraldo,* Barranquilla, January 1950–December 1952 (he also managed the magazine *Crónica* and *Comprimido,* his own invention, 'the smallest newspaper in the world'); *El Nacional,* Barranquilla, October–December 1953, where he worked with his friend Alvaro Cepeda; *El Espectador,* in Bogotá, January 1954–July 1955 (he also wrote a few important articles for his friend Alvaro Mutis's magazine *Lámpara*) and also in Europe July 1955–April 1956 (including *El Independiente,* the replacement for *El Espectador* after it was closed by the military dictatorship of Gustavo Rojas Pinilla); various magazines in Caracas (*Elite, Momento, Venezuela Gráfica*) and in Bogotá (*Cromos, El Espectador, El Tiempo, Acción Liberal*), September 1956–May 1960; *Prensa Latina,* Bogotá and Havana, May 1959–June 1961; and *Sucesos para Todos* and *La Familia,* Mexico City, October 1961–April 1963.

11 For many years GGM purported to believe that he was born in 1928, the year of the banana massacre in Ciénaga narrated in *One Hundred Years of Solitude.* Regardless of this, he has set the events of his novel ten years earlier than the dates on which they actually took place and in doing so has, to a large extent, depoliticised them. In fact, the dating of the novel puts it, symbolically, between his birth on 6 March 1927 and the 6 December 1928 massacre in Ciénaga.

12 This episode is based on an event in GGM's childhood when his grandfather did indeed take him to see the corpse of Don Emilio, a Belgian who lived in Aracataca and had committed suicide, supposedly after watching *All Quiet on the Western Front.* GGM would later recall, 'The gaze of that dead man pursued me in dreams for many years.'

13 *La hojarasca* (Madrid, Alfaguara, 2nd edn, 1982), p. 25.

14 The novel treats *time* in a way which is the exact opposite of GGM's eventual solution – total, intentional inexactitude – in *One Hundred Years of Solitude.* Here there are repeated precise temporal references, all of which can be put together as in a Flaubert or Faulkner novel to work out a plausible timescale.

15 *La hojarasca,* pp. 87–8.

16 See esp. pp. 51–5 for a key version of the GM family founding myth (later repeated in *One Hundred Years of Solitude*) and a subsidiary proof that *Leaf Storm,* 'The House' and *One Hundred Years of Solitude* are family texts with a family likeness.

17 GGM has been especially unlucky with the translations of his titles, in part because they are so well chosen: apparently and deceptively simple, they usually contain a layer of hidden meanings relating not only to the text itself but also to important aspects of life and history out in the wider world. See my 'Translating GM, or, the Impossible Dream', in D. Balderston and M. Schwartz (eds.), *Voice-Overs: Translation and Latin American Literature* (Albany, State University of New York Press, 2002), pp. 156–63.

18 The Prologue is dated 1909 but this seems to be a misprint: 1929 would make more sense. It is a mysterious, rather clumsy and yet evocative piece which is also curiously hybrid: it relates most directly of all to the colonel's vision of history, tinged by myth, but also connects to the child's sense perceptions relating to decay and corruption, and to his mother's apocalyptic vision of the future destruction of Macondo.

19 So, again, why the title? The '*hojarasca*' (leaf-trash) is a word introduced to the colonel by the doctor on page 96, then used with full personal identification by the colonel himself on pages 130, 151 and 168. GGM does not identify with this view of the migrant workers, even in a work as early as *Leaf Storm*, and even with his nostalgia and affection in full flow. In other words, the grandson (who will nevertheless continue until after the Nobel Prize unconsciously rejecting his *father*) has a different world view and therefore shows the grandfather's contradictory patriarchal-humanist perspective in a complex, convincing and not merely 'upper-class' way. (From page 36, indeed, we see clearly the contrast between a patrician vision based on honour and a proletarian vision based on solidarity.)

3 The neorealist turn: *In Evil Hour, No One Writes to the Colonel* and *Big Mama's Funeral* (1956–1962)

1 As mentioned, it has direct autobiographical associations – so not only was he more attracted to the character of the colonel and the story about him than to the characters in *In Evil Hour* but the new novel also had a strong emotional motivation relating to his personal experiences at the time. See my *Gabriel García Márquez: A Life* (London, Bloomsbury, 2008), chapter 10.

2 In *El coronel no tiene quien le escriba*, Sabas says : 'This is a shit town' (p. 55); the barber does likewise in *In Evil Hour* (*La mala hora*, Madrid, Alfaguara, 2nd edn, 1982, p. 169).

3 See GGM's essay on 'The novel of *La Violencia*' in *Obra periodística vol. VI: De Europa y América* 2, ed. Jacques Gilard (Bogotá, Oveja Negra, 1984).

4 The later two-part structure could not function in *Leaf Storm* because of the three-character Faulknerian *As I Lay Dying* technique, though there is, of course, a doubleness in the contrast between the half-hour of the foregrounded action ('now') and all the interior monologue flashbacks into the past ('then').

5 Curiously enough, there is a discussion of such distinctions between the doctor and the colonel in *Leaf Storm*.

6 Most readers have assumed that since GGM's own grandfather was a colonel, this character must be based on him (like the colonel in *Leaf Storm*, who undoubtedly is); but although there are several key aspects of their curriculums which coincide (so that Nicolás Márquez is indeed a *partial* influence), this colonel differs both physically and in terms of his personality from GGM's own grandfather – who, in any case, lived as a respected resident of Aracataca and not as a harassed and humiliated resident of Sucre. On page 45 the colonel observes that Aureliano Buendía's surrender at Neerlandia is 'what put the world out of joint'.

7 *El coronel no tiene quien le escriba*, p. 7.

8 *El coronel no tiene quien le escriba*, p. 60.

9 *El coronel no tiene quien le escriba*, p. 18.

10 We also see references once more to Colonel Aureliano Buendía and the Duke of Marlborough (p. 22), as in his previous novels and as in the later *One Hundred Years of Solitude*.

11 The friends are Alvaro, Alfonso and Germán (pp. 49–53), i.e. García Márquez's friends Alvaro Cepeda, Alfonso Fuenmayor and Germán Vargas, who were sending him money to ease his own poverty during the time that he was writing the novel. His friend the *vallenato* composer Rafael Escalona is also mentioned on page 49.

12 *El coronel no tiene quien le escriba*, p. 85.

13 *El coronel no tiene quien le escriba*, p. 61.

14 *El coronel no tiene quien le escriba*, p. 90.

15 *Leaf Storm, In Evil Hour, No One Writes to the Colonel*, 'Big Mama's Funeral', *Chronicle of a Death Foretold* and *Love in the Time of Cholera* all begin with real deaths and/or burials; *One Hundred Years of Solitude* and *The General in His Labyrinth* begin with apparent deaths.

16 This was foreshadowed when, earlier in the novel, the colonel was confronted, for the first time, by the policeman who killed his son: 'In an instant he felt himself swallowed by those eyes, chewed, digested and immediately expelled' (p. 78).

17 Just as Montiel appeared in 'Balthazar's Marvellous Afternoon', so the ghost of Big Mama appears in 'Montiel's Widow'.

18 It is perhaps significant that the influence here was Colombian Jorge Zalamea's novel *El gran Burundún-Burundá ha muerto* (1952), not a North American book. Most of the stories are pure García Márquez but Zalamea's *Gran Burundún Burundá* is the key to 'Big Mama' itself.

4   *One Hundred Years of Solitude* (1967): the global village

1 No one knows how many died in the Ciénaga massacre: certainly it was fewer than 3,000 but many more than the nine the government claimed, and the killings went on for weeks after the massacre itself.

2 *Cien años de soledad* (Buenos Aires, Sudamericana, 18th edn, 1970), p. 242.

3 *Cien años de soledad*, p. 191.

4 *Cien años de soledad*, p. 300.

5 *Cien años de soledad*, p. 296.

6 *Cien años de soledad*, p. 264.

7 *Cien años de soledad*, p. 329.

5   *The Autumn of the Patriarch* (1975): the love of power

1 The back cover of the English-language *Collected Stories* quotes John Updike: 'The stories are rich and startling in their matter and confident and eloquent in their manner ... They are – the word cannot be avoided – magical' (*New Yorker*).

2   He told an interviewer that he had written these stories in part to entertain his sons and in part to 'disinfect' his style; the Macondo era was over and so too was the style for which he was known until then. After he had completed his fifth story (he does not say which one, but it was probably 'Blacamán'), he had found the style for the new novel, *The Autumn of the Patriarch*.

3   See Emir Rodríguez Monegal, 'Novedad y anacronismo de *Cien años de soledad*', *Revista Nacional de Cultura* 185, Caracas, July–September 1968, 3–21; and Ricardo Gullón, *García Márquez o el olvidado arte de contar* (Madrid, Taurus, 1970).

4   By my – perhaps approximate – count there are twenty-nine sentences in chapter 1; twenty-three in chapter 2; eighteen in chapter 3; sixteen in chapter 4; thirteen in chapter 5; and only one in chapter 6.

5   GGM always insisted that Franco had had little impact on the novel, even though he was living in Spain, under Franco's regime, throughout the period of its writing. While Franco is certainly not the primary influence, it would be unrealistic to accept that he had no impact at all.

6   See Guillermo Sheridan and Armando Pereira, 'GM en México (entrevista)', *Revista de la Universidad de México* 30: 6, February 1976.

7   At one point the dictator laments that he is 'more lonely than a left hand in this country which I didn't choose willingly … with this sense of unreality, this smell of shit, this people without history who don't believe in anything except life, this is the country they forced on me' (*El otoño del patriarca*, Barcelona, Plaza y Janés, 1975, p. 159).

8   *El otoño del patriarca*, p. 46.

9   There are several references in the novel to the Nicaraguan *modernista* poet Rubén Darío, himself a servant of dictators (notably Guatemala's Estrada Cabrera), who visits the Patriarch's country on several occasions. GGM uses verses and images from Darío, the most influential poet in Latin American literary history, throughout the novel.

10 On page 132 we discover that his name is apparently Zacarías, and at the very end of the novel he is addressed by Death as Nicanor, 'the name by which Death knows all men'.

11 *El otoño del patriarca*, p. 58.

12 Paradoxically, 'autumn', like 'spring', is a concept with only limited application – because limited duration – in the tropics. Most tropical countries have only a summer (dry season) and a winter (wet season).

13 This novel is doing so many other things with its labyrinthine, modernist technique – the influences of James Joyce's Molly Bloom soliloquy in *Ulysses* and the techniques of Virginia Woolf's *Mrs Dalloway* on the approach to time and consciousness, both of the Patriarch and the People, are everywhere apparent – that the tendency is not as pronounced as usual, though still unmistakable.

14 *El otoño del patriarca*, pp. 126–7.

15 Note that only sections 7 to 15 are narrated in the novel in true chronological order: all of the rest are flashbacks within flashbacks. And since all of the novel is a flashback from the moment of the Patriarch's second – true – death, this confirms, in effect, that what is narrated chronologically – chapters 7 to 15 – is, precisely, his 'autumn', whose beginning is first glimpsed when Patricio Aragonés, his double, is murdered and he has to become the same person in public that he is in private. (This dichotomy is a theme that became personally important to GGM between the ending of *One Hundred Years of Solitude*, which brought him so much fame, and the ending of *Autumn*.)

16 *El otoño del patriarca*, p. 266.

17 There are numerous themes and images in the novel that could refer to Fidel Castro. The brutal irony is that the picture has increasingly fitted Castro more than twenty years after the novel was written; he too, with the US embargo, had the 'sea' taken away from him, and he too presided over a regime which decayed before the eyes of the world while he himself was apparently oblivious.

18 When he was finally able to turn to the topic of love, in the 1980s, GGM was also able to turn away from his grandfather at last (colonels, however much you may love them, are about power) and turn to his previously unloved father (fathers are also about power but eventually you may accept that they truly loved your mother).

6   *Chronicle of a Death Foretold* (1981): postmodernism and Hispanic literature

1 He began with *El Espectador*, Bogotá, 1980–84 (articles syndicated to *El País*, Madrid, and other Latin American newspapers, including Cuban ones); later, he created and directed practical 'workshops' on journalism like the ones he had directed on cinema – especially on 'how to tell a story' – at the Film School he founded in Havana in 1986; lastly, he became co-owner of the weekly *Cambio* (Bogotá, 1999–2002), through which he finally came to control his own journalism completely.

2 See the book by the author's younger brother, Eligio GM, also a writer, who compares the novel not only with the original events of 1951 but also with the film version made by the great Italian director Francesco Rosi in 1987: Eligio García, *La tercera muerte de Santiago Nasar. Crónica de La crónica* (Madrid, Mondadori, 1987).

3 It might also suggest that he was not the deflowerer of Angela Vicario, merely one of many sexual partners. This possibility has not been mentioned by previous critics of the novel but one can be sure that it was mentioned by the townsfolk of Sucre in 1951.

4 In reality GGM was not in Sucre on the day of the murder of Cayetano Gentile, one of his best friends; but in the novel he is present in the town though largely unaware of what is going on.

5 Kafka, although generally considered a 'modernist', is a different case, closer in many ways to Dostoyevsky: his texts are not primarily interesting linguistically – it is our perception of the world itself, not our linguistic presentation of it, which he wishes to change.

6 *Crónica de una muerte anunciada* (Bogotá, Oveja Negra, 1981), p. 13.

7 *Crónica de una muerte anunciada*, p. 67.

8 *Crónica de una muerte anunciada*, p. 65.

9 *Crónica de una muerte anunciada*, p. 69.

10 The novel has a few technical lapses, though given its narrative conventions most of them can conveniently be attributed to the narrator rather than the author. Santiago Nasar is warned by an anonymous letter very early in the book (p. 23), and there are several other such details which any reasonable person would have taken more seriously than Nasar is shown to do. When on p. 149 he is finally persuaded that he is in mortal danger, he chooses to go out unarmed. An unreasonably rigorous critic might suggest that the whole novel – based on the fact that he dies because no one warns him and that there is no alternative to his death – collapses at this climactic moment, but GGM's narrator and almost all the critics seem unaware of this fact.

7   *Love in the Time of Cholera* (1985): the power of love

1 In fact, it is best for the reader not to delve too deeply into the chronological matters because it is not easy to make them fit very precisely together. Mathematics was never GGM's strong point, and several of his novels have manifest flaws in this direction. Nevertheless, the overall historical trajectory of the book is entirely clear.

2 GGM showed an interest in plagues from early in his literary career ('One Day After Saturday'), and Defoe and Camus were crucial points of reference. *Love in the Time of Cholera* brings Urbino and Fermina together, and at the end of the book it is cholera which isolates Florentino and Fermina on the steamboat and allows them to spend more time together. In the novel, Urbino is said to have studied in Paris with Marcel Proust's father, himself a noted expert on cholera. (Joseph Conrad, whose *Nostromo* may have been inspired by a visit to Colombia, is also mentioned in the novel.)

3 *El amor en los tiempos del cólera* (Barcelona, Bruguera, 1985), p. 467.

4 The novel parodies not only nineteenth-century literature but also twentieth-century popular romances, not to say, above all, Isabel Allende, who imitated GGM, and whom he, piqued, now also copies while pretending exclusively to parody her (beginning with the dead Great Dane on the first page of the novel).

5 Soon after the publication of this novel GGM wrote his first play, *Diatriba de amor contra un hombre sentado* (*Diatribe of Love Against a Seated Man*), on this topic.

6 The author notes that Florentino Ariza's secretary, Leona Cassiani, 'was the true woman in his life although neither of them ever knew it and they never made love' (p. 267).

7 *El amor en los tiempos del cólera*, p. 433.

8 More about power: *The General in His Labyrinth* (1989) and *News of a Kidnapping* (1996)

1 *El general en su laberinto* (Bogotá, Oveja Negra, 1989), pp. 43–4.
2 On the whole the French are treated with scepticism and even hostility in the novel; the English get a good press, in line with Bolívar's own experience of them; and the US is viewed as a land of political hypocrites: 'It's omnipotent and terrible, and its tale of liberty will end in a plague of miseries for us all' (p. 223). On pages 121–4 GGM rehearses again his views on Europe, through Bolívar, and effectively summarises his Nobel address: like GGM, Bolívar pleads: 'Damn it, let us have our Middle Ages in peace!' (p. 130).
3 M. E. Samper, '*El general en su laberinto*: un libro vengativo', *La Jornada Semanal*, Mexico, 9 April 1989, pp. 3–9 (p. 3).
4 It has not been noticed that Bolívar does not actually die in the novel, despite first appearances to the contrary: the date and time of his death are foretold but GGM avoids having to describe the death itself: Bolívar lives on!
5 GGM decided that the title should be in the singular because the kidnappings it deals with were the carrying-out of a single policy by Pablo Escobar. His initial idea was to concentrate only on the kidnapping of Maruja and Beatriz but this proved impractical; it is arguable, however, that the title gives rise to confusion.
6 One thinks of the concessions made by Costa-Gavras, director of the brilliant *State of Siege*, in making the movie *Missing*, about post-coup Chile, for a North American audience and using North American money.
7 *Noticia de un secuestro* (Bogotá, Norma, 1996), pp. 155–6.

9 More about love: *Of Love and Other Demons* (1994) and *Memories of My Melancholy Whores* (2004)

1 *El general en su laberinto*, p. 170.
2 *Del amor y otros demonios* (Bogotá, Norma, 1994), p. 124.
3 When he took over the Colombian magazine called *Cambio* in 1997, he named the company which owned it 'Abrenuncio'.
4 At this time the extent of paedophiliac activities by Catholic priests was much less known about than it subsequently became.
5 This epigraph notes that the old men in Kawabata's novel are not allowed to touch the young women; this is curious, because GGM's ancient protagonist is up against no such prohibitions and does indeed touch 'Delgadina' as and when he pleases. Note another Kawabata quotation in his *La casa de las bellas durmientes*, page 79: 'old people have death and young people have love, and death comes only once and love many times' (my translation). Kawabata is specifically mentioned in GGM's story 'Sleeping Beauty and the Airplane' (*Strange Pilgrims*), which is undoubtedly a

prototype version of the later novel. Compare Italo Calvino's story 'The Adventure of a Soldier' in *Difficult Loves*.
6 The 'Delgadina' theme had previously been referenced briefly in *The Autumn of the Patriarch*.
7 On page 6 he says this is to be the 'memoir of my great love', that is to say, *not* a 'memoir of my melancholy whores'!
8 *Memoria de mis putas tristes* (New York, Knopf, 2004), p. 66.
9 This experience largely repeats that of Aureliano with the young mulatto girl in *One Hundred Years of Solitude* and even more precisely GGM's own first experience as an innocent teenage boy.

10 Memoirs: *Living to Tell the Tale* (2002)

1 And he repeats it here. See *Vivir para contarla*, p. 438: novice writers should keep their activities secret, 'especially in interviews with the press, which are after all a *fictional genre* which is dangerous for timid writers who don't want to say more than they should' (my emphasis).
2 See his somewhat incoherent and unconvincing preface for an explanation of the origins and and dating of these stories.
3 See chapter 10 of my book *Gabriel García Márquez: A Life* (London, Bloomsbury, 2008).
4 In the memoir he reveals the 'fetish … which forces me to calculate in advance the length of the book, with the exact number of pages for each chapter and for the complete book' (p. 472); but he does not reveal the more interesting secret that his fetish extends to dividing the book, and many of the chapters, in half, as we have shown in this study.
5 One might argue that each half ends with success and a kind of graduation: the first half would end with him obtaining his only certificate – as *bachiller*, or high-school graduate – in Zipaquirá in 1946 (chapter 4) and the second with him publishing his first novel and becoming an ace reporter before moving ('graduating') to Europe (chapter 8). If this was the intention, it was probably unconscious: it has certainly not been well highlighted.
6 Another ingredient of this episode is undoubtedly Juan Rulfo's Mexican classic *Pedro Páramo*, in which the narrator Juan Preciado is walking through the dead town of Comala in search of his father. The connection is the more apposite because Juan Preciado has been sent on this mission by his dying mother. On page 30 of *Vivir para contarla* GGM and his mother find a 'dead town … we were lost [in the] swamp of the siesta'.
7 For example, 'my grandfather had twice been mayor', 'my grandmother was nearly a hundred when she died'. Both these statements are entirely false; there are many others.

8 *Living to Tell the Tale*, p. 41.
9 See Dasso Saldívar, *García Márquez: el viaje a la semilla. La biografía* (Madrid, Santillana, 1997), pp. 210–15.
10 GGM asserts that he was reading *Light in August* during the journey with his mother; it might have been more appropriate if he had 'remembered' that he was reading *As I Lay Dying*, which he was about to convert into something entitled *Leaf Storm* but which might have been called *As I Rose Up and Came Back to Life*.
11 *Vivir para contarla*, p. 438.
12 *Vivir para contarla*, pp. 436–7.
13 In 1973 he told Mexican writer Elena Poniatowska, 'I was never conscious of any of it. I am a man who tells stories, anecdotes' (Elena Poniatowska, *Todo Mexico*, vol. I, Mexico City, Diana, 1990, pp. 218–19).

Conclusion: the achievement of the universal Colombian

1 Bakhtin's works on carnival and Mann's *The Magic Mountain* provide invaluable background to GGM's vision of popular impulses and liberation from repression.

Further reading

Works by Gabriel García Márquez (in Spanish)

Literary works (date of first publication; edition used in this book)

La hojarasca (1955; Madrid, Alfaguara, 2nd edn, 1982).
El coronel no tiene quien le escriba (1961; Buenos Aires, Sudamericana, 1968).
La mala hora (1962; Madrid, Alfaguara, 2nd edn, 1982).
Los funerales de la Mamá Grande (1962; Barcelona, Plaza y Janés, 1975).
Cien años de soledad (1967; Buenos Aires, Sudaméricana, 18th edn, 1970).
La increíble y triste historia de la cándida Eréndira y de su abuela desalmada
      (1972; Madrid, Mondadori, 4th edn, 1990).
El otoño del patriarca (1975; Barcelona, Plaza y Janés, 1975).
Todos los cuentos (1947–1972) (1975; Barcelona, Plaza y Janés, 3rd edn, 1976).
Crónica de una muerte anunciada (1981; Bogotá, Oveja Negra, 1981).
El amor en los tiempos del cólera (1985; Barcelona, Bruguera, 1985).
Diatriba de amor contra un hombre sentado (1988; Bogotá, Arango, 1994).
El general en su laberinto (1989; Bogotá, Oveja Negra, 1989).
Doce cuentos peregrinos (1992; Bogotá, Oveja Negra, 1992).
Del amor y otros demonios (1994; Bogotá, Norma, 1994).
Noticia de un secuestro (1996; Bogotá, Norma, 1996).
Memoria de mis putas tristes (2004; New York, Knopf, 2004).

Journalism, interviews, memoirs, etc.

Obra periodística vol. I: Textos costeños 1, ed. Jacques Gilard (Bogotá, Oveja
      Negra, 1983).
Obra periodística vol. II: Textos costeños 2, ed. Jacques Gilard (Bogotá, Oveja
      Negra, 1983).
Obra periodística vol. III: Entre cachacos 1, ed. Jacques Gilard (Bogotá, Oveja
      Negra, 1983).
Obra periodística vol. IV: Entre cachacos 2, ed. Jacques Gilard (Bogotá, Oveja
      Negra, 1983).
Obra periodística vol. V: De Europa y América 1, ed. Jacques Gilard (Bogotá,
      Oveja Negra, 1984).

Obra periodística vol. VI: De Europa y América 2, ed. Jacques Gilard (Bogotá, Oveja Negra, 1984).
Notas de Prensa 1980–84 (Madrid, Mondadori, 1991).
Por la libre: Obra periodística 4 (1974–95).
Periodismo militante (political journalism; Bogotá, Son de Máquina, 1978).
El secuestro (documentary film script, 1982, aka *Viva Sandino, El asalto*; Bogotá, Oveja Negra, 1984).
Relato de un náufrago (documentary narrative, 1970; Barcelona, Tusquets, 29th edn, 1991).
La novela en América Latina: diálogo (with Mario Vargas Llosa) (Milla Batres, Lima, 1968).
El olor de la guayaba. Conversaciones con Plinio Apuleyo Mendoza (1982; Bogotá, Oveja Negra, 1982).
'La soledad de América Latina' / 'Brindis por la poesía' (speeches at Nobel Prize ceremonies, Stockholm, December 1982).
'El cataclismo de Dámocles'. Conferencia Ixtapa, 1986 (speech on the dangers of nuclear proliferation, Bogotá, Oveja Negra, 1986).
La aventura de Miguel Littín clandestino en Chile (documentary narrative, 1986; Bogotá, Oveja Negra, 1986).
'Un manual para ser niño' (essay on children's educational needs; *El Tiempo*, Bogotá, 9 October 1995).
Noticia de un secuestro (documentary narrative; Bogotá, Norma, 1996).
Taller de guión de Gabriel García Márquez. *'Cómo se cuenta un cuento'* (script-writing workshop, EICTV Cuba/Ollero & Ramos, Madrid, 1995).
Taller de guión de Gabriel García Márquez. *'Me aquilo para soñar'* (script-writing workshop, EICTV Cuba/Ollero & Ramos, Madrid, 1997).
Taller de guión de Gabriel García Márquez. *'La bendita manía de contar'* (script-writing workshop, EICTV Cuba/Ollero & Ramos, Madrid, 1998).
Vivir para contarla (memoir; Bogotá, Norma, 2002).

Works by Gabriel García Márquez (in English translation)

Collected Stories (London, Jonathan Cape, 1991).
The Story of a Shipwrecked Sailor (New York, Vintage, 1989).
Leaf Storm (London, Picador, 1979).
No One Writes to the Colonel (includes *Big Mama's Funeral*; London, Penguin, 1974).
In Evil Hour (New York, Harper Perennial, 1991).
One Hundred Years of Solitude (London, Picador, 1978).
The Autumn of the Patriarch (London, Picador, 1978).
Innocent Eréndira and Other Stories (London, Jonathan Cape, 1979).
The Fragrance of Guava: Conversations with Gabriel García Márquez, ed. Plinio Apuleyo Mendoza (London, Faber, 1988).
Clandestine in Chile (London, Granta, 1989).

Love in the Time of Cholera (London, Jonathan Cape, 1988).
The General in His Labyrinth (London, QPD, 1991).
Strange Pilgrims (London, Penguin, 1992).
Of Love and Other Demons (London, Penguin, 1996).
News of a Kidnapping (London, Jonathan Cape, 1997).
Living to Tell the Tale (London, Jonathan Cape, 2003).
Memories of My Melancholy Whores (New York, Alfred A. Knopf, 2005).
'The future of Colombia', *Granta* 31 (Spring 1990), pp. 87–95.
'Plying the word' (portrait of Fidel Castro), *North American Congress on Latin America* 24:2 (August 1990), pp. 40–6.
'Watching the Rain in Galicia', *The Best of Granta Travel* (London, 1991), pp. 1–5.

Works on Gabriel García Márquez

Biographical works

Arango, Gustavo, *Un ramo de nomeolvides: García Márquez en 'El Universal'* (Cartagena, El Universal, 1995).
Bell-Villada, Gene, *García Márquez: The Man and His Work* (Chapel Hill, University of North Carolina Press, 2nd edn, 2009).
Cebrián, Juan Luis, *Retrato de Gabriel García Márquez* (Barcelona, Círculo de Lectores, 1989).
Collazos, Oscar, *García Márquez: la soledad y la gloria* (Barcelona, Plaza y Janés, 1983).
Fiorillo, Heriberto, *La Cueva: crónica del grupo de Barranquilla* (Bogotá, Planeta, 2002).
García, Eligio, *La tercera muerte de Santiago Nasar. Crónica de La crónica* (Madrid, Mondadori, 1987).
    Tras las claves de Melquíades: historia de 'Cien años de soledad' (Bogotá, Norma, 2001).
García Usta, Jorge, *García Márquez en Cartagena: sus inicios literarios* (Bogotá, Planeta, 2007).
Hart, Stephen, *Gabriel García Márquez* (London, Reaktion Books, 2010).
Martin, Gerald, *Gabriel García Márquez: A Life* (London, Bloomsbury, 2008).
Minta, Stephen, *Gabriel García Márquez: Writer of Colombia* (London, Jonathan Cape, 1987).
Plimpton, George, *Writers at Work: The 'Paris Review' Interviews. Sixth Series* (New York, Viking Press, 1984).
Saldívar, Dasso, *García Márquez: el viaje a la semilla. La biografía* (Madrid, Santillana, 1997).
Sorela, Pedro, *El otro García Márquez: los años difíciles* (Madrid, Mondadori, 1988).
Stavans, Ilan, 'Gabo in decline', *Transition* 62 (October 1994), pp. 58–78.

Vargas Llosa, Mario, *García Márquez: historia de un deicidio* (Barcelona, Barral, 1971).

Literary-critical works

Bakhtin, Mikhail, *Rabelais and His World* (Bloomington, Indiana University Press, 1984).
Barth, John, 'The Literature of Exhaustion', *Atlantic Monthly* 220:2 (1967), pp. 29–34.
'The Literature of Replenishment: Postmodernist Fiction', *Atlantic Monthly* 245 (1980), pp. 65–71.
Bell, Michael, *Gabriel García Márquez: Solitude and Solidarity* (New York, St Martin's, 1993).
Bloom, Harold, ed., *Gabriel García Márquez* (New York, Chelsea House, 1989).
Cobo Borda, Juan Gustavo, ed., *Repertorio crítico sobre Gabriel García Márquez*, vols. 1 and 2 (Bogotá, Instituto Caro y Cuervo, 1995).
Fiddian, Robin, ed., *García Márquez* (London, Longman, 1995).
Frye, Northrop, *Anatomy of Criticism: Four Essays* (Princeton University Press, 1990).
Gullón, Ricardo, *García Márquez o el olvidado arte de contar* (Madrid, Taurus, 1970).
Hutcheon, Linda, *The Politics of Postmodernism* (London, Routledge, 1989).
Ludmer, Josefina, *Cien anos de soledad: una interpretación* (Buenos Aires, Trabajo Crítico, 1972).
Lukács, Georg, *The Historical Novel* (Harmondsworth, Pelican, 1981).
Martínez, Pedro Simón, ed., *Recopilación de textos sobre Gabriel García Márquez* (La Habana, Casa de las Américas, 1969).
McGuirk, Bernard, and Cardwell, Richard, eds., *Gabriel García Márquez: New Readings* (Cambridge University Press, 1987).
McMurray, George R., *Gabriel García Márquez: Life, Work and Criticism* (Fredericton, Canada, York Press, 1987).
Moretti, Franco, *Modern Epic: The World System from Goethe to García Márquez* (London, Verso, 1996).
Oberhelman, Harley D., *The Presence of Faulkner in the Writings of García Márquez* (Texas Tech University, Graduate Studies, August 1980).
Gabriel García Márquez. A Study of the Short Fiction (Boston, Twayne, 1991).
Ortega, Julio, *Artes de releer a Gabriel García Márquez* (México, Jorale Editores, 2003).
Ortega, Julio, ed., *Gabriel García Márquez and the Powers of Fiction* (Austin, Texas University Press, 1988).
Oyarzún, Kemy and Magenny, William W., eds., *Essays on Gabriel García Márquez* (University of California, Riverside, Latin American Studies Program, 1984).

Rama, Angel, *García Márquez: edificación de un arte nacional y popular* (Montevideo, Universidad Nacional, Facultad de Humanidades, 1987).

Rentería Mantilla, Alfonso, ed., *García Márquez habla de García Márquez en 33 grandes reportajes* (Bogotá, Rentería Editores, 1979).

Rincón, Carlos, *La no simultaneidad de lo simultáneo* (Bogotá, Editorial Universidad Nacional, 1995).

Rodríguez Vergara, Isabel, *Haunting Demons: Critical Essays on the Works of Gabriel García Márquez* (Washington, OAS, Interamer, 1998).

Sims, Robert L., *El primer García Márquez. Un estudio de su periodismo 1948 a 1955* (Maryland, Scripta Humanistica, 78, 1991).

Swanson, Philip, ed., *The Cambridge Companion to Gabriel García Márquez* (Cambridge University Press, 2010).

Timpanaro, Sebastiano, *On Materialism* (London, Verso, 1980).

Von der Walde, Erna, 'El macondismo como latinoamericanismo', *Cuadernos Americanos* 12:1 (Jan.–Feb. 1998), pp. 223–37.

White, Hayden, *The Content of the Form: Narrative Discourse and Historical Representation* (Baltimore, Johns Hopkins University Press, 1990).

Williams, Raymond, *Gabriel García Márquez* (Boston, Twayne, 1984).

Wood, Michael, *García Márquez: 'One Hundred Years of Solitude'* (Cambridge University Press, 1990).

Index

Abello, Jaime, 115
Abrenuncio, 118, 119, 147
Allende, Isabel, 62, 145
Allende, Salvador, 7, 75
Antonioni, Michelangelo, 62
Aracataca, 3–4, 5, 6, 13, 21, 40, 42, 47, 50, 135–40
Aureliano Buendía, Colonel, 4, 25, 41, 49–53, 67

Bakhtin, Mikhail, 149
Barcelona, 7, 13, 61, 131
Barcha, Mercedes (wife), 6, 7, 20, 56, 96, 100, 122, 124, 131, 140
Barranquilla, 3, 4, 5, 6, 13, 17, 20, 22, 37, 47, 76, 104, 115, 120–7, 137, 140, 141
Barranquilla Group, 5, 47, 58
Barth, John, 145
Bayley, John, 132
Begin, Menachem, 78
Bergson, Henri, 84
Berlin Wall, fall of, 8, 108, 119, 146, 147
'Big Four', 31
Bogotá, 4, 5, 6, 7, 13, 14, 15, 17, 29, 43, 53, 66, 75, 103, 105, 136, 140, 143, 145
Bogotazo, 5, 16, 17, 58, 76
Bolívar, Simón, 8, 85, 102–7, 113, 119, 123, 139, 140, 146, 148
Bonaparte, Napoleon, 105
Book of Good Love, The, 127
'Boom', 7, 12, 27, 48, 49, 57, 61, 82, 119, 144

Buenos Aires, 7

cachacos, 5, 44, 105
Caracas, 6, 13, 32, 33, 42, 64, 103
Caribbean, 3–4, 5, 8, 9, 13, 67, 103, 104, 105, 130, 132, 140
Cartagena, 5, 6, 9, 13, 17, 20, 62, 79, 91–101, 103, 104, 117–20, 132, 139
Castro, Fidel, 8, 42, 74, 75, 85, 91, 102, 130, 144, 147
Chávez, Hugo, 115
Church and Catholicism, 4, 9, 34, 35, 43, 87, 97, 98, 124
Ciénaga massacre, 4, 49, 51, 54–8, 143
Clinton, Bill, 10, 115
Cold War, 20, 31, 145
Colombia, 3, 9, 11, 12, 13, 18, 19, 27, 30, 33, 35, 41, 43, 49–60, 66, 79, 91, 102, 105, 107–16, 143, 145
Columbus, Christopher, 67
communism and socialism, 7, 12, 19, 34, 38, 49, 53, 79, 91, 114, 122, 145, 147
conservatism, 3, 19, 33, 41, 67, 79, 86, 105, 113, 146
Cortázar, Julio, 12, 13, 48, 64
Costa, 3, 5, 15, 20, 66, 145
costeños, 5
Cuba and Revolution, 6, 7, 9, 42, 43, 48, 76, 85, 102, 107, 144, 145, 147

De Sica, Vittorio, 29, 34, 37
dictatorship, 6, 7, 21, 32, 33, 47, 63–74,

75, 76, 77, 108, 145, 148
Duke of Marlborough, 49

Eastern Europe, 6, 31
Escobar, Pablo, 108–12, 146
Europe, 6, 8, 13, 31, 32, 90, 94, 100,
    129–33, 135, 140, 142, 145

Fellini, Federico, 62, 63
France, 19, 29, 91, 93, 98, 105, 108,
    119, 142, 146
Francisco the Man, 49
Franco, General Francisco, 7, 65
Freud, Sigmund, 12, 128, 134, 135, 137
Fuentes, Carlos, 7, 10, 13, 27, 64, 144

Gaitán, Jorge Eliécer, 5, 33, 44, 113, 143
Galán, Luis Carlos, 108
García, Gabriel Eligio (father), 3–5, 22,
    91, 96, 123, 137, 138
García Barcha, Gonzalo (son), 7, 132
García Barcha, Rodrigo (son), 7, 132
García Márquez, Gabriel
  influences and comparisons
    Asturias, Miguel Angel, 46, 59,
        62, 144
      Men of Maize, 46
      President, The, 65, 67
    Borges, Jorge Luis, 13, 49, 144
    Carpentier, Alejo, 46, 59, 66, 144
    Cervantes, 9, 17, 28, 142
      Don Quixote, 53, 95, 97, 127
      Jealous Old Man, The, 126
    Conrad *Nostromo*, 66
    Dante and Beatrice, 123
    Darío, Rubén, 11
    Defoe
      *Robinson Crusoe, Journal of the
        Plague Year*, 30
    'Delgadina' (ballad), 124, 125, 126
    Diego 'Insomniac', 131
    Dumas
      The Count of Monte Cristo, 11
    Faulkner, 15, 22, 28, 42, 83, 143
      As I Lay Dying, 21

Flaubert, 83
  Madame Bovary, 96
  Sentimental Education, 91
Frye
  Anatomy of Criticism, 68
García Lorca, Federico, 11, 86, 87
Garcilaso de la Vega, 12
Gómez de la Serna *greguerías*,
    19, 20
Góngora, Luis de, 12, 125, 126
Hemingway, 16, 17, 28, 42, 45,
    61, 143
  Old Man and the Sea, The, 21,
    40
Joyce, 14, 27, 83, 143
  Ulysses, 123
Kafka, 13, 15, 143
Kawabata
  *House of the Sleeping Beauties,
    The*, 123, 131
Larbaud
  Fermina Márquez, 91, 98
Leandro Díaz
  'Crowned Goddess, The', 96
Machiavelli, 72
Mann
  Magic Mountain, The, 91, 97,
    100
Manrique
  *Verses on the Death of My
    Father*, 105
Munthe
  Story of San Michele, 91
Nabokov
  Lolita, 123
Neruda, Pablo, 11
Nostradamus, 49
One Thousand and One Nights, 11
Poe, 13, 15
Proust
  In Search of Lost Time, 91, 137
Ravel
  Bolero, 89
Roa Bastos, Augusto
  I the Supreme, 66

Rojas
  Spanish Bawd, The, 127
Rulfo, Juan, 13, 144
  Pedro Páramo, 46, 65, 158
Salgari, novels, 11
Shakespeare, 72, 147
Sophocles
  Antigone, 23
  Oedipus Rex, 143
Spanish Golden Age literature,
  12, 86–7, 126
Stevenson
  Treasure Island, 11
Tolstoy
  War and Peace, 13, 88
Twain, Mark, 17, 136
Valle-Inclán, 86
  Tirano Banderas, 65, 66
Vicente, Gil, 79
Woolf, Virginia, 20, 22, 25, 83, 143
  Mrs Dalloway, 20, 21, 64
life, 3–10
  activism, 9, 17, 76
  Alternativa, 8, 17, 75–7, 122, 146
  Blue Lobster, The, 47
  Cambio, 17, 115
  cinema, 6, 16, 17, 21, 22, 29, 32,
    34, 38, 48, 104, 108, 143
  EICTV, 17
  El Espectador, 5, 6, 12, 29, 31, 77,
    77, 115, 129
  El Heraldo, 5, 20, 29
  El País, 77, 129
  El Universal, 5, 18, 29
  FNCL, 17
  FNPI, 17, 115
  Habeas, 18, 76, 146
  human rights, 32
  IAPA, 115
  journalism, 5, 6, 7, 8, 16–21,
    29–32, 45, 75–8, 114–16
  lymphoma, 9, 116
  MacBride Commission, 18, 77
  Momento, 6, 32, 42
  Montessori school, 11

Nobel Prize, 8, 77, 90, 133, 146, 148
poetry, 11–12, 140
Prensa Latina, 7, 43, 45, 144
QAP, 107, 114
Russell Tribunals, 18, 76, 146
short stories, 12–13, 29–30, 40–4,
  47, 61–3, 129–33, 140
80th birthday Cartagena 2007, 9
techniques and styles
  autobiography and memoir, 7,
    49, 56, 73, 78, 81, 82, 94,
    128–42, 145, 146
  crónicas, 16, 18, 77–8, 129
  first-person narrative, 24, 30, 65,
    81, 84, 95, 125, 133–42
  humour, 34, 83, 88, 136
  hyperbole, 48, 67, 136
  irony, 9, 44, 80, 81, 87, 88, 95, 122,
    130
  journalistic approaches, 9, 78,
    108, 109
  magical realism, 4, 13, 16, 43, 46,
    48, 58–60, 136, 141, 144,
    145, 148
  modernism, 14, 21–8, 34, 58–9,
    64, 71, 82–3, 139, 143, 148
  neorealism, 6, 21, 29–44, 82–3,
    143, 145
  postcolonialism, 49
  postmodernism, 49, 50, 58, 64,
    78–89, 94, 95, 119, 148
  realism, 21, 40, 41, 82–3, 94, 141–2
  short story versus novel, 13
  storytelling, 11, 17–18, 30, 86,
    114, 142
  structural *enjambement*, 36, 39,
    85, 93, 120, 126
  structure in two halves, 35–6,
    39, 52–3, 69–70, 85, 93–4,
    104, 105, 110–13, 120, 126,
    136–7, 139
  surrealism, 59, 132
  thriller, 109–14
  titles, approach to, 8, 73, 88, 104,
    125, 133

García Márquez, Gabriel (*cont.*)
  themes
    absurdity, 15, 84, 87
    burial, 15, 23, 39, 71, 94
    childhood, 3–4, 21–8, 47–60
    colonialism, 26, 46–7, 67
    communication, 19, 35, 83–5,
      99–100
    death, 15, 26, 27, 28, 39, 43, 88–9,
      94, 96, 100, 101, 105, 107,
      131, 148
    dignity and justice, 38, 39, 41, 149
    dreams, 15, 35, 62, 86, 87, 120,
      131
    fame, 63, 75, 77, 95, 106, 109–10,
      144, 145
    fate and destiny, 27, 35, 78–89, 106
    genealogy and identity, 14–15, 20,
      28, 47, 50, 57, 82, 106, 144,
      145
    history and memory, 12, 14, 17,
      24, 38, 39, 53–60, 67, 82,
      102–7, 135, 136, 139, 146,
      147
    honour, shame and machismo,
      23, 33, 39, 41, 50, 89, 97, 121,
      146
    incest, 3, 50–5, 59
    legitimacy, 5, 14, 20, 145
    Lolita syndrome, 117–27
    love, 3, 8, 39, 70–1, 73, 87,
      90–101, 105, 111, 113,
      117–27, 138, 147, 148, 149
    marriage, 40, 91–101, 121
    myth, 24, 27, 28, 34, 39, 57, 59,
      66, 68, 82, 89, 105
    nostalgia, 4, 5, 9, 55, 58, 70, 139,
      146
    old age, 36–40, 90–101, 120–7
    perception, 14, 15, 26, 139
    plagues, 29, 55, 118
    politics, 8, 12, 19, 21, 33, 34, 38,
      39, 43, 107–16, 122, 138,
      143, 145, 147
    popular culture, 20, 95, 98–9, 146
    power, 8, 23, 34, 35, 63–74, 83,
      90, 101, 102–14, 121, 146,
      147, 148
    sexuality, 9, 24, 63, 68, 70,
      92–101, 106, 117–27, 131
    solitude, 8, 19, 39, 50, 53–60, 83, 90,
      101, 106, 121, 122, 141, 148
    the body and materiality, 14
    time, 25, 51, 67, 82, 86, 136, 139
    truth and sincerity, 19, 72, 73,
      130, 134, 136, 147
    violence, 8, 37, 39, 47, 50, 83, 86,
      88–9, 107–14
  works
    90 Days Behind the Iron Curtain,
      31
    Autumn of the Patriarch, The, 7,
      18, 40, 47, 48, 61, 63–74, 79,
      94, 122, 124, 140, 145, 146,
      147, 148
    Big Mama's Funeral, 6, 13, 16,
      40–4, 48
    'Big Mama's Funeral', 27, 40, 44,
      46, 47, 48, 82, 145
    'Chile, the Coup and the Gringos',
      76
    Chronicle of a Death Foretold, 8,
      78–89, 91, 92, 94, 95, 100,
      109, 111, 122, 146, 148
    Clandestine in Chile, 78, 108
    *Diatribe of Love Against a Seated
      Man*, 143
    Eyes of a Blue Dog, 13–16
    General in his Labyrinth, The, 8,
      17, 74, 102–7, 114, 117, 123,
      139, 146, 148
    'House, The', 5, 21, 48, 135
    In Evil Hour, 6, 21, 38, 48, 49, 79,
      82–3, 92, 121, 145, 146
    Innocent Eréndira, 13, 47, 61–3,
      123
    Leaf Storm, 5, 16, 21–8, 30, 34, 37,
      49, 50, 80, 82–4, 95, 96, 104,
      111, 112, 136, 139, 141, 145,
      147, 148

Living to Tell the Tale, 9, 120, 121, 125, 128–42
Love in the Time of Cholera, 8, 86, 90–101, 117, 123, 124, 125, 137, 146
Memories of My Melancholy Whores, 9, 78, 120–7, 130, 133, 136, 137, 148
'Monologue of Isabel Watching it Rain in Macondo', 16, 22, 46
News of a Kidnapping, 9, 78, 107–14, 133, 146
'Night of the Curlews, The', 13, 16, 46
No One Writes to the Colonel, 6, 21, 30, 32, 33, 36–40, 48, 49, 54, 73, 79, 82–3, 93, 94, 123, 145
Nobel Prize speech, 54, 67, 84, 90
Of Love and Other Demons, 9, 114, 117–20, 124, 140
'One Day After Saturday', 30, 33, 40, 41, 48
One Hundred Years of Solitude, 7, 9, 21, 28, 29, 33, 40, 46, 47–60, 73, 79, 82, 83, 85, 90, 94, 95, 100, 122, 123, 136, 138, 144, 145, 148
'Other Side of Death, The', 12, 15
'Sea of Lost Time, The', 47, 48
Story of a Shipwrecked Sailor, 30, 78
Strange Pilgrims, 9, 13, 129–33
'Third Resignation, The', 5, 12, 15
'Tuesday Siesta', 22, 33, 41, 42
García Márquez, Luis Enrique (brother), 3
García Márquez, Margarita ('Margot', sister), 4
Garcilaso de la Vega, 120
Gaviria, César, 107–13
Geneva, 6, 130
Gentile, Cayetano, 79, 80
González, Felipe, 9, 76, 102

Gramsci, Antonio, 147
Guajira, 3, 6, 13, 25, 50, 62, 92

Havana, 17, 43, 144
Hutcheon, Linda, 84

Iguarán Cotes, Tranquilina (grandmother), 3, 4
Isaacs, Jorge
  María, 98
Italy, 29, 31, 32, 131

Latin America, 6–8, 16, 19, 27, 32, 43, 49–59, 65–6, 84, 85, 90, 94, 122, 142, 143, 145
liberalism, 3, 12, 19, 29, 34, 37, 41, 51, 67, 108
London, 6, 13, 32, 40, 64
Lukács, Georg, 103

Machado de Assis, Joaquim Maria, 13
Macondo, 4, 6, 13, 21, 23, 24, 25, 26, 27, 29, 34, 40, 41, 42, 46, 47, 48, 49, 50, 60, 61
Magdalena River, 3, 5, 93, 100, 103, 104
Márquez, Colonel Nicolás (grandfather), 3–4, 19, 22, 37, 50, 57, 76, 96, 135, 137, 138, 145
Márquez Iguarán, Luisa Santiaga (mother), 3–4, 22, 96, 100, 135–40
Martínez, Tomás Eloy, 10
Masetti, Jorge Ricardo, 43
Medellín, 30, 108, 111
Melquíades, 50–7, 100
Mendoza, Plinio Apuleyo, 6, 32, 32, 43
Mexico, 7, 8, 9, 33, 45, 47, 144, 145
Mitterrand, François, 9, 102
Mutis, Alvaro, 6, 103

Nicaragua, Sandinistas, 8, 77
Nixon, Richard M., 32

Otero Silva, Miguel, 131

Padilla Affair, 7
Paris, 6, 32, 37, 91, 92, 132
Pérez Jiménez, General Marcos, 6, 32,
    64, 65
Pinochet, General Augusto, 78, 108

Quintana, Tachia, 37, 96
Quiroga, Horacio, 13

Riohacha, 3, 137
Rolland, Romain, 147
Rome, 6, 34, 40, 47, 131
Rushdie, Salman, 145

Sáenz, Manuelita, 106
Saldívar, Dasso, 139
Salgar, José, 30
Santa Marta, 62, 104, 137
Santander, Francisco de Paula, 105,
    113
Spain, 7, 9, 61, 65, 103, 105, 145
Stockholm, 8
Sturrock, John, 132
Sucre ('the Town'), 4, 6, 13, 32, 36, 40,
    44, 47, 78, 79, 95
Sucre, Antonio José de, 105

Suez crisis 1956, 37, 54

Third World, 37, 49, 50, 59, 144
Timpanaro, Sebastiano, 147

United Fruit Company, 4, 51, 55
United Nations, 31, 77, 115
US, 7, 19, 26, 31, 32, 43, 46, 47,
    51, 67, 103, 105, 108
USSR, 6, 31, 85, 90

Vargas Llosa, Mario, 7, 13, 58, 64,
    66, 144
Velasco, Luis Alejandro, 30
Venezuela, 6, 33, 43, 62, 66, 67, 100,
    102, 103, 145
Violencia, 5, 20, 33, 41, 56, 58,
    79, 143

War of the Thousand Days, 3, 4, 37,
    113, 143
White, Hayden, 84

Zabala, Clemente Manuel, 18
Zalamea Borda, Eduardo, 12
Zavattini, Cesare, 29, 34,
    42, 131
Zipaquirá, 4, 5, 11, 12, 136

Cambridge Introductions to ...

AUTHORS

Margaret Atwood Heidi Macpherson

Jane Austen Janet Todd

Samuel Beckett Ronan McDonald

Walter Benjamin David Ferris

Chekhov James N. Loehlin

J. M. Coetzee Dominic Head

Samuel Taylor Coleridge John Worthen

Joseph Conrad John Peters

Jacques Derrida Leslie Hill

Charles Dickens Jon Mee

Emily Dickinson Wendy Martin

George Eliot Nancy Henry

T. S. Eliot John Xiros Cooper

William Faulkner Theresa M. Towner

F. Scott Fitzgerald Kirk Curnutt

Michel Foucault Lisa Downing

Robert Frost Robert Faggen

Gabriel García Márquez Gerald Martin

Nathaniel Hawthorne Leland S. Person

Zora Neale Hurston Lovalerie King

James Joyce Eric Bulson

Thomas Mann Todd Kontje

Christopher Marlowe Tom Rutter

Herman Melville Kevin J. Hayes

Milton Stephen B. Dobranski

Sylvia Plath Jo Gill

Edgar Allan Poe Benjamin F. Fisher

Ezra Pound Ira Nadel

Marcel Proust Adam Watt

Jean Rhys Elaine Savory

Edward Said Conor McCarthy

Shakespeare Emma Smith

Shakespeare's Comedies Penny Gay

Shakespeare's History Plays Warren Chernaik

Shakespeare's Poetry Michael Schoenfeldt

Shakespeare's Tragedies Janette Dillon

Harriet Beecher Stowe Sarah Robbins

Mark Twain Peter Messent

Edith Wharton Pamela Knights

Walt Whitman M. Jimmie Killingsworth

Virginia Woolf Jane Goldman

William Wordsworth Emma Mason

W. B. Yeats David Holdeman

TOPICS

American Literary Realism Phillip Barrish

The American Short Story Martin Scofield

Anglo-Saxon Literature Hugh Magennis

Comedy Eric Weitz

Creative Writing David Morley

Early English Theatre Janette Dillon

Eighteenth-Century Poetry John Sitter

English Theatre, 1660–1900 Peter Thomson

Francophone Literature Patrick Corcoran

Literature and the Environment Timothy Clark

Modern British Theatre Simon Shepherd

Modern Irish Poetry Justin Quinn

Modernism Pericles Lewis

Modernist Poetry Peter Howarth

Narrative (second edition) H. Porter Abbott

The Nineteenth-Century American Novel Gregg Crane

The Novel Marina MacKay

Old Norse Sagas Margaret Clunies Ross

Postcolonial Literatures C. L. Innes

Postmodern Fiction Bran Nicol

Russian Literature Caryl Emerson

Scenography Joslin McKinney and Philip Butterworth

The Short Story in English Adrian Hunter

Theatre Historiography Thomas Postlewait

Theatre Studies Christopher B. Balme

Tragedy Jennifer Wallace

Victorian Poetry Linda K. Hughes